BEYOND THE TWO-STATE SOLUTION

BEYOND THE TWO-STATE SOLUTION

A JEWISH POLITICAL ESSAY

YEHOUDA SHENHAV

polity

First published in 2012 by Polity Press
First published as במלכודת הקו הירוק (*Entrapped by the Green Line*) in 2010 by הוצאת עם עובד (Am Oved Press).

Polity Press
65 Bridge Street
Cambridge CB2 1UR, UK

Polity Press
350 Main Street
Malden, MA 02148, USA

ISBN-13: 978-0-7456-6028-8
ISBN-13: 978-0-7456-6029-5(pb)

A catalogue record for this book is available from the British Library.

Typeset in 10.75 on 14 pt Janson Text
by Servis Filmsetting Ltd, Stockport, Cheshire, SK2 5AJ
Printed and bound in USA by Edwards Brothers, Inc.

The publisher has used its best endeavours to ensure that the URLs for external websites referred to in this book are correct and active at the time of going to press. However, the publisher has no responsibility for the websites and can make no guarantee that a site will remain live or that the content is or will remain appropriate.

Every effort has been made to trace all copyright holders, but if any have been inadvertently overlooked the publisher will be pleased to include any necessary credits in any subsequent reprint or edition.

For further information on Polity, visit our website: www.politybooks.com

CONTENTS

FOREWORD: YEHOUDA SHENHAV'S *BEYOND THE TWO-STATE SOLUTION*

In his book *Beyond the Two-State Solution*, Yehouda Shenhav makes an unusual and unsettling argument. It is an argument that targets the Israeli left in the English-speaking world and those who take their heed of them. Shenhav argues that what appears on its face a "progressive" position on the question of Israel and Palestine, is in fact censorial and duplicitous. The Israeli left's sanctimonious insistence in the face of the Jewish settlers of the West Bank that the settlements were illegal and that the proper borders of Israel are those of *1967*, is nothing short of an ideological maneuver. The purpose of the maneuver is to obfuscate the fact that Israel itself is nothing short of a huge settlement project that was founded upon the displacement of hundreds of thousands of Palestinians and the systematic expropriation of the land they left behind.

The ideological maneuver is accomplished, according to Shenhav, through a shift in terminology from "The Green Line" to "The 1967 borders": "The Green Line" signified the borders Israel fell upon in 1949 following the 1948 war, but after the 1967 war when Israel occupied the West Bank and Gaza, these very same borders came to be called "The 1967 borders." They were the same borders but they were now called something different. This transmutation in sign from "Green Line" to "1967 borders" in the language of the left is premised on a moral distinction: the 1948 war and the outcome it yielded was legitimate – not so with 1967 and the occupation/settlement in its aftermath.

The translation of Shenhav's book into English is a welcome intervention because it is not just the Israeli left that doesn't want to "touch" 1948. The Jewish left and its allies in the US also insist, often vociferously, on dating Israel's injustice to 1967. Any Palestinian who has attempted to enter coalition politics with the progressive forces in the US on the question of Israel and Palestine feels the heavy-handed, almost authoritarian manner in which such moral distinctions are made. There is a demand by one's allies that one should forget 1948, that one should split one's own diasporic experience, one's uprooting, one's trajectory over time, so that it tracks that of the moral judgement of the Israeli left. Many of us Palestinians, who have attempted (and stubbornly refuse to despair of) such coalition politics, whether on the streets, in activist organizations, in media interventions, in academia as activist students or professors, have had the experience of "stepping on someone's toe" by evoking 1948 – the very hint of it, it would seem, causes a meltdown of sorts, a denunciatory rage, a charge that we have misunderstood our well-deserved and "self-inflicted" banishment, that we should just get on with the international (read "Western") consensus, that the national(ist) division premised on theirs in 1948, ours in 1967, is a just and rightful one; in short, a demand that we should "put up and shut up already" about 1948.

In the academic literature in the US, the situation is just

as dire, and the defense of the moral distinction as tight. In legal scholarship, for instance, the farthest to the left on the political spectrum one can get is a law review article that denounces Israeli occupation of the "territories," declares the "transfer of the occupier's nationals to the occupied territories" as violating international law, and demands the dismantlement of the "settlements" and the "return to the 1967 borders." Such an author might marvel at the Israeli occupation's tenacity: an occupation that has stumped the International Law of Occupation with its duration, persistence and the legal adroitness and resourcefulness of its administrators and national apologists; and one that has, ironically enough, by transferring half a million of its own nationals into the occupied "territories," proven itself absolutely correct in denying it's an "occupation."

From this position on the left, one can only move to the right. The progressive author insisting on "withdrawal from territories occupied in 1967" is then dragged into a debate with the apologist for Israel. Such an apologist would insist that these territories could not be considered occupied in any legal sense since no legitimate sovereign authority controlled them when they were occupied by Israel in 1967. This was no-man's-land, according to the apologist, and therefore the rule prohibiting transfer of population doesn't apply. This was no man's land and therefore there was no rush for the Israeli authorities to leave. This was no-man's-land and therefore the humane and humanitarian standards limiting the conduct of the occupier vis-à-vis the occupied population do not apply, though the Israeli authorities could choose to follow them out of generosity, rather than by rule of law. The author might go as far as adopting the Israeli term "Judea and Samaria" in referring to the "territories," thereby completing in sign what the author had made in argument.

Then there is the never-failing argument about "security" and "terrorism," with reference to which everything from building a fence, to dismembering territory through checkpoints, to waging a war on Gaza, to passing a discriminatory legislation, to building yet another settlement, is justified – a discourse that "confuses cause and effect" as Shenhav so rightly puts it.

From left to right, no robust political position exists in the US that would be based on the injustice of 1948. One can appreciate, in this light, the radical-ness of Shenhav's insistence on evoking politically the injustices of that year. It would seem by doing so he is pushing the left to be more left.

But Shenhav might not be too pleased with this characterization of the politics of his project. As you reach the last part of his book, you find that he aims at nothing less than confusing the political spectrum of left to right altogether on the issue of Israel/Palestine.

Shenhav doesn't just charge the Israeli left with selective morality (obscuring 1948 and highlighting 1967), he also contends that the move to settlements in the territories that the Israeli left finds so objectionable was in large part a convenient resolution of an ethnic/class conflict internal to Israel (among its Jewish population) that the ruling elites welcomed and in which their victims found comfort and respite. The "Third Israel" – Mizrahim, ultra-orthodox Jews and poor Russians – found "migrating" to settlements in the new land an escape from racism and marginality in Israel proper, and their racial superiors (the Ashkenazi) found in such migration an easy solution to the social and economic crisis that had intensified over the past three decades due to Israel's adoption of neo-liberal economics. In fact, Shenhav stresses that the settlement project has been most profitable for the ruling elites of Israel – the left being members of this class – in the most convenient and self-serving ways. It has, on the one hand, allowed the elites to profit economically from building the settlements while waxing eloquent and nostalgic for an Israel that was morally unburdened by their existence. They have built walls and highways to protect the settlers while blaming them for obstructing the way to a two-state solution. They have provided military support for the settlers while decrying their increasing political influence in Israel.

If the Israeli left is duplicitous, and the settlers – a good part of them, at least – are migrants from oppression, then, surely, one should get off one's moral high ground and develop some sympathy for the latter. This would only complete the "flip" that Shenhav started by describing the Israeli left as not so left. In this case, then, the right, classically sympathetic towards the settlements, might not be so "right."

Shenhav points, for instance, to the ways in which Mizrahi participation in the administration of the occupied territories given their mastery of the Arabic language – his own family, of Iraqi origins, being an example – was liberating for them. It provided opportunities for upward mobility for this community, otherwise doomed to manual labor or lower-rung jobs inside Israel, through managerial work in the military administration of the territories. It has also allowed them to interact with other Arabic-speaking people who have experienced, as migrants from the Arab world to Israel, a diminution in value of their Arabic language and culture by the general Ashkenazi public.

He also points to the deconstructive sensibility of some of the settlers themselves who bring to light what the Israeli left keeps hidden through its moral high ground: there is no real difference between the settlement project in the occupied territories and the settlement project that is Israel proper, those settlers would insist. Indeed, some settlers, as Shenhav points out, are far more attached to the land of Israel than the state of Israel itself, and would rather share the land with the Palestinians from sea to river, including returning refugees, than be forced out of biblical "Judea and Samaria" to go to live in the state of Israel. If the left is not so left, then surely the right is not so right and there is some left to be gleaned from its positions?

Of course, Shenhav is perfectly aware that, even if there are understandable reasons for settlers to move to the West Bank, they have done so at the expense of the Palestinians. Some Jews win more than other Jews in this ongoing settlement project called Israel, but there is this one consistent loser: the Palestinians. Shenhav doesn't argue with that at all; he is happy to accede that not only has the Ashkenazi Jew built his empire on the grand larceny of Palestinian land in the aftermath of 1948, but also his brethren less-esteemed Jews were complicit in no less of a crime in the West Bank, even if they were running away from sibling tyranny. Still Shenhav wants us to sympathize with at least some of the settlers; even more, he's arguing that those settlers should just stay put!

That the settlers should stay comes as a surprising twist in Shenhav's otherwise on-its-face-radical argument insisting on the injustice of 1948. At this point in your reading, you will start to move uneasily in your chair!

If you had, especially as a Palestinian, imagined a land-free-of-the-Jews, even if it were a fragment of Palestine, on which you could project your Volksgeist, and call it a state, or if you were a progressive Jew who had always thought that a just solution would necessarily require "unsettling" the settlers, evacuating the settlements, so that *you* would have a land to attach your Volksgeist to, Shenhav doesn't offer such a place. That settlers should stay – a classically right-wing position – acquires with Shenhav a different political resonance, though what kind takes a bit of work to comprehend.

Shenhav's argument for settlers to stay is premised on an implicit trade-off: recognition of Nakba and the return of refugees. Settlers should stay in all the areas in Palestine, from river to sea. No areas of Jewish habitation should be disturbed, no matter what the historic inequities. That is Shenhav's position, for which the return of refugees is traded. But if this is so, where would the refugees return, you might ask? Everywhere else is Shenhav's answer. Why? Because a wrong cannot be remedied by another wrong. "Villages that were destroyed and resettled by Jews will not be destroyed again," he declares.

Instead:

> new communities may be constructed – in the Galilee, in the Negev and in the West Bank and Gaza. The refugees' resettlement will be on individual basis (for example, in big cities like Haifa) or on communal basis, by rebuilding some of the destroyed communities on new sites. The building of new sites will be based on a general outlined plan negotiated by the two peoples, and the redistribution of space will not harm the existing and already settled population. The refugees will be rehabilitated and afforded broad-based affirmative action. Those who will choose not to return will receive financial compensation. The eradicated communities will be mentioned in all official signposting. Some communities will retain their mono-national characters if they request it.

Such a proposal would require, according to Shenhav, that Palestinians give up, on the one hand, "the narrative of destruction and redemption" and replace it with the idea of return as a "multivalent process." On the other, it would require of the Israelis giving up "the land regime that gives Jews exclusive preference."

But it is not just the idea of prohibiting the undoing of a historic wrong through the commission of another that inspires Shenhav's proposal. It is something far more affirmative than that. Shenhav is inspired by what he calls "consociational democracy," which he describes as "a model of partnership that presupposes the national and religious rights of both peoples, which will be expressed through dividing the space into smaller national spaces and into religious and secular communities, canton/federation-like." The presence of historic wrongs – no empty land to inherit, as Zionism had claimed, but a land encumbered by a people who had to be expelled so the land could be inherited – all this doesn't deny that Jews *also* have "national and religious rights" to the land, and it is in accommodation to these rights, as well as to those of the Palestinians, that Shenhav proposes a form of joint-living-based "consociational democracy" as a solution.

Shenhav's solution is an intermediate one, between a one-state solution – which he opposes because it "does not consider the fact that most of the population of the area concerned is both religious and nationalist," irreducible to a "homogeneous public with individual interests" – and a two-state solution which ignores the fact that the respective communities' nationalist and religious interests are spread across the whole land of Palestine and cannot be coercively divided through arbitrary borders. This is an interesting proposal that I would like to briefly un-pack to determine whether the political "flip" which Shenhav has attempted can be done. I will do so by asking how it would line up with the interests of the Palestinians.

How the Palestinians, the biggest losers in the drama of Jewish settlement of Palestine, would fare under Shenhav's consociational democracy is an interesting question. We don't really have much to go on by way of a proposal from Shenhav, merely a sketch and an outline. But whether one is discussing a one-state, two-state or consociational democracy, the distributional consequences for Palestinians in relation to Jews simply depends on the details of the institutional structures being proposed and the extent to which they respond to historical inequities by opening up the current regime. After all, the current Oslo regime could very well be described as "consociational democracy" that is premised on an idea of "joint sovereignty," which Shenhav makes much of. The trouble of course, is that under Oslo, land, wealth and power are tilted so much to one side at the expense of the other – so that one, the Jews, gets a "surplus" in nationalism and sovereignty, and the other, the Palestinians, a gross deficit of both.

Shenhav does propose an amendment of the land regime to remove the in-built preferences for Jews, to allow for land the refugees can return to. He, however, conditions transfer of land to considerations of keeping Jewish communities "undisturbed" as communities. This is a general formula premised on a kind of balancing, and, depending on how it is legally and institutionally worked out, could either turn out badly for the Palestinians (giving them little in return for stamping Jewish settlements with legality) or turn out well for them (the reward for recognition of legality of settlements would be well worth their while).

It would seem to me that there are two primary challenges to Shenhav's consociational democracy model. The UN Resolution 194 (December 11, 1948) grants the Palestinians right of return to properties they lost in 1948, a right that they can exercise by returning to their actual homes wherever these might be, and if they choose not to, they are entitled to compensation for the "loss or damage to [such] property."[1] If this is the case, why would Palestinians accede to a regime, such as the one proposed by Shenhav, that would limit the exercise of that right to a "chosen" few (in the cities) and balances its exercise with the consideration of not disturbing the Jewishness of established communities? Even if they accede to not returning to those properties, would they be able to rent them out to their current Jewish occupiers? Can they become landlords in Jewish cities? If so, do they have the right to sell those properties and buy others inside Jewish cities? In other words, if they themselves cannot physically inhabit and reside in Jewish communities, can they become investors and capital owners in them? This question is deeply related to the second challenge.

If returning refugees can only reside in "Palestinian" communities, and the current structural relationship – spatial and economic – of Palestinian to Jewish communities is the outcome of the latter swallowing up and appropriating the material and symbolic resources of the former over a long period of time, to what land exactly is the returning refugee returning? To be cramped along with other fellow Palestinians in the Galilee? To replace the Jews in competition for land spaces claimed by the Bedouins in the Negev? To the towns and villages outside the ones they had lost in 1948, as outsiders looking in? Hadn't their relatives who survived 1948 done that already?

If the contemporary structure will remain in general unperturbed in the name of preserving the Jewishness of

---

[1] The Resolution resolves "that the refugees wishing to return to their homes and live at peace with their neighbors should be permitted to do so at the earliest practicable date, and that compensation should be paid for the property of those choosing not to return and for loss of or damage to property which, under principles of international law or in equity, should be made good by the Governments or authorities responsible": UN General Assembly Resolution 194 passed on December 11, 1948, (Article 11).

current communities, wouldn't the returning refugees simply become themselves the new settlers of Palestine, this time settlers in an essentially Jewish state? But unlike the Zionist settlers who came to Palestine unimpeded by law or custom, would they not find themselves bumping against the limits of the Jewishness of the Jewish communities, by law, custom and history? Wouldn't they be better off staying where they are, settlers in Lebanon, Syria and Jordan – at least there they are settlers in a land cohabitated by fellow Arabs?

If, realistically speaking, the only spaces available for them to settle are the hills of the West Bank not already claimed by Jewish settlers, where they can dig roots in a community they can claim organic bonds with and an economy they can participate in as "owners" and not just as workers, wouldn't Shenhav's consociational democracy have essentially reverted to a "two-state" solution with "large land swaps???"

In the end, Shenhav's consociational democracy, an attempt at flipping the current line-up of left to right, simply depends on the "quality" of return this form of democracy offers the Palestinians.

Lama Abu Odeh
January 5, 2012

ACKNOWLEDGMENTS

Although this book is based on academic sources, it is essentially a political essay that seeks to reach a broad audience and make a political statement. I wrote it with strong political passion and I would therefore like to spell out my political motivations in writing it. As a Jew of Iraqi origin living in Israel, I am concerned with the state's non-democratic practices towards the Palestinian population under Israel's control, including those holding Israeli citizenship. I am deeply concerned with the violation of the political rights of the Palestinians, but no less so with the future political rights of the Jews themselves. I believe that the combination of a persistent foundational state of emergency and blatantly racist legislation – which grows more restrictive and barefaced day by day – poses a threat not only to the Palestinians, but also to the very existence of the Jews in the Middle East. For this reason, I wish to unpack the Jewish–Israeli discourse on the conflict, to highlight the dangerous political zones within which it roams, and offer an alternative political vision in which the rights of both Jews and Palestinians are intertwined and co-determined.

By and large, Jewish thought on the Israeli–Palestinian conflict is fixated on binary and banal oppositions of "right" and "left" and draws simplistic lines between "good" and "bad," "hawks" and "doves." While criticism regarding the violence of the Jewish right wing has been heard, the ideas promoted by the left are still considered, progressive and liberal. Yet I believe that, although the liberal left harks back to seemingly progressive ideals, its views and practices often reinforce, rather than weaken, Israel's non-democratic rule. It is for this reason that I turn a critical spotlight on the ideas and practices that the liberal left clings onto. In particular, I argue that the so-called "two-state solution" in the form proposed by the Israeli liberal left not only is unrealistic, but in essence is based on false assumptions that sustain and reinforce the non-democratic Israeli regime and mask the essence of the conflict. Instead, I offer a different vision for Jewish political thought, which is not based on state terror or Jewish supremacy. My suggestion to leave most of the settlements intact – which seems contradictory to my position, since I believe these settlements are war crimes – becomes clearer, I hope, throughout the book.

The ideas presented in this book were developed in the course of my interaction with many others in the last twenty years. I have had the privilege of the company of wonderful friends, colleagues, students and fellow activists, from whom I learned a great deal. In 1999–2010, I edited the Jerusalem Van Leer Institute's journal *Theory & Criticism*, and I benefitted tremendously from both the writers and reviewers of the journal. Some of the ideas comprising the book were initially spelled out in my editorials during this period. I would like to thank the Jerusalem Van Leer Institute for providing a canopy under which the journal's complete political freedom was vigorously upheld. Some of the ideas were also published in various essays in the "Books" supplement of *Ha'aretz*. I wish to thank its two consecutive editors: Michael Handelsatz and Dror Mishani, for their invitations and encouragements. I am thankful to Nir Bar'am and Yaron Sadan for providing me a home at Am Oved, the publishing house which published the first version of the book in Hebrew. Thanks also go out to Benny Nuriely, for his insights on the "New Nostalgia," and to Rivi Gillis who first helped me to develop some of these ideas in our class on "Society in Israel" at Tel Aviv University; and thanks go to Professor Amnon Raz Karkotzkin and Dr. Hillel Cohen, for their original thoughts regarding the rights of the Jews. Thanks to those who have read the manuscript and gave me wise comments: Shlomit Benjamin, Dr. Hagai Boas, Professor Gil Eyal, Ella Glass, Yuval Evri, Uri Misgav, Regv Nathansohn, Professor Adi Ophir, Dr. Alexandra Kalev, Tom Pessah, Professor Haggai Ram, Areej Sabbagh Khouri, Talia Shif and Mati Shmueloff. Special thanks go to Efrat Weiss, who translated the first chapter into English. Deepest thanks go to Dimi Reider who translated the rest of the manuscript into English, and provided eloquent comments that improved the quality of this text.

I had the wonderful opportunity of working with Professor John Thompson, the Editor at Polity Press, and of benefitting from his intellectual insights. His suggestions on editing and articulation of ideas were marvellous and contributed a great deal to the final shape of the book. I am also grateful to the two anonymous reviewers, who helped remove unnecessary obstacles.

I am particularly grateful to Professor Lama Abu Odeh of the faculty of Law in Georgetown University, for her insightful and critical Foreword for the English-speaking world. Her criticism is part and parcel of the book itself, and

needs to be read carefully. Her emphasis on the rights of
the Palestinians comes as a complementary balance to my
emphasis on the rights of the Jews. Many thanks to Dr.
Jennifer Jahn, Editorial Assistant, who made the experience of working with Polity Press an enjoyable one. She was
always there with remarkable patience and astuteness. Lastly,
thanks go to the book's copy-editor, Leigh Mueller.

I could never thank enough the many individuals who
influenced me intellectually and politically during these long
years. In particular, I wish to thank my friends at the Mizrahi
Rainbow Coalition, from whom I learned so much during
the 1990s. Lastly, I owe my deepest love to Hannan Hever
and Effi Ziv. Both urged me to write the book without delay,
read versions of the manuscript and helped me in organization, articulation and the writing of the ideas.

INTRODUCTION AND OVERVIEW: THE CRISIS FACING ZIONIST DEMOCRACY

For over two decades the Israeli liberal bloc has attempted, with massive international support, to implement the two-state solution: Israel and Palestine, partitioned on the basis of the Green Line, which would serve as a territorial signifier for the resolution of the conflict. This solution has been advanced in various imagined adaptations – "disengagement," "border corrections," "including/excluding settlement blocs." Yet even as the two-state idea traveled through European and North-American capitals as an enticing solution, in the political practice of the Middle East it has remained a remarkably hollow slogan. In fact, all the spectacular peace summits – from Oslo to Camp David, from Taba to Annapolis – ended in failure. The widely accepted explanation for the failure in Israel has been the lack of a Palestinian partner to end the conflict.

In this essay, I offer a different interpretation. I suggest that the two sides use different historical languages which do not converge: the language of 1967 and the language

of 1948. For the majority of Israelis, 1967, the year of the
"Six-Day War," is the watershed around which they shape
their memory of the conflict as well as the vista for its resolution. On the other hand, the majority of Palestinians
– including those who support the two-state principle –
interpret the conflict and define the political horizon for its
resolution through the lens of the 1948 war. Examining the
solution through the language of 1967, whilst denying the
1948 question, eliminates the chances for sincere dialogue
with the Palestinians and does not offer a genuine solution
to the Israelis, denying as it does the core issues pertaining to the conflict. This is the main reason for the failure of
the Oslo Accords, a procedural mechanism that sentenced
the historical origins of the conflict (e.g. the Palestinian
refugees, the Jerusalem question, the problem of the Jewish
settlements) to oblivion. The Israelis will need to muster the
courage to deal with the 1948 question – it will not disappear
without recognition. To achieve that, many segments of the
society in Israel will need to abandon the 1967 language as
well as its border perception based on the "Green Line." As
I argue below, the Green Line is a cultural myth, harnessed
to advance the economic–political and cultural interests of a
broad liberal Jewish stratum of society in Israel. This is the
source of the paradox: the principal obstacle for a shift in the
historical language resides with the liberal classes frequently
referred to as "leftist," who have a significant impact in shaping and offering solutions to the conflict.

This liberal "left" offers an outlook on the conflict derived
from a cultural and politico-economic position which is both
sectorial and conservative. In fact, among the Jewish political
right there has long been broad agreement that the 1948 war
is the pivotal question which needs to be addressed – rather
than concealed. Consequently, a renewed thinking about a
solution to the conflict calls for redrawing the Israeli politi-

cal map – including reshaping the conventional distinction between "left" and "right" – in a manner which may produce surprising new alliances. These are the tasks I undertake in this essay.

In a broader perspective, I wish to offer an option for alternative Jewish political thinking. I refer to it as "Jewish" because I write it as a Jew, who holds Jewish political privileges, who is concerned about the future of the Jewish collective in the Middle East and fears that the present path may lead to the annihilation of the Palestinian people and to collective Jewish suicide. Instead of counting on the violence of the nation-state as Zionism's primary mechanism of emancipation, we should return to the discussion about political rights of the Jews themselves, which started during the emancipation in Europe.[1]

My proposition to lay the ground for political thinking based on the 1948 paradigm is not, therefore, an attempt to deny the Jewish collective its right to self-definition. It is rather the opposite: I propose returning to a historical and epistemological time which will enable the formulation of a new political theory and ensure the position and future of Jews in the region. The Jews will need to formulate a new political vision which will take into consideration other peoples in the region, and at the same time define political rights for themselves.

A LINE DRAWN WITH A GREEN PENCIL

The Green Line is the eastern armistice border determined in 1949, at the end of a war between Israel and its Arab neighbors: Jordan, Egypt, Syria and Lebanon. It served as an administrative borderline of cease-fire and a snapshot of the status quo at the end of the 1948 war. The line was termed "green" because it was drawn with a green pencil on the Rhodes Agreements debate maps. In January 1949, first Israeli Prime Minister David Ben Gurion summoned the "Temporary State Assembly" in order to discuss the border outline and responded to his right-wing opponents – among whom was poet Uri Zvi Grinberg, who called the outline a "Jewish tragicomedy . . . a Purim farce"[2] – that the line was needed to cement Israel's military achievements. We may note, however, that even Ben Gurion, who represented the more moderate hegemonic faction, expressed indecisiveness concerning the drawing of the Green Line:

> The Bible contains various definitions of Israel's borders and so does our history. The topic is therefore endless. No border is absolute. If the border is a desert – it may include the other end, and if it is a sea – it may include the opposite shore. This has always been the way of the world – only the terms were different. If we will find a path to other planets – the earth may not be enough.[3]

The Green Line was sketched by politicians, diplomats, measurers, cartographers and geographers and was seen as the war's greatest Jewish achievement, because it secured Israeli rule over a far greater territory than the one allotted to it in the UN Partition Plan (Resolution 181, also referred to as the November 29 1947 Resolution). The Green Line allocated to Israel 79 percent of Mandatory Palestine, as opposed to the 55 percent assigned to it in the Partition Plan.

The Palestinians were not involved in the armistice agreements and never asked about the border, despite the fact that it shaped their lives and changed their societies beyond recognition. At the time, the Palestinians were not recognized as a national group – neither by the international institutions nor by the Arab states, nor by the State of Israel. As Tom Segev writes: "When Israelis referred to 'Arabs' they meant mostly Egypt, Jordan, Syria, Lebanon and Iraq; not the Palestinians." He adds:

> Since their flight and expulsion in the War of Independence, the Palestinians were no longer considered a part of the enemy forces, and were almost only mentioned as a diplomatic nuisance: Refugees whose case was discussed by the United Nations once a year. Terrorist acts were also largely attributed to the Arab states rather than to the Palestinian national struggle.[4]

The Green Line was therefore an arbitrary border. It ignored the existence of a Palestinian society, overlooked its political, urban and social infrastructure, cruelly dismembered its villages, towns and urban societies, separated families and sentenced the history of the conflict between Jews and Palestinians before the 1948 war to oblivion. "Whatever happened, happened, and the past cannot be revoked," explained the Jewish Governor of Jerusalem Dov Yosef to members of the UN Truth and Reconciliation Committee.[5] That position was fixed as a starting point for the culture and politics of the new regime.

Later, the Green Line – although it was determined in 1949 – was labeled the "1967 borders," and became a signifier for the "legitimate" (or "proper") Israel. Moreover, the Green Line has metamorphosed over the years from a territorial–material signifier into a deeply rooted cultural and politico-economic paradigm. The more it was eliminated in practice by the Jewish settlement enterprise in the West Bank after 1967,[6] (proving again that Zionism is a settlers' movement), the more its mythological significance grew.[7] The arbitrary border drawn with a green pencil in Rhodes colored the historic time of four generations of Israelis who lived it and imagined it in their literature and culture.

TIME AND SPACE

Time is a political concept and, as such, it is a tool for the formation of cultures, populations and identities. As Michael Young has suggested, every year can be seen as Year Zero. The key step is the framing of several events into a certain fragment of time and their declaration as "ours."[8] In other words, every social hegemony chooses a "beginning" and endows it with mythical cultural meanings.[9] There are considerable differences between various cultural perceptions of time: secular and religious time, linear and circular time, agricultural and industrial time, biological and social time, or majority and minority time. Political groups struggle over perceptions of time, arrange it, and wed it to cultural and historical meanings. When human societies lack a common language of time, it is difficult for them to find meeting points for political dialogue or a shared existence. [10]

In classical mechanics, time and space existed as two separate and independent entities. The theory of relativity, however, bound the two into a knot which cannot be untied. The modern (as well as postmodern) Quantum Physics which followed recognizes terms like the "shrinking" and "expansion" of time, "time loops," "multiple parallel worlds" and "time travel," which is also travel through space – all of which classical mechanics was unable to recognize. This insight is important as it enables us to look into the manners in which time organizes space as well as the ways in which divisions of space verify the cosmology of time.

The practice of juxtaposing time and space can be found in literary theory – for example, in the works of Mikhail Bakhtin, who formulated the theory of the "chronotope," which viewed the history of the novel as a point of convergence between time and space; in the political thought of David Harvey who rephrased the need to view the global structure as one unit of time/space in economics, culture and politics; or in the anthropological works of Johannes Fabian, who showed how different conceptions of time among Europeans and indigenous populations created racial hierarchies and justified imperialist conquests.[11] Scientific evolutionism enabled imperial anthropologists to define the meeting point between imperialist and colonized native as an encounter in time, through which the native is perceived as an early precursor of modern man, prior to his socio-cultural evolution.[12]

Therefore, space is also the result of the definition of time applied to it, an idea that can be described as "spatialized time." In the words of psychoanalyst Jacques-Alain Miller, "Spatialized time [is] the time identified with a line, represented by a line – this geometrical time is a result of the control enforced over time."[13] The time of the Green Line is thus a spatialized time expressed in what has been defined as the 1967 paradigm.

THE DEGENERATION OF THE 1967 PARADIGM

A paradigm is an epistemological and social framework through which a certain reality is defined. In the early 1960s Thomas Kuhn published *The Structure of Scientific Revolutions*, in which he explains how scientific paradigms described as "normal" create a dogmatic structure of consciousness and awareness which continues to exist by the force of inertia until its eventual collapse.[14] This dogmatism is expressed through entrenchment and power struggles, which serve to preserve power structures through the knee-jerk dismissal of more successful alternatives. Each paradigm busily creates structures of denial for the circumvention of anomalies – deviations, digressions and maladaptations – that it itself continuously generates by its very existence.

However, as noted by Kuhn, the anomalies are destined to defeat the paradigm, which will collapse and be replaced by other alternatives.

The 1967 paradigm – with the imaginary spatial time of the Green Line at its core – is based on numerous "political anomalies." Until the early 1980s these anomalies were invisible to the public in Israel, having been blurred by an ideological discourse that constructed the conflict as divorced from Israel's own actions. The injustices and distortions created by the Green Line were justified by a discourse of "security," which forever presented Israel's wars as inevitable wars of self-defense.

And still, these "anomalies" deepened over the years, leaving Jewish Israel in a state of deep melancholia. At the same time, international criticism grew, even among Jewish thinkers, arguing that Zionism, emerging from a just attempt to solve the problem faced by Jews in Europe, has turned into a problem, even for the Jews: not only because Israel has become one of the least safe places to live in, but mostly because Zionism has metamorphosed from a political movement, legitimate for its day and age, into a destructive war machine which justifies its immorality with circular arguments and fossilizes its own thinking.[15]

The crisis comes to emphatic expression in political thought in Israel: in the absence of a democratic tradition detached from emergency regulations (some call it "ethnic democracy"), political thought has long been afflicted with paralysis. Symptoms of the malaise include a blurring of boundaries between society and state, the active work of self-censorship mechanisms, the lack of a political alternative and the creation of vacuous oppositions (mainly between left and right).[16]

The degeneration of present-day Zionist thought is revealed through an apocalyptic discourse, an ever-growing escapism, and in the sense that "the political reality and moral atmosphere in Israel have begun to show a distressing resemblance to that of Europe between the two World Wars."[17] One should note, for example, the increased demand for European passports among Israelis during the past five years. It is true that this frenzy is partly due to the opportunities which opened in Europe, but at the same time many of these passport holders seek an insurance policy for fear that one of the apocalyptic prophecies will materialize.[18]

Jewish-German-American sociologist Herbert Marcuse calls a society based on political paralysis while upholding well-developed mechanisms of self-censorship a one-dimensional society.[19] Such a society sustains pseudo-democratic regimes, including formal (or procedural) democracy and freedom of speech. But at the same time, on the central issues of the political agenda, the thought is paralyzed and almost uniform.[20] The symbiosis between left and right is the cause and effect of the one-dimensionality which rejects any type of discourse that strays beyond the boundaries of consensus. Despite the discord, which creates an illusion of pluralism, the democracy produced within the framework of the paradigm is fractionalized, in a perpetual state of violent conflict (with Israel's expansive reliance on emergency legislation and states of emergency as one of its quintessential expressions), thus turning the State of Israel into a gigantic security corporation.

A one-dimensional society of this sort came to exist in Israel, among other reasons, because it denied the 1948 question, closeting skeletons which may threaten its morality and justification. As Stanley Cohen suggested, historical skeletons are kept in closets due to the political need to be free of disturbing facts.[21] The skeletons kept in Israel's closet, as well as the near-total lack of investigative curiosity about them, are symptoms of the crisis in the Zionist democracy expressed in the Green Line and the 1967 paradigm. Liberal Israel will need to "come out of the closet" and formulate its positions and responsibility vis-à-vis the 1948 question, which the 1967 paradigm conceals and blurs.

The 1967 paradigm constructs the memory of the conflict relying on three distinct historical periods:

1) 1949–67. The first period is the State of Israel's historical time up until 1967 and includes the nation-building processes (e.g. the writing of Israeli law, the division of space and lands and the dispersal of population) which have created the Green Line paradigm and upheld it with the help of a cultural, economic and political infrastructure.

2) 1967–93. The second period, which commenced in 1967 is, in the mindset of the Israeli liberals, the "Archimedean point" of the conflict. Although the period marked the gradual erasure of the spatial presence of the Green Line, mostly as a result of the occupation and the Jewish settlement enterprise, the cultural imagination began to thicken the spatialized time of the Green Line into a mythical entity. In other words, it was extracted from history and gained an independent standing all of its own. The time of the Green Line carried nostalgia for a "just" Israel, as it was alleged to exist within the realms of that line. Well-known Israeli author David Grossman's *The Yellow Wind*, written in the late 1980s, was a foundational text for this nostalgia, which views the post-1967 conquests as a regrettable accident in Israel's political history and as a temporary condition which would be resolved upon the state's return to the June 4, 1967 borders.

3) 1993 and onwards. During the third period, which budded during the first Intifada in 1988 and matured during the Oslo Accords (1994), the term "separation" was added to the "Green Line." Although separation is colorless, it

is based on the transformation of the Green Line into an imaginary time/space, which later received various epithets such as the "Fence of Life" and the "Security Fence." Thus, despite the fact that the Green Line was wiped out in reality, due to the colonial settlements in the West Bank, its fundamental cultural principle was maintained as an instrument for the preservation of separation between Jews and Palestinians.[22]

These are the primary historical pillars of the 1967 paradigm. Through these three periods, liberal Israelis imagine their state as a democracy which went astray after 1967 and would regain its glory upon the retreat to the 1967 borders. Paradoxically, the anchoring of the 1967 borders as a cultural myth coincided with their de-facto blurring, almost to the point of their total annihilation in the daily lives of Jewish settlers, as well as in maps which depict the territory of Israel's sovereignty.[23] In the following pages I will describe the socio-political and economo-political infrastructure of the Green Line and will suggest diverting the discussions pertaining to the conflict from a paradigm anchored in the Green Line to the conflict's earlier roots, which were normalized and blurred in Israeli law from 1948 onwards. Accordingly, I will refer to them as the 1967 paradigm and the 1948 paradigm.

The 1967 paradigm is the paradigm which Israel deploys whenever it engages in negotiations with the Palestinians. But the 1967 paradigm is an illusion which will not yield a resolution to the conflict, as its core issues – principally the Palestinian refugees, Israel's Palestinian citizens, the settlement enterprise and the theological demands of Jews and Arabs – are either denied in it or, at best, defined as political anomalies.[24]

These "political anomalies" express radical resistance to

the Green Line paradigm, upheld by four primary groups: (1) 1948 refugees, for whom the Green Line stops the historical time in 1948 – for some of them, 1967 not only constitutes a moment of occupation, but also one of liberation and the opening of space for the reunion of cities, villages and families; (2) supporters of the idea of a "Greater Israel" (among whom there are many notable differences) – these can be found in strong political parties, and are an effective lobby in the Knesset (the Israeli parliament) and in the successive governments; (3) the "Third Israel" – Mizrachi (Jews from Arab countries, sometimes referred to as "Arab Jews"), settlers represented mostly by Shas, Haredi (Ultra Orthodox) settlers, and poor immigrants from the former Soviet Union, represented largely by current Foreign Minister Avigdor Lieberman;[25] (4) a politically radical spine of 1948 Israeli Arabs, such as the Abnaa al-Balad (Sons of the Land) movement, segments of the Palestinian groups that do not accept the Green Line, and Palestinian intellectuals who have been advancing this agenda in recent years.[26] Each of the groups, who identify themselves as "Arabs of 1948" opposes the definition of the Green Line, as well as its observance, and all view it (in all its imagined versions) as an arbitrary and violent border.

It is true that there are other forces at work among Israeli Palestinians (Arabs of 1948), some of whom accept the 1967 paradigm and use it to struggle for their position within the society in Israel.[27] Moreover, in the Palestinian territories, Palestinians like Abu Mazen and Salam Fayyad recognize the 1967 borders and strive to reach within them a decent resolution for their plight, with massive international support. At the same time, however, Abu Mazen has never accepted Israel's "border corrections" in the West Bank and has never consented to Israel's demands for recognition as a Jewish State.[28] Recently, voices began to be heard in the

Fatah movement, calling for the relinquishment of the "two states for two peoples" model in favor of one state.[29] Meron Benvenisti argued – and I fully agree with him – that even the Palestinians beyond the Green Line will gradually begin to view themselves as "Arabs of 1948," a definition so far used to describe Palestinians who carry Israeli citizenship.[30]

The 1967 paradigm – as manifested in politics, culture, society and economy – is the main obstacle faced by Israelis confronted with the conflict and its historical sources. This paradigm creates a "beginning" to the conflict through a truncated and fragmented time–space perception, which locks out the 1948 problem; each attempt to return to 1948, or to express such a desire, is blocked by a taboo. The "entries" to critical engagement with the history of the conflict have been barred: the 1948 war has turned from history to myth with the help of elaborate mnemonic technologies operated on all levels of state, society and culture.[31] Israeli text books, for example, do not contain a comprehensive history of the war, and instead describe only the Zionist perspective. The conflict of 1948 is deeply presented in Israeli culture as a war between David (the Jews) and Goliath (the Palestinians). The 1948 question was further blurred in the conception of Israeli citizenship and in the political thinking that produced the model of the "Jewish and Democratic State" through the use of intellectual acrobatics and complex justification regimes. The assumption that 1948 is closed and sealed rests firmly on a variety of interrelated causes, e.g. fear, political interests and the prospect of relinquishing cultural, economic and other privileges.[32]

I believe that the political anomalies embedded in the 1967 paradigm will lead eventually to its collapse, and the repressed question of 1948 will resurface on the agenda in its stead – also among Jews.[33] Signs of such reappearance are already evident in the public discourse on the conflict. The questions of the 1948 law and the Israeli citizenship regime, including the violence the latter embeds, will resurface with full force over time.[34] The return to the 1948 question will force the Jews living in Israel to confront the painful fact that the war is not yet over[35] and millions of refugees await a discussion of their fate as well as that of the lands and property expropriated by the State of Israel.[36] The 1948 paradigm will allow Israeli Jews to reconsider the epistemology of the conflict and the division of space, and may tackle some of the anomalies brought about by the present situation. It will require complex thinking about the future, including the production of more creative models which will enable both Jewish and Palestinian sovereignties over the space.

The replacement of the 1967 paradigm with the 1948 alternative will alter the contours of the political map in Israel. The present political division into "right," "left" and "center" is simplistic and is determined solely on the basis of the position vis-à-vis the Palestinian territories conquered by Israel in 1967: those who believe that all or some of the territories occupied in 1967 should be returned to the Palestinians for the establishment of a state alongside the State of Israel, are perceived as the political "left," and vice versa. I would like to show that this distinction is false and that the liberal left in Israel holds political and social views which, in any other context, would be considered nationalist, conservative and even right-wing.

The liberal (and white) Jewish left focuses on the war against the settlements in order to preserve the Israel of the Green Line, thus sentencing the 1948 question to oblivion. The 1948 paradigm would suggest, for example, that some of the settlements within the Green Line (for example, Jewish Nazareth which was founded to expedite the Judaization of the Galilee) are no less repressive to the Palestinian society than the settlements in the West Bank. Moreover, the 1967 paradigm fails to provide a solution to the settlement enterprise and is even more oblivious to its broad ethnic and class aspects. The fact that the Green Line was erased in practice by the settlers, and in consciousness by the state and society, is absent from the political thinking of the Israeli liberal left and the solutions it offers to the conflict. Although over 40 years have passed since the "Six-Day War," the liberal left continues to view the June 4, 1967 lines as Israel's imagined borders. The occupations which followed 1967 and the settlement enterprise are seen as a temporary situation – an accident in Israel's political history. At the time, the 1967 war also created an agenda for the Zionist left as it enabled a shift of the (im)moral space beyond the Green Line and the cemented depiction of the 1948 injustices as irreversible. This position has allowed the denial of the colonial practices exercised by Israel prior to 1967 (e.g. the oppressive military regime over the Palestinians and the use of emergency regulations until December 1966) and has disguised the fact that Israel is already a bi-national society with a regime based on apartheid policies.

THE ZIONIST-LIBERAL LEFT AND THE PEACE ACCORDS

The liberal left in Israel has entrenched itself in the 1967 paradigm, and has turned the Green Line (which now includes "border corrections" to annex a big block of Jewish settlements in the West Bank) into a symbolic Maginot Line and a political fetish, despite its gradual erasure from the Israeli consciousness and from the maps which present Israel's territorial sovereignty.[37] For example, in 2006 Minister of Education Yul Tamir – a Labor MK (Member of Knesset) – asked for all new textbook editions containing maps to clearly indicate the Green Line.[38] Zeev Sternhell, a spokesperson for the Israeli liberal left argued emphatically that the Green Line is "The Border" and that "it is necessary to deepen and establish the status of the armistice line [the Green Line] in the consciousness of young Israelis."[39] He does not say how Israel will pull out 500,000 settlers, and does not discuss its moral ramifications.

This perception attributes autonomous and mythical qualities to the Green Line, so much so that the political consciousness of the liberal left ascribes the term "occupation" only to the 1967 conquests.[40] This practice has also a politico-economic foundation. The left (also referred to as "moderate")[41] wing of the Zionist Labor movement – including Mapam and Hashomer Hatzair – swallowed lands and Palestinian property appropriated after the 1948 war and have profited from them. The Jewish "left" was always active in normalizing the injustices created by the Israel of the Green Line.[42]

Thinking through the language of the Green Line has allowed Israel to claim that "there is no partner" to talk to, sentencing Israel to a long period of bloodshed. When in 2000 the Palestinians declined Ehud Barak's "generous offer" in Camp David, many Israelis, as well as members of the international community, interpreted it as the ultimate proof of the lack of a Palestinian partner.[43] However, the basic assumption with which the Israelis were equipped when they arrived for the negotiations, encouraged by the United States and the international community, was limited. It was based on the sterility of the 1967 paradigm, which erased the question of the Palestinian refugees, blurred the historical sources of the conflict and limited them to border corrections along the Green Line.

Israel's Foreign Minister in 1999–2000, Shlomo Ben-Ami, a Tel Aviv Professor of History, describes the negotiations with the Palestinians on the basis of the Green Line: "As far as I know, before Camp David we received a 2% deposit from the Palestinians. We therefore assumed that we would go beyond 90 percent and they would reach beyond 4 percent, and that we would eventually meet somewhere in the middle."[44] And he concludes: "Throughout the process the Palestinians did not accept our most basic parameters. I therefore concluded that we should not continue to produce back-door diplomacy papers. They do not obligate the Palestinians and serve them only for the preparatory weakening of the target."

Shlomo Ben-Ami, a historian, comes here to an a-historical conclusion. Drawing on the time of the Green Line, his inference sentences the history of the conflict to oblivion and reduces it to the 1967 question (including "border corrections" and an inventory of territorial percentages).[45] In response to a question about a Palestinian counteroffer, he states the following: "No. This is the heart of the matter. There are never any Palestinian counteroffers. There never was one and there never will be." Palestinians' unwillingness to offer border corrections is perceived as a fraud – "a gigantic camouflage behind which he [Arafat] has exercised political pressure and terrorism." Ben-Ami's conclusion regarding the Palestinian "deception" reveals an essential failure in the understanding of the conflict and its sources. Later, with the hindsight of eight years, Ehud Barak formulated the reason for the fact that "there are never any Palestinian counteroffers" and did so with greater historical awareness than that expressed by Ben-Ami: "I went to Arafat and discovered that he does not wish to resolve the '67 problem, but rather the '47 one. Arafat is dead, but I am still held responsible. I am not forgiven for having revealed a truth that collapsed the secular religion of the left."[46]

This quote should be read with great care, as it is symptomatic of the fallacy in which political thought in Israel is ensnared. Barak's words are accurate: there is indeed a disconnect between the 1967 paradigm held by the Jews and the 1947/8 paradigm of the Palestinians. However, instead of exposing a "lack of partner," Barak in fact revealed that the 1967 separation paradigm could not serve as a basis for conflict resolution. It is not for nothing that Barak ridicules the left's continuing and fruitless attempt to achieve an agreement with the Palestinians based on 1967, and refers to it as a "secular religion." In hindsight, Barak and his Camp David partners moved in a circular motion: they proposed the 1967 paradigm to the summit only in order to dismiss it.[47] In retrospect, Barak acknowledged the Israeli delegation left for Camp David while laboring under the basic fallacy of the separation idea. But that same Barak continues to lead himself and his friends on the same unsuccessful path of the 1967 paradigm ("with border corrections"), whether as a political tactic aimed at camouflaging his considerably more hawkish views, or as a result of the very same blindness he described.[48]

Israel's "no partner" claim is a clear product of the 1967 paradigm and the primary reason for the establishment of the Kadima Party by Ariel Sharon, which sought to continue the process of "disengagement" with an additional plan referred to as the "convergence plan."[49] The plan to "converge" on a permanent border did not signal an end to the Occupation, but rather the opposite: it aimed to reap its fruits in order to annex the large settlement blocs under the guise of the end of the 1967 occupation. The plan was based on the annexation of large parts of East Jerusalem and the division of the West Bank into four large cantons, thereby preventing the establishment of a Palestinian sovereignty with territorial continuity. This unilateralism is Israel's prime existential strategy.

One prominent example of this position is the unfounded

claim that Israel withdrew from Gaza in 2005. As colonial history has taught us, occupation can be administered from a distance, without permanent military presence and without settlers. Israel is still operating an occupation regime in Gaza, as it denies the Strip a legitimate government, controls its economy, held the border crossings exclusively until 2011, prevents access from the sea and air and wages an ongoing campaign for the elimination of the leaders of the struggle. Up to 2011, each week, Israel's Ministry of Defense decided how many calories a Gaza subject would consume and which products would enter the Strip. The alleged end to occupation in Gaza, and the disengagement which accompanied it, only mark the continued colonization by other means. The pretense of ending occupation in Gaza has only deepened the political and humanitarian disaster which Israel has brought upon it.[50]

Meanwhile, desperate Israelis are fed with the dangerous "no partner" approach, in which cause and effect interlock into a circle. We should therefore examine the discourse around the rockets fired from Gaza on the south of Israel. The central claim in this discourse is that for eight years Israel's south had been subject to constant rocket fire whereas Israel held back for a long time before it attacked. Yet the conflict did not begin eight years ago and was not born in the area surrounding Gaza: its roots go back to the time before the War of 1948. In 2009, Israel declared war on the Gaza Strip. In the three weeks of that war, it killed approximately 1,400 people – many of them offspring of Palestinian refugees who fled to the Gaza Strip in 1948 or in the following years – and committed other war crimes. The euphoria in Israel at the onset of the war was great, only to discover that the destruction and havoc wreaked in Gaza did not stop the Palestinian armed struggle.

As in other cases in which Israel declared an essentially

one-sided war on the Palestinians (one prominent example is that of Lebanon in 1982), the assault on Gaza did not take place because "Israel had no other choice." The war resulted from a systematic choice made repeatedly by Israel's decision-makers to deny the 1948 question as well as any Palestinian nationhood that does not lean on the barrels of Israeli guns. The extent of the destruction in Gaza in 2009 astonished liberal Israel, but its moral questions were whitewashed by a militaristic discourse of security experts who eviscerated ethical questions and replaced them with a security logic that persistently confuses cause with effect. Terrorist attacks were presented as the cause of the war instead of a symptom of the political crisis and a response to Israel's colonial rule over the space. This vicious circle will inevitably lead to another Israeli attack which will destroy further parts of Palestinian society (houses, mosques, schools or public institutions) without, however, halting its struggle against Israel. The outcome may be the slow but systematic destruction of Palestinian society, in which Israel continues to act as an aggressive war machine.[51]

The staggering "peace process" is part of a sterile simulation-game of peace, which has gone on since the early 1990s, all around the 1967 paradigm. The sad fact is that the peace industry, including the Geneva Initiative for a two-state solution, engages neither in peace nor in conflict resolution, and its most notable result to date was providing a living for dozens, if not hundreds, of non-governmental organizations (NGOs), without any real political result. This industry ignores the fact that the actions taken beyond the Green Line merely emulate what happened within that same line for two decades before the Occupation. It further disregards the fact that the settlement enterprise is rooted in a political-economic system which cannot be catalogued in the traditional distinction between political "left" and "right."

One issue that needs to be explored is the ethnic and class make-up of the Jewish population settled in the territories. It should be asked why the inhabitants of the periphery of the settlement movement, in Maale Edumim or in the area surrounding Jerusalem, would generally fall under the category of the Third Israel:[52] Mizrachim (Jews from Arab countries), immigrants from the former Soviet Union and the poor ultra-Orthodox Jews, who all improved their living conditions through the erasure of the Green Line. Will the Third Israel agree to relinquish its economic achievements, if only in the settlements' periphery, in order to pacify white liberal peace politics? After all, this particular route of the "peace process" was shaped by the interests of the white elites, associated largely with the liberal left.

This context may also help us to understand the price of the "secularity" embedded in the 1967 paradigm. The position advancing a secular liberal Israel within the 1967 borders overlooks the fact that the majority of the population, from the Mediterranean Sea to the Jordan River, Jewish or Palestinian, is not secular and does not accept a mechanical form of sovereignty which is not imbued with theological contents.[53]

For example, Eliaz Cohen, a settler from Kfar Etzion, calls for a theological dialogue between settlers and Hamas towards a division of space detached from the principles of the liberal left:

The ascent of Hamas tore the camouflage from the Israeli–Palestinian conflict: it is a religious-national conflict at its very core. As evident in the choice that they made, the Palestinians are already aware of this. And where do the Israelis stand on this matter? They are still entrenched in dogmatic, anxious – one may even say post-traumatic – thinking, and were recently captivated to no small a degree by escapism – as demonstrated by the mandate-monster known as the Kadima Party.[54]

The Jewish liberal left refuses or finds it difficult to see "the elephant in the room": present-day Israel is, de facto, a bi-national entity which spans from the Mediterranean Sea to the Jordan River. This reality no longer allows a just two-state solution and forces the liberal left to detach itself from its nostalgic attitude towards pre-1967 Israel. This nostalgia – in fact a delusion – which I term the "new nostalgia" is one that denies the historical sources of the conflict.

THE LIBERAL NEW NOSTALGIA

The Green Line defines a moral system according to which Israel was a moral and just democracy prior to 1967. This view allows one to ingest the moral and political distortions which had taken place within the Green Line before 1967, and creates an agenda which outsources the moral and political issues from within the Green Line to the territories outside of it. This agenda points out the political distortions outside the Green Line, but is blind to political distortions within it. In other words, the moral stance which is "looking out" is a reversed mirror-image of the denial of the political distortions within the 1967 borders. This is one of the reasons for this position's disregard of the erasure of the Green Line and the persistent imagination of Israel within its earlier borders.

This position has been emphatically expressed in what I would like to refer to as the new nostalgia: a literature of nostalgia for the Israel of the Labor Zionist movement, for the sense of morality and righteousness, for a European Israel, a "melting pot" Israel – the "beautiful Israel" which ostensibly existed before the Jewish peripheries invaded the heart of its political map and before the Occupation of 1967. This nostalgia is represented in Ashkenazi Jewish white identity politics of a wide liberal stratum, which will be discussed in greater detail below. At this stage, I will simply quote Yossi Beilin, one of the prominent architects of the two-state solution, who longs for the decade before 1967 – "the most beautiful decade of our existence" – and wishes to bequeath the time of the Green Line to the next generations: "All I am trying to do is to ensure that my grandchildren will be able to live in this country as I did during the most beautiful and peaceful decade in its existence, 1957–1967 . . . For two thirds of my life, I have been trying to return to the Israel I was robbed of in 1967."[55]

The new nostalgia has created a synthetic and false distinction between pre-1967 Israel and the one that followed it. Was Israel so beautiful and just in the eyes of the hundreds of thousands of Palestinian refugees deprived of their homes during the War of 1948, and barred from returning to them afterwards? And of the Palestinians within the Green Line, who had to live under oppressive military occupation until 1966? And of the Mizrachim, who were forced to live outside the urban centers and turned into the spine of what we refer to as the Second Israel?[56]

The new nostalgia expresses yearning for pre-1967 Israel, when it still appeared that the political hegemony was secular, Jewish and Ashkenazi. This was the era before Jewish political-theological movements broke into the heart of the political arena and challenged the liberal culture, with Rabbi Kook's messianic Hassidim dancing in Sebastia (a settlement in the West Bank); the educational network of the Shas movement beginning to preach for an Halacha theological state; the Baba Sali's holy water in Netivot; the sermons of Shas spiritual leader Rabbi Ovadia Yossef; the charm and amulets of Rabbi Yossef Kaduri; the assaults on the Supreme

Court and on the (relatively) large number of Mizrachim in the political sphere.[57] The new nostalgia longs for a Jewish-Ashkenazi-secular Israel within the 1967 borders, thereby upholding a violent, distorted political model which denies the ethnic cleansing of 1948, the military regime over the Arabs of 1948, the state of emergency which pervaded until 1967 within the Green Line, and the Jewish takeover of Arab privately and communally owned lands.[58]

The new nostalgia is a cultural sentiment of the Jewish elites from the liberal middle class and the majority of professionals: technocrats, public servants, jurists, academics of the humanities and in the social sciences, diplomats, retired Israel Defense Force (IDF) generals and journalists – most of whom voted for the Kadima Party, the Labor Party or Meretz. It is the population which can be referred to as "the half of the nation that supports the peace process," or, according to a more operative definition – the population which supported the Oslo Accords.[59] This part of the population is well represented in the media, civil service, IDF, cultural sphere and academia. Among the paradigm's key thinkers, one may find prominent journalists, e.g. Amos Elon, Ari Shavit, Tom Segev, Yoel Marcus, Yossi Sarid, Nahum Barnea, Amos Shoken, Yoel Esteron, Amnon Dankner and Dan Margalit. The list could further be enriched with vocal academics such as Amon Rubinstein, Alex Jacobson, Nissim Kalderon, Yaron Ezrahi and Dan Shiftan,[60] and often-quoted legalists like Ruth Gabison, Aharon Barak, Talya Sasson and Mordechai Kremnitzer. Demographers such as Arnon Sofer and Sergio Della Pergola also belong here, as well as prominent (allegedly moderate) politicians like Haim Ramon, Yossi Beilin, Ehud Olmert, Dan Meridor, Tzipi Livni, Amram Mitzna, Avraham Burg and Ehud Barak, and retired generals such as Matan Vilnai, Shaul Arieli, Uzi Dayan and a veritable parade of generals in the Council for Peace and Security. The nostalgia of the Green Line has been the organizing principle of post-1967 historiography, academic research, liberal journalism and canonical cultural products like the ones produced by Amos Oz, A. B. Yehoshua, David Grossman, Joshua Sobol and Shmuel Hasfari.[61] It is the nostalgia of a political group which is identified with the left but advances the nationalistic ideas anchored in the time of the Green Line.

Underneath this cultural-political layer lies a political-economic one, of interest groups and financial networks, agricultural landowners, kibbutzim and *moshavim*.[62] This is a class which is maintained by the Israeli land regime. Many of its sons and daughters supported Kadima; Kadima was established by Ariel Sharon, who for many years and in various positions held sway over all manner of infrastructures as well as the allocation and expropriation of lands, through absolute power over the Israel Land Administration and funds raised through the Jewish Agency and the Jewish National Fund (JNF).[63]

The central control mechanisms of this political-economic stratum are the "regional councils" – an Israeli mutation of the system shaped in settlers' societies and used as a model for the Occupation of land during the colonial era.[64] Through these regional councils, Israel has upheld a distorted privilege-based regime of land allotment, based on racial, ethnic and class discrimination. In this framework, exclusively Jewish villages and communities were established on expropriated Palestinian lands, producing inflated judiciary councils intended to ensure control over the land rather than distributive justice. For example, Dror Etkes, from Yesh Din – Volunteers for Human Rights, explains that the Gush Etzion regional council was meant to "legitimize the takeover of hundreds of thousands of dunams of Palestinian lands." There are presently 16 official settlements in the Gush Etzion regional council, as well as Efrat and Beitar

Illit (settlements in the West Bank which are considered separate councils), but also 17 semi-official settlements.[65] As I will show below, the regional councils serve as instruments for the territorial mechanisms of the privilege regime and the segregation it cultivates. The councils ensure the position of the settlements not only beyond the Green Line, but also within its borders.

SEPARATION

The year 1967 was not only the one in which Israel started to annex territories beyond the Green Line, but also the year of the establishment of the Public Council for Demography, which has sought to manage the ethnic and racial profile of Israel as a Jewish state within the Green Line. This is in light of the "demographic threat" which Israel faces.[66] The demographic logic is a product of the time of the Green Line and the cause for the demand for "separation," just as "separation" has become the cause for the demographic struggle. Israel's present separation policy – known in Israel as "hafrada," a Hebrew word which can mean both segregation and separation – is a natural continuation of the cultural-political position designed by the new nostalgia and of the demographic project, which constitutes "the continuation of the war through other means."

The separation wall, under construction since 2002, was charted unilaterally in order to produce border contours for the future, based on Ariel Sharon's "Stars Program" – a plan aimed at separating Israelis and Palestinians while annexing more occupied land. The first result of the separation wall is the ongoing transfer of Palestinians trapped between the Green Line and the wall – through economic and bureaucratic pressure – and the disruption of Palestinian territorial continuity in the West Bank. The International Court of

Justice in the Hague and the international community had no difficulty seeing through the warped logic of the wall, which enables continued occupation through a discourse of separation. One prominent example is the 1,700–meter section running along the village of Bil'in. The Supreme Court ruled that the route was designed to include in the "Israeli" (western) side of the wall parts of Matityahu East, a neighborhood of the settlement Modi'in Illit (Kiryat Sefer). The court said "Israel expropriated Palestinian land for the construction of the wall, in the guise of a security necessity."[67] The result was that the route of the separation barrier – as charted by political, military and judiciary officials – acquired a life of its own whilst creating territorial mazes and inflicting human tragedies. One of the striking and revealing facts is that the construction of the wall, which began with great pomp and ceremony, was never completed.[68]

From the staggering and incomplete route of the separation wall we learn that fences do not guarantee proper borders, on either side of the Green Line. Separation walls were also built in Lod and in Ramla – both inside the Green Line – to demarcate territorial separation between Jews and Palestinians within "Israel proper." In other places within the Green Line, walls were built to segregate Jews from Palestinians, rich Jews from poor ones, and Mizrachi, Russian and Ethiopian Jews from Ashkenazim, and so on. The Israeli space is criss-crossed with all forms of separation walls.

The separation principle is a product of ghetto-state thinking, which has gained momentum in the liberal political discourse following 1967. It gained even greater force during the Oslo Accords, which deepened Jewish colonialism in the area between the Mediterranean Sea and the Jordan River, assisted the Israeli bourgeoisie in accumulating wealth and widened the socio-economic, national ethnic and gender gaps.

Interestingly enough, and unlike the Zionist liberal left,

some of the settlers – much like the radical leftists – oppose the separation principle. Ruti Ben Haim, a Jewish settler from Ginot Shomron and an activist against the fence, states: "Those who constructed the fence wanted us to run away. They thought we could not bear the idea of life outside of the State. But I do not live in the State, I live on the Land. Why then should I care if there is a fence running through it?"[69] Vered Noam explains, in the settler monthly *Nekuda*, why the liberal left (also referred to as "Zionist left") supports the separation:[70]

> The reason is . . . a network of barriers which revives the Green Line . . . The left views a barrier as a didactic means, an accelerator of the Jewish recognition in the need to separate between the populations, an exercise in Palestinian statehood . . . However, the central motivation is not the concern for the civil rights of the Palestinians. The continued suffocation and starvation of two million people does not sit well with such a concern. It seems that even yearning for peace is not the true motivation of the left. Those who seek peace would insist on open borders and reciprocal economic ties . . . rather than on separate economies and hermetic borders. But the true stimulus of the left is separation from the Arabs. The closure exposes a surprising similarity between the majority of leftists and the extreme right which upholds the idea of the transfer. The central aspiration of both is to dispose of Arab presence.[71]

Amnon Raz-Krakotzkin offers a similar explanation, from the opposite side of the political map (at least in the map's simplistic definition in Israel):

> The separation principle continues to serve as the basis for Israel's policy in all its shades, and it is also the foundation

for the "peace process" and the basis for its failure. In the eyes of the Israelis the process is not perceived as the basis for reconciliation founded on Palestinian rights and mutual recognition, but rather as a way to dispose of the territories in order to get rid of the Arabs. Rather than a clear political stance, the support of peace is a cultural position which emphasizes the need for a homogenous Jewish state, while ignoring the position of its Palestinian citizens.[72]

THE SETTLERS

The political sterility of the liberal separation paradigm is especially clear when contrasted with the systematic and coherent political thinking in the Israeli political right, which understands all too well the malfunction of the 1967 paradigm and the anomalies it creates. While the liberal left denies the connection between the wars of 1948 and 1967, the political right declares it openly. In his last tenure, Ariel Sharon stated that Israel's war against the Palestinians is that of 1948, or, as he described it, "the second part of 1948."[73]

Many segments of the political right oppose the idea of two states for two peoples and wish to control a single territory spanning from the Mediterranean Sea to the Jordan River. With the cooperation of mainstream Zionist institutions, the political right advanced its solution to the 1948 question: a Jewish state under an apartheid regime. The exploitative and repressive settlement enterprise in its present-day form – led in the past by all Israeli governments, right and left – is the spearhead of this model.

The Jewish settlements in the West Bank and the Jerusalem area started immediately following the war in 1967 and have accelerated since 1974 when the messianic Gush Emunim movement was established. Today, there are approximately 120 settlements which comprise approximately half a million settlers. All Israeli governments, left and right, supported the settlement project, by omission or commission. The Israeli Supreme Court has accepted the settlements as legal, provided that they are not based on the annexation of private Palestinian land. Yet, on the ground, this ruling is hardly effective. It should be noted that the settlements and settlers are not all cut from the same cloth. Nearly half of the settlements are a product of Gush Emunim, as well as ideological movements associated with the Labor movement. The rest are Jewish settlers who belong to Second and Third Israel, who migrated to settlements to reap the benefits of the "Welfare State," which offers employment, cheap housing and lavish education and health benefits for Jews only.

If we examine the entire space from the river to the sea, we learn that all Jews and some Palestinians hold citizenship cards. The remaining Palestinians are subjects without citizenship, under an apartheid regime which uses military, legal and administrative tools to preserve colonial control over them. The fact that Israel did not enact its political sovereignty in the West Bank and in the Gaza Strip by no means alters the picture.[74] The majority of the former colonial powers avoided the imposition of full sovereignty on occupied territories and created legal arrangements to support a form of control which was devoid of legal sovereignty, based on "sovereignty gaps."[75]

The liberal perception of the Green Line enables an imagined "schism" between settlers ("the bad guys") and the liberal left ("the good guys").[76] Gadi Taub's book *The Settlers* is a clear demonstration of this double standard, based on a simplistic and embarrassing distinction between liberal secular and messianic Jews.[77] Former Labor Party minister and veteran *Haaretz* columnist Yossi Sarid also formulates an unfounded and artificial political divide between two countries which ostensibly exist side by side, the "State of Judea" (consisting of the West Bank settlements) and the "State of Israel" (Israel within the Green Line).[78]

Are there indeed two states? If so, who provides the settlements with economic and physical infrastructure? Who provides them with telephone lines, sanitation, electricity and water? Who provides them with health care and education? And what of the role of organizations such as the Histadrut Federation of Labor Unions, the JNF, the Jewish Agency and the United Jewish Appeal as subcontractors of the Occupation? Why is there a special council for higher education (for Jews only) in the occupied territories in the West Bank? Who provides the legal infrastructure for the expropriation of lands? Who provides the engineering and construction services for the roads which cross the West Bank? Who drives on apartheid road 443 from Tel Aviv to Jerusalem, and back? As journalist Amira Hass has taught us, the settlements are not a spontaneous and random undertaking by eccentrics, but rather a national project of the Israeli state.

No less importantly, the 1967 paradigm has blurred the changing reality of the past decades, and Israel is no longer either able or willing to evacuate the majority of the settlers from the West Bank.[79] The Israeli position referred to as "border corrections" and adopted by many of the Zionist left seeks to include the majority of West Bank settlers within the borders of Israeli sovereignty. This includes Ariel, the area surrounding Jerusalem and Ma'ale Adumim; these corrections are also referred to as the Blue Line, the line that marks the municipal judicial territory of the "settlement blocs."

Nonetheless, all organizations on the left side of the political map – including radical extra-parliamentary bodies such as Gush Shalom and Yesh Gvul – support the evacuation of settlements on the basis of the 1967 borders or their correction. One of leftist organization Gush Shalom's recent advertisements stated that "the settlers' children must understand: You will not be able to build your house on occupied land. Seek your future in Israel. Your parents will soon join you."[80]

This is a fantasy that denies the political reality. The return of 350,000–500,000 settlers to within the Green Line is not a realistic option. Many of the settlers hold prominent positions in the Israeli army and are controlled by their rabbis. What's more, the liberal left is not dealing at all with the moral questions and violent practice pertaining to such an evacuation. Would it be possible to cast out members of the third generation because their fathers and mothers ate sour grapes? The settlement issue requires more serious consideration.[81]

My position on the evacuation of settlements is neither axiomatic nor a priori. Although I have been part of the struggle against the settlements in the last 25 years, I believe that in the case of a just agreement, most settlements could remain, although the expansion of these settlements should be halted momentarily. I also believe that the settlement project, both within and outside the Green Line, opens the door to the return of the Palestinian refugees, both within and outside the Green Line.

THE POLITICAL RIGHTS OF THE JEWS

One neglected aspect in the discourse about the conflict is the rights of the Jews in the region. Already in the 1930s and 1940s, Jewish intellectuals such as Martin Buber, Judah Leib Magnes, Ernest Simon and Hans Cohen, who were part of the circles of Brit Shalom and Ichud, cautioned that Jewish rights should be ensured in the context of Arab surroundings. At the 1921 Zionist Congress, Buber proposed[82] – as did Magnes in 1929 – that the rights of Jews should be formulated: "Just as Arab rights should not be reduced under any circumstances, so should the right of the Jews be recognized to develop uninterruptedly in their ancient homeland, according to their national selfhood/independence, and to share that development with as many of their brothers as possible."[83]

Amnon Raz-Krakotzkin is presently reformulating the importance of dealing with the political rights of the Jews under the current historical circumstances, in which the discourse of rights is aimed solely at the Palestinians due to the political asymmetry in the region:

> The political discourse usually focuses on the rights of the Palestinians. This is both understandable and natural, as it is the rights of the Palestinians which are systematically and continuously violated. However, in principle, and especially since the point of departure is Palestinian rights, the picture should be upturned and we must discuss Jewish rights as well. Palestinian rights are clear and cannot be denied. The problem is created by the issue of Jewish rights ... Only in a bi-national context can we discuss Jewish existence in terms of a democracy.[84]

The rights of the Jews must further be formulated because rights based on violence and apartheid could never be ensured over a long period of time. The lesson learned from global history is that such regimes are doomed to be defeated or to defeat themselves. Israel may one day find itself in the midst of a political revolution reminiscent of the ones which took place in South Africa or Zimbabwe, accompanied by a bloodbath and international embargo. With such violence it would be difficult to shape a discourse of rights, particularly Jewish rights, which in such a scenario may regrettably end up as a mirror image of Palestinian rights today. Although, before 1948, the Palestinians may have rejected an appealing option such as the Partition Plan,[85] there is presently a possibility for fruitful dialogue on the re-division of space and the decentralization of sovereignties, while upholding the rights of the Jews. I believe that a return to a fair and sensible discussion of the 1948 question will enable a long-term political perspective and "outside the box" thinking, while creating new political coalitions and discovering new political horizons.

1

THE ROOTS AND CONSEQUENCES
OF THE LIBERAL NEW NOSTALGIA

THE "NO PARTNER" APPROACH

One of the main flaws of the 1967 paradigm is its basic premise of the lack of a Palestinian partner. We tend to identify the "no partner" approach with former Prime Minister Ehud Barak and the Camp David talks, but Barak wasn't the argument's main architect; he merely put it to a test, which produced the desired result. The "no partner" approach was the axis of the geopolitical strategy of Ariel Sharon, who had done more than anyone else for the elimination of the Palestinian partner and the establishment of a policy of Israeli unilateralism.

The circular conception of "no partner" has guided many politicians and journalists over the years. One of the more vocal among them, *Haaretz* columnist Ari Shavit, reported with great empathy and conviction on the disengagement plan and endorsed its unilateralism: "There will be no possibility to reach a peace agreement that will end the conflict in the next decade. This should be the working assumption of the partition project, which means partitioning Western Eretz Israel even without peace."[1] And he concludes:

> The idea of partitioning the country along the 1967 borders . . . requires Israel to withdraw to the 1967 border and the Palestinian not to demand anything beyond the 1967 border. So long as the Palestinians insist upon the right of return, they do not accept the entire 1967 [approach]. So long as this is the situation, we cannot expect Israel alone to remain committed to the idea of 1967.[2]

In a different article several years later, Shavit offers a frustrated reading of the uselessness of speaking to the Palestinians, playing on the popular leftist slogan, "It won't be over till we talk":

> Even if we talk, it won't be over. The fact is that we spoke at Oslo and it wasn't over, we spoke at Camp David and it wasn't over, we spoke at Annapolis and it wasn't over. We talked and we talked and we talked and all this talk didn't produce a thing. Shimon Peres, Ehud Barak and Tzipi Livni offered the whole world to the Palestinians, and the Palestinians were not satisfied.[3]

Shavit reinforces the same fundamental assumptions put forth by the historian and former Foreign Minister Shlomo Ben-Ami during the Camp David talks; his perception of time is rooted in the "secular" political ideology of Jewish liberals ready to digest the violence of the Jewish and "democratic" state sovereignty model and to legitimize it through convoluted justifications. One result of the distorted political horizon of the 1967 paradigm was the gradual mental colonization of the occupied territories by the liberal left. This was the process by which the 1967 paradigm was formulated and put into practice in terms of "separation," without a concrete geographic border. Over time, the Green Line transformed from a thin and narrow border to a wide and consistently expanding strip of land, and the "separation," divorced from a specific territorial line, became a floating marker for the term "Green Line." The supporters of separation express fear of the opening up of the space, of the erosion of the European cultural model that Jewish Israel has aspired laboriously to construct, of losing the monopoly over the political economy and land economy, and, finally, of losing the cultural hegemony. But the eradication of the Green Line has unabashedly brought forth the question of opening up the space between the river and the sea, a question which the Zionist left has not yet found the courage to confront. Shavit formulates this paradigmatic confusion as follows:

> We urgently need a novel idea. The paradigm of the right is outdated. But the paradigm of the center-left is also no longer relevant. Two states for two peoples is the right slogan, but it's no working plan. It cannot be immediately implemented, not in the real world. Instead of repeating and reiterating the model like a religious chant, it's time to review its fundamental premises . . . it's time to think outside the box. It's time to think outside both boxes.[4]

And indeed, the time has come to think outside both of these boxes. We can begin by acknowledging that we already live, even today, in a bi-national reality.[5] Ben Gurion University geographer Oren Yiftachel describes this reality as "an ethnocratic apartheid" – an apartheid based on the domination of one ethnic group (rather than on skin color, as in South Africa)[6] – and invites us to revisit the question of the sovereignty established in 1948. I agree with Yiftachel, and I suggest we begin rethinking the question of sovereignty and the obvious implications of asking this question in a bi-national reality: creating new spheres of overlapping political, communal, municipal and theological sovereignties. This kind of thinking just might produce creative new solutions that are not rooted in the paranoia and racism that saturate the "new nostalgia".

A new political theory must be grounded in a new sovereign structure that I call "post-Westphalian": a structure that rejects the traditional definition of sovereignty as an exclusive monopoly of territory, and the "need" to homogenize identity over that territory, in favor of a more appropriate model of joint intersecting sovereignties organized in a manner reflecting the complexity of actual communal existence and heterogeneity of populations. We need first to examine the problems associated with the "new nostalgia".

CHASING THE YELLOW WIND

David Grossman's 1987 collection of essays *The Yellow Wind* is an important landmark in the new nostalgia of imagining Israel as a liberal democracy prior to 1967 and of yearning for the political morality that ostensibly characterized Israel in its first two decades. In this form of consciousness, occupation of Palestinian territories only began in 1967: "I belong to the generation that celebrated its Bar Mitzvah during the Six Day War. Then, in 1968, the surging energy of our adolescent hormones was coupled with the intoxication gripping the entire country: The conquest, the confident penetration of the enemy's land, his complete surrender, breaking the taboo of the border . . . Afterwards, everything happened."[7]

"Afterwards, everything happened," Grossman writes.

The "Afterwards" traces a path to a "beginning," the beginning of a new time:

> I could not understand how an entire nation like mine, an enlightened nation by all accounts, is able to train itself to live as a conqueror without making its own life wretched. What happened to us? . . . So I also became an artist of sublimation. I found myself developing the same voluntary "suspension" of all questions about ethics and occupation . . . like the walls of a penitentiary I built around a reality I do not want to know . . . like jailers I stationed in order to protect myself from a grey world now repugnant to me . . . It turns the matter of the territories from an immoral matter to an amoral matter. It corrupts and anesthetizes us. One day we will wake up to a bitter surprise.[8]

When Grossman writes about the time of *The Yellow Wind* he actually introduces the time of the Green Line as the wind's diametric opposite; and any discussion of the immorality of the time of the yellow wind is also a discussion of the morality of the time of the Green Line that preceded it. The position is expressed directly in another book by Grossman, the *Present Absentees*: "Our identity fills up the Green Line borders of the State of Israel in its full validity and force, and there we have moral strength as well – and there the collective message radiating from us is unequivocal."[9] As if the conflict between Jews and Palestinians only began in 1967, as if there existed a mutually agreed border before 1967, as if this border was impenetrable, as if occupation and colonialism were irrelevant terms before 1967, as if occupation was not practiced within the land of the Green Line. Here is how Grossman phrases his position: "Giving up the territories will bring the Israeli Jews into the authentic experience of their identity, the true feeling of true Israeliness of the new era. For the first time in years, there will be an overlap between the political borders and the borders of identity."[10]

This fragmented perception of time relies on a historical disconnect between the question of 1948 and the 1967 paradigm. The formulation offered by Grossman marks the moment of completion for the 1967 paradigm and the cementing of the Green Line in a culture of nostalgia – exactly as if it became a kind of a zombie category, a walking dead: something that doesn't exist on the ground anymore but is forever there in the collective memory.[11] Grossman cuts, as if with a surgeon's knife, the historical continuity between the Arabs of 1948 and the Palestinian Arabs living in the West Bank, Gaza and the diaspora, as if 1967 was the first year of encounter between Palestinians and Jews. One clear testimony comes from Orly Yadin, daughter of the acting Chief-of-Staff of the IDF in the War of 1948, Yigal Yadin: "Up until the Six Day War my generation never even knew there was such a thing as Palestinians. We grew up in a country that had Arabs, but before 1967 I never met a Palestinian and didn't even think that it was strange."[12]

Orly Yadin echoes the Jewish discourse in which the Arabs of 1948 were not perceived as part of the larger Palestinian people. Even Gideon Levy's important work in documenting the wrongs of the Occupation leans on a position that marks 1967 as the year the Occupation began. In 2004, he collected his reports for the daily *Haaretz* into a book called *Twilight Zone*, which opened thus: "For 15 years I've traveled to the Occupation [*sic*] territories . . . drawn like a moth to the flame to where the greatest story of the State of Israel since its establishment is taking place . . . the state has lived with the Occupation for two-thirds of its life and there's hardly a day when the Occupation is not on the agenda."[13] Levy's positions are established firmly in the ideological infrastructure and the epistemology of the Green Line: he calls the areas beyond that line "Occupation Land," arbitrarily distinguishing "there" from "here," which sanitizes the greater story of the Occupation of the country in 1948, and reproduces its historical denial and the new nostalgia.

This nostalgic approach is a secular liberal epos on what Edward Said would have called a "beginning." The beginning is a secular idea created by secular thought in theological clothing. Walter Benjamin wrote of the "beginning" that it determines the form in which "the idea confronts time and again with the historical world, until it arrives at its full historical perfection."[14]

We may argue that in 1967 the idea of the Green Line had arrived at its historical perfection, with the forgetting of 1948 resting underneath it as an unbreakable principle. The two-state solution is a product of that thought. This kind of moral approach is a natural sequel to *Soldiers Talk*, a book of testimonies by the veterans of the 1967 campaign released soon after the war; the liberal discourse canonized the book as proof of the morality of the Israeli army before 1967, and held it up for decades as a moral standard for the Labor Zionist movement. Similarly, former MK and historian Meir Pa'il wrote of the Israeli just state "which was disrupted after the Six Day War."[15]

The fundamental premise of the time of the Green Line as a "beginning" also predetermines the end result: a return to the Green Line would solve the conflict, ending the "bad phase" in the Jewish–Arab relationship. This is the moral stance of the liberal left, fed by ignorance and blindness forced on the Israeli public for decades in regard to the history of 1948, and by the international support for the political model created in 1949.[16] Marking 1967 as the turning point and as a political crisis seals the questions of 1948, while ignoring the question of the Palestinian refugees, the anomalous status of the Israeli Arabs, and the anomalous status of the Jewish settlements in the West Bank. The spatialized time of the Green Line presupposes the conflict as extraneous to Israeli society, and therefore as a matter of fate; as historian and journalist Amos Elon puts it in his seminal book *The Israelis*: "Sorrowfully ... the Israelis awaited the next war, like one awaits the visit of a tiresome, bothersome mother-in-law."[17]

Another stark example of the new nostalgia consciousness can be found in a book by former Meretz leader, minister and long-time *Haaretz* columnist Yossi Sarid, one of the key figures of the moderate left. The book, entitled *And So We Gather Here: An Alternative History*, offers a biographical narrative, partly imagined, partly told through other characters, which begins with the foundation of the state in 1948 and ends, bowing to the genre, in 1967. For Sarid the problems started only in 1967: "The second decade of the state was a decade of normality ... who would believe in 1965 that soon, in less than two years, the country would lose its mind."[18]

But 1967 is cast here as a dramatic year from yet another perspective: the beginning of the end of the "secular" state.[19] Even when looking at events that happened after 1967, Sarid holds them up against the model of secular liberalism. He uses the character of Ben Gurion in his book to express surprise at the appearance of

> Jewish Jihadists, reminiscent of the fanatics of the second temple that brought about its destruction. This was the first time he [Ben Gurion] met face to face with the wild weeds that sprang on the flowerbeds of religious Zionism. He didn't know they were like that – devoted, messianic. He wasn't aware of the underground currents that trickled for years in the depth of the religious nationalism, and are now threatening to break forth in all their might, like simmering

lava; the stream of secular Zionism will soon merge into a greater river.[20]

The new nostalgia, which outsources moral questions to beyond the Green Line, is also a form of Ahskenazi, white, identity politics, founded on a demographic struggle against the "other" within, the Mizrachi Jews – a demographic struggle waged by the same elite who holds up the time of the Green Line as a political horizon.[21] In 1966, on the eve of the Six Day War, author Shabtai Tevet warned for all to hear: "The greater the part of the sons of those who come from Africa and Asia in [our] population, the lower the level of education will drop and the gap with Europe will grow." He went on:

> With a relatively high growth of descendants of Asians and Africans, this group will surely become prevalent among the teachers ... can we possibly be certain that a teacher born in Asia or Africa, or born in Israel to parents who come from Asia and Africa, will be able to maintain the same teaching level established by teachers of European origin? ... We should prevent dwindling of the share of those of European and American origin.[22]

Amos Elon, who, in his book *The Israelis*, articulated the early foundations of the 1967 paradigm, also thought of Israel as a branch of the white, liberal Europe. In the last decade of his life he left Israel and settled in Tuscany, to become once again, in his own words, a European Jew. Like Yossi Beilin, who longs for "the most beautiful decade in our lives," Elon, too, yearns for a different, European Israel: "There was provincialism here. There was the slave becoming king. I'm not surprised about the population. We know where it came from. Either from the Arab lands or from Eastern Europe."

Or, as Ari Shavit put it in an interview with Elon: "This is probably the reason why Amos Elon was with us and then left us. He turned back the wheel of time. He went back to being a Jewish European."[23]

One of the main spokesmen of this liberal elite is Amos Oz, who never hid his revulsion at the introduction of the religious settler movement of Gush Emunim into mainstream politics after 1967. The back cover of Haim Be'er's book *The Time of Trimming* carries the following notes, attributed to Oz:

> An epic, wide reaching work . . . on the time of the emergence of the messianic worldview . . . which does wonders to depict the dreams of the students of religious-nationalist education which urged them, to borrow from Amos Oz, to rise and abandon their traditional roles as Kosher keepers in the dining car of the train and rush forth to the engine to grab the wheel.

We should note the patronizing – and distancing – description of religious Zionism as a movement that extricated itself too quickly from its role as a restaurant-car employee on the train driven, traditionally, by liberal Zionism. This is a constitutive text, which washes the liberal Zionism clean of its messianic elements and presents religious-nationalist theology as an accident in the supposedly secular history of Zionism. Oz's perception forcibly denies that Zionism, in all its streams and on all its levels, carried and carries still a substantial Messianic baggage.

The landmark elections of 1977, in which the Likud Party won for the first time in nearly 30 years of Israeli history, and in which the right, the Mizrachi and the religious took over the very heart of Israeli politics, was experienced by the liberal Zionist elite as a powerful identity crisis.[24]

Here is what Oz wrote about the lost dream of liberal white Israel:

> And after all it is evil days that are upon us. The petite-bourgeoisie, which already ruled our lives for the past few years, will now become the official code of conduct of "grab what you can." It will be accompanied now more and more by the tam-tam drums of muffled tribalism, ritualism, blood and soil and passions and intoxicating slogans.... the world is against us, Israel trust God, wars of the pure and the impure, fanaticism ridden with dark fears, the suppression of the mind in the name of inflammatory visions, and high above it all will hang the almighty roar of "Hey-hey, what's the news Israel haters gonna lose" . . . And over all that will hang a cloud of self-pity, self-righteousness, exile-misery in the guise of uprightness with heads held high and erect, tough, steadfast standing on one's own, male sexuality, the disease of persecuted Jews disguised as impeccable Hebrew glory . . . and us, what shall we do, what will we be from now on?[25]

Oz sneers at supporters of the Movement for Greater Israel ("tribalism, ritualism, blood and soil and passions"), at Jews and Jewish theology ("Israel trust God"), at immigrants from exile and at exile mentality ("exile-misery"), and at the rabble, whether the rabble is Mizrachi and right-wing or simply not white and liberal. The mechanism employed by Oz borders racism, and is known in sociology as "racism without a race." It is a pattern of discourse on racism, that was born in Europe after 1945 and replaced the traditional biological indicators – skin color, eyes, facial structure, hair type, smell – with sociological indicators, in seeking to respond, among other factors, to the trauma of the Nazi racial state. But despite this blurring, the parallels between the two kinds of discourse are near-perfect.[26] We should note that none of the expressions used by Oz (the tam-tam drums, the ritualism, blood and soil and passions, Israel trust God, and, most poignantly, the mob chanting "Hey-hey, what's the news") are biological, but the linkage between the indicators and just who they indicate could not be more clear. Oz embeds in his nostalgia the identity of the white Israeli sabra (Israeli-born youth) as the opposite of all of these: a socialist secular man, not an exile Jew, not one of the rabble, upright. We can also sense a phobia here, a fear of the exile, his supposedly wimpy masculinity, and a fear of the Oriental, whether a Jew or otherwise. Four years later, in a campaign broadcast for the Labor Party in the 1981 elections, Oz appeared on the screen, upright, in white trousers and a white shirt, a loyal icon of the white values dominant before 1977.[27]

Oz's novel, *Black Box*, published a decade later still, in 1987, completes this ethos and uses identity politics to demarcate the whiteness of the new nostalgia, as observed by literary critic Dror Mishani. Although *Black Box* was written a decade after the revolutionary elections of 1977, it still engages with them through the character of Sumo, who represents the new, theological, Mizrachi right. In the words of one of Israel's pre-eminent literary researchers, Dan Miron:

> When fleshing out the character of Sumo, Oz was tempted into a stereotypical and utterly simplistic representation of Israel's "New Right." Sumo distills nearly all of the characteristics required for this role: He was born in North Africa to a poor family, a student of the French Beitar, a born-again religious Jew, a former Yeshiva student, motivated by communal frustration, class insecurity and, of course, a deep-seated hatred of Arabs.[28]

As Ofra Yeshua-Lyth put it in her review of the novel in the daily *Ma'ariv*:

> Oz is remarkable in a work that provides literary legitimacy for the racist anti-Mizrachi myth, popular on many levels among Israelis of Eastern-European origin. *Black Box* was, for Oz, the death of secular Zionism and the rise of a different social layer. In this Israeli novel, that other social layer is no less terrifying than the portrait of the Jew in classical European literature.[29]

In 1982, the year of the total war on the Palestinians of Lebanon, Oz set off on a journey as a white ethnographer in the new Israel, and reiterated once again that both the Occupation of 1967 and the elections of 1977 were breaking points and deviations from classical (i.e. his) Zionism.[30]

In an article entitled "From 'Death to the Arabs' to Death of the Arabs," Anat Rimon-Or makes the following argument regarding the sensitivities of liberal Zionism:

> Sometimes, one gets the impression that the chants of "Death to the Arabs" [chanted by the mostly Mizrachi fans of the Jerusalem Beitar soccer club] concern the Israeli public considerably more than actual deaths of actual Arabs caused by Israelis within Israel and beyond its borders. Slurs of left-wing public figures and of Arabs are usually identified with Mizrachi right wingers of a lower social status, while the killing itself, when carried out in an institutional and sanctioned manner, rewards the perpetrator with prestige; for many years, this activity was reserved for the social elites normally identified with the left.[31]

The "Death to Arabs" chants, Rimon-Or argues, remind the Israeli mainstream what is supposed to be concealed in the liberal secular discourse: that killing of Arabs is something that is practiced regularly.

Some of the liberal academic discourse responded to the change of power in 1977 similarly to Oz. Speaking at a panel on the rise of the right with the support of the Mizrachi population, Hebrew University's Professor Shlomo Avineri, former General Manager of Israel's Foreign Ministry, opined that the Mizrachi arrived in Israel from the Third World, from an ethnocentric environment a far cry from universalist and egalitarian ideas, an environment that has not gone through processes of secularization and democratization. If Israel's main achievement, Avineri went on, is sustaining a democratic regime, why then "the eruption of a population with traditional patterns of thought and behavior from the periphery of political life into its center means changing the very face of this [political] life." [32] Avineri has some reservations, noting that political intolerance should not be blamed on the Mizrachi (and their Arab background) alone, but states that "there's no doubt that intolerant, fanatical position fall on particularly fertile ground in many layers of that population," for these are groups for whom "ideas of equality, humanitarian liberalism and universalism are not part of the intellectual baggage that characterizes their traditional patterns of behavior."[33] Avineri does not draw these ideas from Zionist theology itself; rather, it is the Mizrachim themselves that serve him as a canvass on which to draw the links between religiosity and political and cultural irrationality.

A few years later, journalist Boaz Evron will phrase it more clearly still: "The fact that part of the Israeli population comes from proto-political societies ... especially Muslim countries – may also have helped the nationalist idea to be swallowed by religion, a co-optation that was a vital factor in the appearance of Gush Emunim."[34]

The 1967 paradigm of the liberal left does not, therefore, stem only from a fear of the Palestinian demographic growth, but also from a fear of Israel becoming a Mizrachi-majority society. Journalist and politician Yosef "Tommy" Lapid, who ran for the Knesset on an exclusively secularist platform, and served as Minister of Legal Affairs in the government, had this to say, ahead of the 2002 general elections:

> [I am concerned because] we reside in the corrupt, lazy, retarded environment of the Middle East . . . what holds us above the water is our cultural difference. The fact we are a forepost of Western civilization. But if our Westernness is eroded, we won't have a chance . . . if we let the East-European ghetto [of religious Zionism] and the north-African ghetto [the Shas Sephardic Party] take over, we won't have anything to float on. We will merge into the Semitic region and will be lost in a horrific Levantine mire.[35]

This is the language of the Green Line: a language through which Israel is described as a liberal democracy, while the Arabs (and Mizrachi and religious Jews to boot) are described as inferior and undemocratic. This is the language of someone who came to the Middle East for a short while, not to integrate but to exist here as a guest. The position it expresses is not only immoral with regard to Palestinians, but also potentially disastrous for the Jews. It commits them to life in a ghetto with a limited idea of democracy based on racial laws and a perpetual state of emergency. It is utterly astonishing that there is no public cry in Israel for the abolition of legal emergencies. In contrast, such claims are currently put forward by protestors in Egypt or Syria.

But next to these voices there have been, and there are still, the voices of Israelis who criticized the crusader-like conduct of the Zionist movement. There was Uri Avnery, who in his

newspaper *This World* [*Ha'olam Haze*] attacked Israel's cooperation with European imperialism and called for Israel to
find its place in the "Semitic region";[36] and political organizations, including Matzpen and the Canaanites, who sought
to open up the space and called for a joint Semitic revolution by both Arabs and Jews.[37] One of them, prominent
translator and author Aharon Amir, who had memorably
called upon Israelis to liberate themselves from the shackles
of the Jewish-Zionist entrenchment behind the borders of
the Partition Plan, joined the Movement for Greater Israel.
Opening up the space was, to him, a possibility for making it
a secular, egalitarian state for both Jews and Arabs.[38]

It's interesting to look, in this context, at the manner in
which some Mizrachi Israelis worked to blur the distinction
between pre- and post-1967 Israel and between Jews and
Arabs, if even for completely contradictory motives. One
prominent group among these are the Mizrachi Jews (or
Arab Jews – that is, Jews from Arab countries) of the political, diplomatic and military establishment, fluent in the Arab
language. For them, 1967 opened up possibilities of profes-
sional, social and cultural prosperity. These were the Arabic
teachers, the translators, the military officers and Civil
Administration employees, the security organization officers
– especially the Intelligence Corps or the Mossad – the curriculum inspectors in the Education Ministry, the bankers,
the lawyers, the agricultural advisers and the Arabic-speaking
workers of the Broadcasting Authority and Israeli Radio.
Their cultural and linguistic background became a social
and economic resource, and they became "experts" on Arab
affairs.

My father, the late Eliyahu Shaharabani, was one of them.
As a boy of 14, I would join him from time to time on raids
to confiscate textbooks from West Bank schools soon after
the end of the 1967 wars. In my own school bag, one could

find back then notebooks, pencils and pens with Arabic writing, which my parents would carefully conceal with tape.

A similar transformation was in store for the late Nissim Evri, who overnight went from being a temporarily employed renovator in Beer Sheba garage to a career state official – namely, an officer in the employment headquarters in Gaza, charged with issuing work permits for Palestinian laborers. Van Leer Institute fellow Yuval Evri, Nissim's son, recalls how his father, an officer with the Civil Administration, would appear at Beer Sheba's Fourt Quarter with a car and a driver, and sometimes even give televised interviews in Arabic. Later on, Nissim's wife Edna Evri recalled how she helped her husband to reacquire literary Arabic for his new role.

The War of 1967 gave independence, status and promotion opportunities to an entire generation of Arab Jews, who celebrated the reopening of the space. It enabled a redefinition of the Mizrachi identity in Israel, not as a direct antithesis to Ashkenazi identity, but as an option for integration in the newly opened space, even if the circumstances made this integration an oppressive one.

Jewish-Arab authors like Samir Nakash, Shimon Balas and Yitzhak Bar Moshe testify that the opening of the space greatly increased their ability to write and publish in Arabic outside Israel. Their moral position was also rather different from the one formulated by Grossman. Shimon Balas, who first identified himself as an Arab Jew in the Israeli context, was in touch with Aharon Amir's milieu and shared some of its ideas, but distinguished himself from Amir and formulated independent positions after the latter declared himself a supporter of Greater Israel.[39] Immediately after the war, Balas wrote that "A new wind is blowing: The wind of the East," and that "Overnight, we were yanked from our tiny, bothersome, quarrelsome world and were put face to face with our reality – Israel as part of the region in the past, present and future."[40] This wind was quite different from that of Grossman in *The Yellow Wind*.

My parents – born in Baghdad – and their friends also developed ties with Arab musicians and singers after 1967 and celebrated the newly reopened Arab space; even if they accepted the cosmology of the Green Line, they gently expanded its margin. Philphel al-Masri, Filfel al-Georgi, Saleh and Daoud al-Kuwaity, Salah Al Kuwaiti, Faiza Rushdi, Mousa Halala, Abu-Yman, Abdo Saada, Zuzu Mousa, Mouhammad Balan and Ibrahim Azam sang and played together in Arabic at Jewish parties, in private homes and in coffee shops, and imagined their past in the Arab cultures.[41]

But voices like that of Balas resided on the cultural margins. Most Israelis – and Jews around the world – were not exposed to them, internalizing instead the time of the Green Line, which had become a fundamental part of the core curriculum of the Education Ministry, of the cultural industry and of Israeli political thought.[42] This worldview imposes ignorance of the history of the Israeli–Palestinian conflict, denies a solution to the refugee problem and does not allow one to confront the main theological, and political-theological, questions that are paramount today in Judaism, Islam and Christianity.[43]

THE ACADEMIC AND INTELLECTUAL DISCOURSE

The canonical academic research is also subjugated to the 1967 paradigm and is rooted deep in the epistemology of this nostalgic approach. Specifically, researchers in social sciences have endorsed the premises of the two-state solution, and have conceptualized sovereign Israel as confined by the Green Line, even 40 years after it was breached.[44]

When Zeev Sternhell calls on us to "stop the radical right, marginalize it, and prevent Israel from becoming a colonial state sprawling from the river to the sea and leaning upon perpetual discrimination on national, religious and ethnic basis,"[45] the sincerity and morality of his intentions are without a doubt. But this is the very same Sternhell who wrote otherwise about the founding myths of the Israeli state. Sternhell notes that, while the historic Labor Union and the Israeli Labor movement in general have continued using socialist rhetoric, they have long since given up on the values of social and political justice in favor of militarist nationalism.[46] However, he forgets to apply the same lessons to events within the Green Line. Moreover, he also misses the devastating aspects of the racialized political economy of the 1967 paradigm within the Green Line, as I will demonstrate later on, and misses the line's blurring by the Third Israel. He fails to see the political-economic and ethnic motives underlying the Occupation of the West Bank. We should take note here of the arguments of Chaim Gans, who chooses and defends the Green Line as the preferable option. He says he supports the Green Line because of historical reasons and international recognition: "The reason here is not that these are objectively just borders, but the lack of a clear answer . . . to the question of what is the right territorial division of the Western Land of Israel."[47] Yet he addresses neither the question of who the victims of this territorial division are, nor the more fundamental question: is it necessary to divide the space in such a way?

Researchers associated with the radical left have also accepted the epistemology of the Green Line, reproducing directly or indirectly the 1967 paradigm and its model of sovereignty. In his work *Israel's Occupation*, for example, Neve Gordon analyzes the Occupation of Gaza in the West Bank while assuming the Green Line as Israel's imaginary border and the Occupation as only having started in 1967. The perception of Israeli citizenship within the Green Line is at the core of the book by Ariella Azoulay and Adi Ophir, *This Regime Which Is Not One*, which investigates the control system of the Occupation after 1967.[48] Azoulay and Ophir's position on the linkage between Israel and the occupied territories is more complex than that of Gordon, as they also look at the political segregation between the Arabs of 1948 and the Palestinians of 1967 as part of the control mechanism over the latter, and point out the blurring of the links between the Nakba of 1948 and the 1967 conquests. Expressions like "Israel itself," "this democratic rule," "the meaning of Israeli democracy itself" and "the active participation of its citizens" base their analysis firmly on the category of formal citizenship within the Green Line. The Occupation is described as being against "the Israeli democracy," and, in their own words, "the backyard of the democratic rule" as opposed to "its façade."[49] Thus, they demarcate between 1948 and 1967. One notable exception is Eyal Weizman's book *The Hollow Land*, which does not distinguish the conquests of 1948 from the conquests of 1967 and calls the Israeli communities within the Green Line "settlements."[50]

2

WAS 1967 A REVOLUTIONARY YEAR?

In this chapter I set out to argue that, while 1967 is considered a watershed of the conflict in the eyes of Israeli Jews, it was in fact a "natural" continuation of Israel pre-1967. Zionism from the start was a colonial project of land settlements. Zionism from the beginning was founded on a Jewish identity which is both ethnic and theological. Yet liberals in Israel deny these theological and colonial roots of their own ideology, and treat 1967 as a watershed moment.

THE "INEVITABILITY" OF THE 1967 OCCUPATION OF PALESTINIAN TERRITORIES

"To our mind, the Six Day War was not a watershed moment but rather an integral part of the continuous, century-old Arab–Israeli conflict," argue Yagil Levi and Yoav Peled. They criticize the 1967 paradigm and its representation as a sudden rupture in the "normal development process of society" around the principle of "a Jewish and democratic

state." This flawed perception, the two say, demands special attention because most of the sociologists who imagined
the "Jewish and democratic" model of the state "belong to
the liberal left and believe that Israel is capable of ending the
Israeli–Arab conflict." They attribute this approach to the
fact that the conflict has been outsourced to the occupied
territories, becoming "external" to Israeli society itself.[1]

If we endorse the perspective offered by Levi and Peled,
we may see that the conquests of 1967 are no historical accident, as argued by proponents of the 1967 paradigm, but an
integral part of a historical continuity operating on particular
cultural, military and theological premises. In this chapter, I
seek to re-read 1967 as the realization of a purpose rooted
earlier in the 1940s (possibly from the Biltmore convention
in 1942), although the realization was not always a conscious
one.

It is more and more evident that many of those who
fought in the War of 1948, known in Israel as the 1948
Generation, saw the conquests of 1967 as a "natural" continuation of their war. Yigal Allon, one of the key generals
of 1948, once reflected that "I've never forgiven the Ben
Gurion government – it didn't let us finish the job in 1948–
49."[2] Finishing the job meant expelling all Palestinians from
"proper" Israel. A year before the Six Day War, in June
1966, the daily *Yedioth Ahronoth* ran a feature entitled "A
Weeping for Generations," in which Ben Gurion biographer
and historian Michael Bar-Zohar disclosed a scoop: Ben
Gurion told him that he had suggested the Occupation of
the West Bank before, but the proposal was rejected by the
Cabinet.[3] Just over a month before the 1967 war, the daily
Maariv published an interview with Yigael Yadin, a former
Chief of Staff and Deputy Prime Minister in the 1970s, in
which he said he regretted the Old City of Jerusalem and
other areas were not conquered in 1948.[4] In May 1959, the

IDF Chief Education Officer distributed blue plastic folders among the troops, containing materials entitled "Israel
from Dan to Eilat" (both are places within the Green Line).
Yet two of the booklets were concerned with the Gaza Strip,
and a third with Judea and Samaria, or the West Bank. The
folder also contained 20 photographs of Jerusalem, only
two of them taken in the Israeli Western side of the city.[5]
Children who played Rikuz, an Israeli version of Monopoly,
bought and sold houses and hotels in the West Bank cities of
Hebron, Jenin and Nablus, and in Gaza. The land stretched
across the game board as one borderless entity.[6] Azaria Alon,
who hosted a nationwide popular radio show on hiking and
walking, would send his listeners on hikes across the Green
Line. In June 1963, when Levi Eshkol took office as Prime
Minister, Chief of Staff Tzvi Tzur and his deputy Yitzhak
Rabin presented him with Israel's desirable borders: the
River Jordan, in the depths of the Jordanian West Bank;
the Litani River, 30 kilometers into Lebanon; and the Suez
Canal, beyond the Egyptian peninsula of Sinai. They did not
accompany the presentation with a ready plan for a military
campaign to reach these borders, but stated that it constituted
a military and a diplomatic option. A few months later, the
IDF proposed to Prime Minister Eshkol Operation Whip,
aimed at occupying the West Bank and East Jerusalem.[7] In
1966, the newly elected Mayor of Jerusalem, Teddy Kollek,
canceled a plan to move the Jerusalem city hall from the partition line, arguing that "one day the city will be united."[8]
The city's outline plan ensured new roads were paved in a
manner that would allow them to be linked to roads in East
Jerusalem (Hebron Road is one such example). In a lecture
before the National Security College, Foreign Ministry
official Mordechai Gazit stated that there was a possibility
Israel would occupy the West Bank, while Major General
Elad Peled warned of the demographic risks in such a move.[9]

In April 1966, Prime Minister Levi Eshkol announced that "our demand for access to the Western Wall is eternal."[10] An article in the daily *Maariv* in that same year described the Wall and other Jewish holy sites as "stolen."[11] This was all before the 1967 war.

The reopening of the space by the 1967 war sharpened the messianic-militant ideology and the appetite for more land. Generals have become celebrities, entertained by all the most important military figures; Moshe Dayan, the Defense Minister during the war, has become a cult figure – "like a Caesar returning to Rome after a grand victory," Chaim Herzog wrote.[12] Dayan himself likened the war to rebirth, before adding: "The death of combat is not the end of combat but its apogee." Shabtai Tevet's heroic epos *Exposed in the Turret* became the most popular book among Israel's teenagers. Israelis flooded the markets of Nablus, Hebron and Jenin, and many secular Jews tasted religious elation. Levi Eshkol said he wanted to keep Gaza in Israeli hands because of his own strong feelings for the story of Samson and Delilah.[13] This was also the time in which the enormous bureaucracy of the Civil Administration was set up, and the IDF produced manuals for governors of the occupied territories, which included information on the legal basis and organizational structure of the Occupation regime. In 1968, Gazit took the office of Coordinator of Government Activities in the "Territories." He sought to avoid reusing the military regime model applied to Israel's Palestinian citizens before 1966; he described it as reeking with corruption, cronyism, favoritism and deliberate instigation of conflicts between various clans. Gazit himself recalled the difficulties he had to overcome to find the appropriate administrative model: "The basic premise was that this would be a repeat of the [brief occupation of] Gaza in 1956, but in 1968 this attitude has changed . . . the major experience we had at our disposal was the Nazi occupation of Norway. We didn't want to learn from it, although there have been mechanisms of a Nazi civil administration. Our structure was essentially similar."[14]

Around that time, the Israeli Education Ministry took on the task of educating the 200,000 Palestinian school students in the occupied territories. Major General Uzi Narkiss asked then-Education Minister Zalman Aran: "Will we teach our curriculums? [Hebrew authors] Bialik, Tchernichovsky, Shalom Aleichem?"[15] The IDF education officers reviewed the textbooks used in the territories and banned 49 of them as "inappropriate."

Meanwhile, Palestinian land was being expropriated for the building of a Jewish Jerusalem, but the state instructed its officials to write "acquired for public needs" rather than "expropriated" in the registries. The West Bank was renamed Judea and Samaria. But, much to the chagrin of Israelis, whether messianic or secular, the lands occupied in 1967 were not empty; or, to put it in the words of Levi Eshkol and Golda Meir, the important dowry came with an unwanted bride:

> In September 1967, three months after the expansion of Israel's borders, the ruling party of Mapai held an interesting discussion of the future of the area then called "the currently held territories." Levi Eshkol told Golda Meir that he understands that she likes the dowry, but not the bride. The "dowry" was the matter, the land, the "territories." The human factor, the "unwanted bride," was the Palestinians. "This is so," Meir responded, "but have you ever heard about someone getting the dowry without the bride? . . . yet this is something each of us would want. My soul yearns for the dowry, and to let someone else take the bride . . . but these go hand in hand." [16]

Ada Sereni, the widow of famed Jewish World War II para-trooper Enzo Sereni, was appointed as chair of a "transfer committee," set up to encourage the residents of Gaza to leave their lands. Once a week, Eshkol would call Sereni to inquire: "How many Arabs did you get out so far?"[17]

The disparaging, arrogant approach to the occupied population ("let someone else take the bride") was also breaking to the surface in contemptuous orientalist statements. Here is what Chaim Herzog, a major general and a future president, wrote about the "bride" entrusted to his custody as the military governor of the West Bank after the war: "The unbridled psychological warfare of the Arabs reached heights unknown in the enlightened world … the Arab [world] … leapt into unbounded Oriental ecstasy. The Oriental imagination was ignited."[18] Side by side with the derogation of the Oriental, Herzog was praising Israeli glory to high heavens. Here is how Herzog, no Gush Emunim acolyte, spoke of Israel's new borders: "The political map of the world was changed completely by the IDF triumph and so was, obviously, the political map of Israel. We have obtained borders the likes of which the people of Israel never had in all their long history … facts that are more important than statements are being set on the ground every day."[19] This position cannot be understood without engaging with the theology that lies at the base of Jewish "secularism" in Israel, and the manner of its denial. This theology forms a continuity between 1948 and 1967, and offers a new interpretation of what is seen as a rupture in the secular approach taken up by the Israeli liberal left.

THE DENIAL OF POLITICAL THEOLOGY

Liberal secularism's purification from theology is at its clearest in the politological narrative of the breach between "The

State of Israel" and the "State of Judea," a nickname awarded by liberal commentators on the settler movement. This narrative seeks to get rid of the religious-national Zionism, which violates the rules of the liberal game. But we should note that the result of the purification process is not the complete elimination of religion, but rather the creation of two polarized models of nationalism. To establish the Zionist-Ashkenazi nationalism as "secular," its spokesmen need an alternative and an antithesis – the religious-right-wing-Mizrachi nationalism, seen as zealous and primordial.

As mentioned earlier, many Israelis were moved and inspired by the vast new space opened up before them. Gradually, the Zionist left split away from that and formed a critical position against retaining the territories. But the Israeli mainstream still held on to theological positions on the Occupation. Territorial ambitions mingled with racist consciousness and the practices of an apartheid regime: military regime, civil administration, governors, checkpoints, segregated roads, political apartheid, and an economic and ideological settlement program. The Israeli liberal stratum – writers, poets, intellectuals, academics, publicists and entire political movements – were busy purifying themselves of Jewish political theology and the responsibilities that it entails.

If we look at Zionist history from a theological perspective, we should remember that it was the "secular" Labor movement that carried the messianic spirit of the conquest of the land and cemented it onto political theology.[20] Much of the research on political theology in Israel has focused on Gush Emunim and its messianic message, but in recent years attempts have been made to engage with the ideology and politics of the Labor movement as theology-ridden.[21] Historian Amnon Raz-Krakotzkin argues that despite its self-proclaimed secularism, secular Zionism did not lose its deeper theological roots:

Zionism was unique by the fact its national consciousness was from the start an interpretation of a religious myth. It was a new interpretation of the Judeo-Christian theological myth, which was adapted to the European perception of history, especially accepting of the European perspective on history. The Jewish "Returning to history" – as it was – meant integrating as Jews in the European narrative . . . this is particularly relevant for the thought described as secular, which renounced the commitment to halacha discourse and the theological discussion that it entails. The trend of secularizing religious consciousness was expressed not in it neutralizing or disconnection from the myth, but in the national interpretation of the myth. The secularization was expressed through nationalizing religion on the one hand, and in attributing theological meaning to political activity, on the other.[22]

Jewish nationalism in the form it took in liberal circles serves as a substitute for religion, but this secularity is loaded with deeply theological terminology and a leaning towards Europe. Jewish philosopher Gershom Scholem understood early on the power of the religionization of the supposedly secular revived Hebrew language. In 1926, during the great cultural war for Hebrew as a spoken language in mandatory Palestine, Scholem wrote to fellow philosopher Franz Rosenzweig:

The people here [in Palestine] do not understand the implications of their actions . . . They think they have turned Hebrew into a secular language, that they have removed its apocalyptic sting. But this is not the case . . . Every word that is not created randomly anew, but is taken from the 'good old' lexicon, is filled to overflowing with explosives . . . God will not remain mute in the language in which he has been entreated thousands of times to return to our lives.[23]

The attempt to create a secular terminology using a sacred language, Sholem warned, was destined for failure. Hebrew was never a secular language, and using it brings the holy scriptures into our lives. Much of today's everyday Hebrew uses highly charged theological terms to describe things like mission, atonement, community, crowd, public space, regret, guilt, redemption, salvation, Tikkun Olam and more. Raz-Krakotzkin describes the pretense of secular Zionism in regard to theology.

> We should note that Sholem saw the risk in the actual reality created and shaped by secular Zionism . . . he does not argue the danger lies in the religious mythology, but that it lies in the possibility of interpretations arising against the backdrop of a reality shaped by the national, ostensibly secular mythology. In other words, that secular Zionism itself prepares the ground for messianism with which it disagrees.[24]

We find a similar phenomenon in nearly all fields of knowledge in Israel. Hebrew University literary scholar Hannan Hever has been tracing the theological origins of national Hebrew literature, and found that the process of secularization was never completed. He argues that the "Worship of the Present" of secular Zionist Ahad Ha'am, which means setting up a cultural center that will correct the nation and form an infrastructure for national identity, was charged with profound theological perceptions.[25] Adi Ophir also stresses that the ideology of occupation is not merely a side-effect of a historic accident Israel experienced in 1967, but flesh of the flesh of the political theology at the basis of Israeli nationalism.[26] This observation challenges the secularization thesis of the Israeli liberalism, and proves that secular Zionism is not an autonomous entity but a response to orthodox Judaism, and, therefore, resides deep within the theological discourse; Shlomo Fischer described it as Jewish heterodoxy.[27]

Historian Anita Shapira writes about the link between the "secular" Labor movement and religiosity when she describes one of the ardent "secular" leaders of the Labor movement, Berl Katznelson: "In a text less than five rows long, Katznelson crammed in the following terms: Vision, shekhina, sparks, revelation, winds of salvation, seers and foreseers, true prophets."[28]

Only through the prism of the theology ingrained in the Zionist thought, whether conservative or liberal, can we interpret the insistence of Ehud Barak, as secular a prime minister as Israel has ever had, that the "holies of holies" must remain in Israeli hands. Barak aspired to be remembered in Jewish history as the leader who secured Israeli sovereignty over Temple Mount, and after Camp David he was heard to say that the Palestinian refusal to acknowledge the Jewish link to the Mount was similar to refusing to acknowledge Jewish ownership of Israeli land, including Haifa and Tel Aviv.

Arie Naor, historian and former secretary for the Menachem Begin government in the 1970s, traces the theological sources of the Labor movement itself.[29] After the "Six Day War," secular author Moshe Shamir, a former member of the labor Zionist Mapam Party, traveled from Ben Yehuda Street in West Jerusalem to the Lions' Gate in the Old City walls, a 20–minute drive. Shamir, author of the epic novel *He Walked through the Fields*, who completed in 1967 his transition to the rightist Revival (Ha'tchiya) movement, described the war of that year as "a great cloud, and a fire unfolding itself, and a brightness was about it, and out of the midst thereof as the color of amber, out of the midst of the fire," quoting the book of Ezekiel. And he writes: "The world was made with the words let there be light. The light doesn't merely illuminate things – it creates them. Jewish history not only seems different. Now – it has become different. A thousand years narrowed into a moment";[30] and later: "The State of Israel . . . is the fruit of two things that are by definition absolute – the spiritual vision and the sacrifice made by those who lived and have fallen for it to come true. The vision is entirely absolute. It speaks of complete redemption."[31] "Secular" Shamir saw the six days of the war as symbolizing the six days of creation, and its results as the end of times and salvation. Haim Hefer, in his poem "We Were as Dreamers," borrows a line from Psalms, while former Mapai MK and publicist Eliezer Levin wrote of Ezekiel's consolation prophecy and suggested a theological explanation for the war and its results. Levin attributes the world of political phenomena to divine intervention into history and its instruction towards a purpose which is beyond the visible. To him, "the military operation constituted an internal, spiritual achievement . . . in which the people was restored from the dust and reconnected from the crumbles of its soul."[32]

In other words, the War of 1967 is perceived as reestablishing the political existence of the Jewish people, since it restored that people from dust and made it come alive again. Terms like "kingdom and government," "gathering of exiles," "salvation," "peace," "the rock of Israel" and "redemption of the land" are secularized theological terms that have penetrated the modern Hebrew language. As promised by Ghersom Sholem, a veritable dormant volcano lies underneath the vocabulary of secular Hebrew. *Bitachon,* "Security" in its oldest Hebrew meaning, is "faith and placing one's entire trust in G-d." *Haapala,* the term used to describe illegal Jewish immigration during the British Mandate, means "a prohibited and disastrous breach," while the Hebrew name of the JNF, *Keren Kayemet Le'Israel*, signifies a link with the afterlife.

After the war, Yisrael Galili, then a government minister, announced that he was an active partner in settling the occupied territories: "The diplomatic situation still commits us to cautiousness and patience with regard to publishing too many details on the settlement initiatives in the new territories."[33]

We should also note the famous petition for a Greater Israel, signed by 57 of Israel's leading intellectuals; leading poet Nathan Alterman was the petition's living spirit, and he secured the support of such central literary figures as Haim Guri, Moshe Shamir, S. Y. Agnon, Haim Hazaz and Uri Zvi Greenberg. They stated that no government in Israel has the authority to give up the commitment to the Land of Israel. Dan Miron described it thus: "The petition reflects the theological elements . . . which has forever bubbled underneath the surface of [secular] Zionism."[34]

Literary critic Baruch Kortzweil also argued that the modern Jewish-secular world was a parasite heir to theology. He interpreted the War of 1967 as "the ripping of the secular mask from the face of Zionism."[35] To him, the new conquests were "the realization of the underground streams of Zionism, which are nothing but religion in a secular dressing."[36] For this reason, Kortzweil asserts, withdrawal would be impossible, because it would constitute an admission of the failure of Zionism as the voice and executor of Judaism.[37]

This is why 1967 was not necessarily a watershed moment. It provided a moment of opportunity, but the ideological roots for the theological and colonial expansion of the West Bank and Gaza were much earlier and much deeper.

Ghersom Scholem, who coined the term "the price of

messianism," would often ask: "Will Jewish history be able to stand at the [Zionist] gate into material reality without consuming itself in the messianic demand, risen from its depths?"[38]

This, then, is the character of the Jewish-secular state as a theological-political perfection: the messianic demand has indeed risen from the depths – and it consumes it.

3

THE "POLITICAL ANOMALIES" OF
THE GREEN LINE

The rigidity of the 1967 paradigm, for which the Green Line serves as a spatial indicator, turns it into a contrarian paradigm that forever fails to acknowledge four major issues of the conflict: the refugees of 1948, the Arabs of 1948, the settlements project, and what I referred to earlier as the Third Israel. The paradigm that the Israeli government took to Camp David and to every convention and summit bars all four of these crucial issues from the agenda. I would now like to look into what the Green Line means for each of these issues, and to demonstrate why, for them, the Green Line is a violent and arbitrary solution.

THE REFUGEES OF 1948

When the United Nations decided to endorse the Partition Plan, Mandatory Palestine had some 1.5 million inhabitants; 600,000 Jews and 1,200,000 Palestinian Arabs. In the summer of 1947, when the British announced their intention to pull out, there was no authority or organization shared by the two peoples that would take their place. This created a vacuum that could be filled in with political powers.[1]

Hundreds of thousands of Palestinian refugees were forced to leave or were directly expelled in the course of the War of 1948, by Jewish forces, in a move that can be described, in international terminology, as ethnic cleansing.[2] Without ethnic cleansing it would have been impossible to advance the model of a Jewish state. Ethnic cleansing does not mean genocide; it refers to the use of military and bureaucratic violence to reduce as much as possible the numbers of Palestinians in the sovereign borders of the Jewish state.

Over 700,000 men and women were severed from homes and homeland overnight. The refugees and their descendants are scattered today in camps across the Middle East, mostly in Lebanon, in Jordan and in other countries, including Israel.[3] The War of 1967 also produced refugees, some 175,000 according to Israeli sources, 250,000 according to Jordanian ones.[4] Overall estimates for the current numbers of refugees speak of 6 million.[5]

The main moral problem facing Israel is not just the expulsion or escape of hundreds of thousands of Palestinians, but primarily the purposeful prevention of their return after the war. Palestinian refugees still yearn for the stolen homeland, and many Palestinians still retain the keys to their old homes. The experience of being a refugee occupies most of the bulk of the Palestinian discourse on the Nakba; it includes demands to return to and resettle the homeland, for compensation for the property looted by Israel (which the Jewish discourse describes as "abandoned"), for an opportunity for the return of "internal" refugees – i.e. long-term internally displaced persons within Israel – to their communities, and for the release of the bank accounts frozen in 1948.[6]

The demand for return is the main reason why Israel

never acknowledged its moral and political responsibility for the refugees – for their property, lands and homes. In the first few years after the war, Israel made vague commitments to pay compensation for the "abandoned property," and, after some American pressure, agreed reluctantly to allow the return of 100,000 refugees as part of a peace agreement.[7] This was "forgotten" as the years went by, and Israel meanwhile launched a war that lasted from 1949 to 1956 – dubbed "Israel's border wars" by historian Benny Morris, this long chain of military operations was aimed at preventing the refugees from coming back to their lands, homes and families.

In the summer of 1949, Jordan transferred to Israel a strip of land stretching from the south of Wadi Ara to west of Tul Karm and Qalqilia, and then further to Kafr Kassem, which contained the cultivated lands of dozens of Palestinian villages on the east side of the border. Benny Morris observes: "Thousands of villagers in the West Bank thus lost a significant part of their cultivated land, their source of livelihood. The infiltration by these fallahs to work 'their' lands and collect 'their' crops was nearly unavoidable."[8]

Israel took harsh measures to prevent this "return" and dubbed it "infiltration." Most of the "infiltrators" in the first few years were refugees trying to get back to their families and properties. Morris writes:

> Most [of the refugees] settled in areas near the borders with Israel; most of them wanted to come back home; many of them were willing to cross the border and try and at least salvage their abandoned property, or their ripening crops, from the hands of the Jews that disowned them. Nearly all of them were penniless. Inevitably . . . many began infiltrating the border to support themselves; some infiltrated to resettle in Israel or visit family members; some infiltrated to take revenge.[9]

In October 1953, "infiltrators" threw a hand grenade towards a house on the eastern outskirts of the town of Yahud, murdering a woman and her two children. In response, Israel launched a raid on the village of Kibia in Jordan. An IDF force brought 700 kilograms of explosives into the village and blew up 45 homes with their residents still inside them, many holed up in basements and attics. Most of the dead were women and children.[10] Speaking to the nation by radio after the raid, David Ben Gurion said:

> For over four years now, armed forces from beyond the Jordan and from other Arab countries break into Jewish communities close to the borders and into the city of Jerusalem, intent on murder and robbery . . . the Arab governments have directly and indirectly endorsed these acts with a clear political purpose: To cause Israel to collapse . . . they have used the Arab refugees for this reason, preventing them from settling down in their countries . . . and didn't extend them the help Israel extended to the Jewish refugees from Arab countries who came to settle here.[11]

But Ben Gurion chose to lie: he proclaimed to Israel and the whole world that it was the residents of the Israeli border areas, the Mizrachi and Holocaust survivors sustaining the border of the Green Line, who carried out the retaliatory killings – quite on their own.

> The residents of the Israeli border areas, most of them Jewish refugees from Arab countries or the survivors of the Nazi concentration camps, have for years been a target for this murderous harassment . . . the Israeli government gave them weapons and trained them to protect themselves . . . the Israeli government utterly rejects the fantastical, ludicrous idea that 600 men of the Israel Defense Forces took

part in an action against Kibia. We have run a thorough check and found that not even the smallest military unit was absent from its base on the night of the Kibia attack.[12]

Moshe Sharett later said: "I would resign if I was charged with standing before a microphone and broadcasting to the ears of the people a fictitious account of something that had been done."[13]

The Kibia military act was not exceptional. It was one on a long list of "retaliatory" actions Israel carried out during these years against the 1948 refugees, after disowning them.[14] One of the clearest conclusions in Morris's book *Israel's Border Wars* was that "an overwhelming majority of the refugees in the second half of 1948, 1949 and 1950, returned unarmed, from which it follows that their purpose was not, it would seem, political violence."[15] Morris shows that less than 10 percent of "infiltrations" in 1949 to 1953 were "politically motivated" or "for violent purposes." Of those crossing the borders, 90 percent were refugees trying to get back to their lands and families. Only in 1954 to 1956 did the Palestinian resistance movements (dubbed "terrorist" by Israel even before 1967) begin "organized [armed] infiltration."[16]

Israel's border wars were also performative, to put it in the words of sociologist Adriana Kemp.[17] Beyond their specific goals, they had the broader role of symbolically reaffirming Israel's sovereignty over territory. Kemp indicates two border discourses used in Israel before 1967: one was territorial sovereignty, the other spatial expansionist. The territorial sovereign language presented the Green Line as a steel wall hundreds of kilometers long, through which the establishment of border communities by Israel can be understood: they were meant as a shield against the returning refugees, a hermetic plug against the infiltrators and, later, the Palestinian national resistance movement. Kemp also describes the reasons why the more veteran, Ashkenazi population did not migrate to the border areas, and speaks of the violence through which the border areas were settled, mainly by Mizrachi Jews (Jews from Arab countries).[18]

At the same time, Kemp suggests, Israel was using a spatial discourse that allowed it to disregard the Green Line and avoid committing itself to permanent borders. The spatial-expansionist language described the border areas as porous, blurring the distinction between "here" and "there," and raising the act of crossing it to the level of a state-sanctioned cult. The existence of a sealed border was never meant to apply to Israelis who wished to cross it. Crossing these borders was pursued with a passion by the sons and daughters of the Labor liberal movement, not by crazy settlers.[19] In Israel's spatial practice, the border wasn't a one-way valve or a thin line defining the limits of legitimate sovereignty, but a place, a voluminous space in which military and political activities were taking place.[20] It's enough to take a look at the various cultural names for this area: "No man's land," "the border area" and so on. Crossing the border had become a symbolic practice and a spatial ritual with a feeling of mastery over the land across the border. The military magazine *Bamahane* ("The Camp") wrote, before 1967: "We passed by the sign 'Danger! Border ahead!' as if we were passing by a national lottery poster."[21] It continued: "When we used to go on deep tours, driving for hours or going on foot even at night, in the cold, and getting to know areas and taking control over spaces and learning to find our way in them, I had a feeling we could go on like that forever."[22] So penetrable was the border that it was often invisible to the Israeli eye. In 1966, a reporter for the daily *Yedioth Ahronoth* recalled visiting the border near the Valley of Ara (Wadi Ara): "The border itself is invisible, and it's hard to say where exactly the State of Israel ends and the Kingdom of Jordan begins."[23]

Israel used this dual border regime to prevent the return of Palestinian refugees, and, at the same time, crossed it and operated beyond it as if it was completely open.

At the political level, Israel recanted on its promise to contribute to an international fund for the solution of the refugee problem, and even prepared a new position offering a deduction calculated on the basis of the numbers of Jewish refugees arriving in Israel from Arab countries and the value of the Jewish property confiscated there.[24] The Israeli negotiators have told their Palestinian counterparts in the past that, if "Israel was to recognize its responsibility for the creation of the refugee tragedy, it would be stained with the mark of Cain of a country born in sin, and doubts will be cast on its moral legitimacy."[25] The moral worldview of the 1967 paradigm is thus based on the eradication of the refugee problem.[26]

The denial of the refugees' problem is repeated in the manner in which Israel arrived at negotiations with the Palestinians in 1999 to 2000. Israel refused to discuss 1948 and restricted the agenda to the question of 1967, in which no solution can be found for the refugee problem. Here was the explanation in Israel's internal discourse: "The Israeli leadership came to believe, therefore, that if Israel relents to Palestinian demands on the issue of the refugees, the international foundation of the state in its current form will tremble, and eventually collapse."[27] Astonishingly, Israel does not run a single multi-year, long-term project tasked with developing solutions for the refugee problem, despite this problem being the root and key of Israel's security, or lack thereof.

THE ARABS OF 1948

The ethnic homogeneity of the Jewish state model set down in law in 1948 necessitated the violent reinforcement of the state's territorial and identity borders, following the arbitrariness of the Green Line. The Palestinians who stayed within the line were denied the label "Palestinians" and officially called "The Arabs of Israel," some of whom were legally defined as "Present Absentees,"[28] a reference to the May 1948 census, conducted under curfew to reset the demographic zero point of the newly born Jewish state.[29] Out of the 150,000 Palestinians remaining in the country after 1948, 143,000 were granted citizenship under the Citizenship Law of 1952.[30] The state conquered the Palestinian space and Judaized it through land expropriations, setting down unequal jurisdiction areas between Jews and Arabs and setting up regional councils that controlled the land through the Interior Ministry, the Israel Land Administration and international Jewish funds, such as the JNF. The border work included defenses against "infiltrations," and the suppression of the political aspirations of the Palestinian minority within it, seeing those as a threat to the homogeny of the Jewish state.[31]

I would like to go back for a minute to what was known in Europe in the second half of the nineteenth and the first half of the twentieth century as the "Jewish problem," and to the debates of Jewish emancipation. The debates were originally stirred by a Prussian government effort to extend an identical status to all Jews under its rule; in 1841, it released a draft law concerned with the need for maintaining "the wondrous essence" of the Jews without "intervening with the Christian state."[32] Bruno Bauer wrote that, in a state where Christianity was the official religion, Jews could not be truly emancipated. Religious freedom necessitates the privatization of religion and eschewing it away from the public sphere, but Judaism, being a religion of (public) law rather than of faith, cannot be reduced into a "private religion." The Jews therefore faced a choice: Accept the rules of the game or set up a national organization of their own which will resolve the "Jewish problem."

The relationship between Judaism as a religion (and a nationality) and the Christian space in which the Jews operated came to a fascinating expression in the move conceived and carried out by Theodore Herzl. His first essay on the Jewish question (in 1893) offered a "free" and "honorable" conversion of Jews to Christianity:

> Free and honorable by virtue of the fact that the leaders of this movement – myself in particular – would remain Jews, and as such would propagate conversion to the faith of the majority. The conversion would take place in broad daylight, Sundays at noon, in Saint Stephen's Cathedral, with festive processions and amidst the pealing of bells. Not in shame, as individuals have converted up to now, but with proud gestures. And because the Jewish leaders would remain Jews, escorting the people only to the threshold of the church and themselves staying outside, the whole performance was to be elevated by a touch of great candor.[33]

Herzl's proposal can be read as a diagnosis of the Jewish question that reflects the "trap" facing the Jews in the liberal-Christian state. Whether they retain their Judaism as individuals or assimilate, they would still lose their identity as a Jewish community. The famous expression attributed to Judah Leib Gordon, on being a man outdoors and a Jew at your own tent (or, in Moses Mendelssohn's version, "Be a Jew at home and a human being outdoors"), means, in this context, being a Jew at home and a Christian outdoors, since the space in which the Jews lived and worked was Christian Protestant, not secular.[34] The religious public sphere was meant to blur out the collective characteristics of Judaism and relegate it, like Protestant ethics, to the private sphere, or to an apolitical religious community. It follows that Mendelssohn's statement corresponds with the Christian theology that dictates a separation between the private and the public spheres, and is presented in the public sphere as secularized.[35] This is the succinctness of Herzl's proposition: if the Jews convert but their leaders remain Jewish, their communal connection as Jews remains.

The "Jewish question" in Europe of the time paradoxically resembles the Muslim question of today. Europe has opened up its gates and is threatened with losing its unmistakably Christian character; a French right-winger once quipped that Europe was justly punished for its imperialism by becoming the colony of all colonies. Here is a particularly blatant example of a local Barcelona daily disengaging anti-Semitism from Jews and applying it to Muslims wholesale:

> We killed and annihilated six million Jews . . . replacing them with 20 million Muslims. We destroyed and incinerated culture, thought, creativity and talent in the death camps. We exterminated, at the time, most of the chosen people . . . and in their place, under the guise of tolerance and because we wanted to prove to the world and to ourselves that we were cured from the horrible affliction of racism that consumed us . . . we went and opened our cities to some 20 million Muslims, who brought us stupidity and ignorance, religious extremism and intolerance, crime and poverty stemming from their lack of willingness to work and proudly and honorably sustain their families . . . they made our beautiful cities in Spain and in the rest of Europe into Third World cities, basking in filth and crime . . . holed up in flats they get for free thanks to government welfare, they huddle and plot acts of murder and destruction against their innocent hosts.[36]

The Palestinian question in Israel is not, of course, identical to the Jewish question in Europe. But we can still argue, without being accused of anachronism, that there is a resemblance in that the Jewish state demands of its Palestinian citizens that they live as a minority without collective political rights in the Israeli public sphere, which is not secular but religious and nationalist. Thus, the reasons for emancipation are reproduced in the Jewish state. The Green Line model would have the Palestinians accept the Jewishness of the space; it does not allow for acknowledging a Palestinian identity that is not pliant, and denies collective political rights to Israel's Palestinian citizens.[37] The demand for a "Jewish and democratic" state requires of the Palestinians in Israel that they define their own nationality as Jewish, even if they are Muslims or Christians by creed.[38] We may well say that the state's project in regard to the Druze community was to make them Jews by nationality, if not by faith. This kind of separation of nationality and religion may also develop among non-Jewish immigrants who arrived in Israel from the former Soviet Union in the 1990s. Some of them may be defined as Jewish by nationality and Christian or Muslim by faith (the latter especially among those coming from the Muslim former republics of the USSR). Palestinian citizens of Israel would not define their own nationality as Jewish (try to recall how many European Jews took up Herzl's proposal to convert), especially when their own nationality is seen by the Jewish state as that of the enemy.

Sociologists Alison Brysk and Gershon Shafir use the term "citizenship gaps" to describe a situation in which there's an internal stratification on the grounds of ethnicity, race, gender or class between citizens nominally equal before the law.[39] These citizenship gaps, which cannot be amended by economic or civic equality alone, can be found in the ban on collective representation of Palestinian citizens of Israel, and the amendment to the Citizenship Law barring Israeli citizenship from Palestinians marrying Israelis. Even if one or both can be rationalized, they are still ethnic laws, a reaction to the anomaly of the "Jewish and democratic" model of the state.[40] After the Supreme Court failed to strike down the amendment to the Citizenship Law, which prevents the unification of scattered families, attorney and Adalah leader Hassan Jabareen explained: "The Supreme Court today established three different citizenship tracks, segregated by ethnicity: A direct track for Jews under the Law of Return, an intermediary, phased process track for foreigners, and the toughest track of all, for its Arab citizens."[41]

Citizenship gaps also appear elsewhere. Jewish settlements throughout the country (within the Green Line), such as Manof and Yuvalim in the Galilee, have written their regulations in such a way as to bar "non-Zionist" residents from joining. The regulations explicitly demand of new members to "partake in the renewal of the Jewish settlement . . . through planning, building and sustaining a Zionist community settlement, assuring in every effective way the preservation of the purpose and vision of this association; this, by jointly marking the traditional holidays of Israel, encouraging the children of the members to join Zionist movements and the IDF, and to take part in absorbing [Jewish] immigrants."[42]

Racialized regulations are not merely a whim of a particular group of Jews. They have been at the heart of the state project since 1948, when Israel developed a sophisticated colonial system of controlling the Palestinians that remained in Israel after the war – a system that included, but wasn't limited to, a military regime, extensive emergency regulations, land expropriations, and a tight control of the education system and Palestinian politics within Israel, especially through setting up vast networks of informers and collaborators.[43] The model created in 1948 turned Israel into a racial state in all but name.[44] Sustaining a "Jewish and democratic" state demanded a permanent state of emergency producing "exceptions" in law to deal with "the enemy within" (as the Arabs of 1948 are often termed a "fifth column"). The state inherited the emergency regulations of the British Mandate, and used them to maintain the anomaly of "lawfully suspending the rule of law."[45] The emergency regulations gave birth to such laws as the "Emergency Authority Law," "Search Powers in Emergency Law," "Seizure of Land Law," "Terror Prevention Directive" and "Infiltration Prevention Law." Some of these hinge on nothing more than the "state of emergency."[46]

Hebrew University historian Hillel Cohen enumerates in his book *Good Arabs* the many powers granted to the Jewish military governors ruling over Israel's Palestinian citizens until 1966: governors could limit the freedom of movement, grant business permits, monitor schools and political parties, carry out arrests, prevent the return of refugees and expropriate lands. It was a regime of everyday humiliations, queues and abuse by regime officials. As in many other colonial settings, the military regime here managed to factionalize the Palestinian society according to its needs and control it politically, reinforcing the pacified Palestinian leadership and increasing its dependence on the regime.[47] In the 1950s and 1960s, Israel fostered Palestinian patriarchy and "traditional" leaders by granting lands, weapon licenses, business licenses and travel permits to Palestinians close to the regime.[48] Some such leaders became members of the Knesset, committing themselves, in exchange, to refraining from presenting the establishment with national demands. The various Jewish advisers for "Arab affairs," who play a central part in the Israeli security mechanisms to this day, opined that "nurturing traditions and separation between the various communities of the Palestinian people would be useful to prevent nationalist organizing" and recommended supplying weapons to the Druze: "Giving weapons to Druze alone might be of use to us, creating the desired tension between various parts of the population, and allow us to control the situation."[49]

As noted earlier, Israel sought to prevent the return of Palestinian refugees after the War of 1948 had ended, labeling them "infiltrators" despite the overwhelming majority being local residents trying to go back to their lands and homes. But the hunt for "infiltrators" and the denial of the "right of return" were only partly successful. Some 20,000 refugees managed to return across the Green Line, raising the number of Palestinians in Israel by some 15 percent, in a kind of a crawling return. The closure was non-hermetic not only from the outside in, but from the inside out. Palestinians would often cross the Green Line from Israel to the West Bank and the Gaza Strip. Khawla Abu-Baker tells of her grandmother, Mariam Aaraf, who stayed in Acre after 1948 and acquired an Israeli citizenship:

> Mariam learned to infiltrate what is now called the West Bank through the villages of Wadi Ara. She paid several visits to her brother and sister in the village of Rumana, her daughter in Jenin and her husband's relatives in Yahbad. On one of the visits, she met with her son Muhammad, who moved between Syria, Lebanon and Jordan. On another, she took little Hiam with her, allowing him to stay with her family for an entire week.[50]

The military regime was based on the need to entrench the Jewish regime in the areas closest to the borders, in which a Palestinian majority on the Israeli side could conceivably result in cross-border Palestinian population blocks, which, in turn, would form a basis for irredentist demands.[51]

Accordingly, an internal military regime memo in the 1950s made clear that, in case of war, "we should allow and encourage parts of the population to move to the neighboring countries."[52] A special committee of the Supreme Council on Arab Affairs, set up in 1952 and headed by Mossad chief Isser Harel, operated a well-honed system of sticks and carrots to try to get Arab citizens to leave Israel. In 1965, the number of "willing emigrants" hit 3,000, and the Prime Minister's adviser on Arab affairs, Shmuel Toledano, recommended to the security chiefs to keep up the policy and "to exhaust all possibilities of quiet Arab emigration from Israel."

Immediately after the 1948 war, the state divided the Arab citizens into two categories: "positive Arab elements" and "negative Arab elements."[53] The official security coordination committee minutes said: "Everyone has his own 'Ahmed' . . . any such Ahmed is permitted to move freely across the area."[54] Hillel Cohen uses the term "secrets in the teachers' room" to describe the political apartheid in Israel's education system. He recounts, for example, the story of how 42 teachers – 6 percent of the entire Arab teaching force nationwide – were fired in 1952 alone, because they weren't "good Arabs." To this day, the approval of the security services is required in many Arab schools in Israel in order to appoint a new teacher. Hassan Jabareen wrote in an appeal to the Supreme Court in 2004: "This unworthy regime has produced sheepish teachers, dismal principals, and submissive school inspectors. Many of these have interpreted their work over the years as fulfilling desires anything but pedagogical. Fear, a culture of silence, paralyzing shame . . ."[55]

The unstable citizenship of Israeli Palestinians was exposed and inflamed by the country's great wariness ahead of its first war since 1948, the Suez Crisis of 1956. A few hours before the war began, fearing that Israel's Palestinians might rebel, Moshe Dayan ordered the IDF to prepare secret action plans to evict the Arab population.[56] The plan, known as Operation Mole, was meant to draw Arabs away from the borders and into internment camps in the Israeli heartland, much like the internment of the American Japanese in World War II. Dan Horowitz, then a young reporter for the *Davar* daily, claimed that Operation Mole was meant to provoke the Arab population into illegal actions that would legitimize its expulsion.[57] This plan was not put into action but the status of Israeli Palestinians as a "fifth column" was evident in the Kafr Qasim massacre. Rosenthal describes the massacre:

> At 16:55, four bicycle riders arrived at the entrance [to the village] and told Ofer, "Hello officer." Ofer asked them, "Are you happy?" They answered, "Yes." The guards under Ofer commanded got off the truck and ordered the laborers off their bicycles, upon which Ofer gave the order to "cut them down." Ahmed Farij and Ali Taha were killed on the spot. "Enough," Ofer said, "They're already killed. Spare the bullets." At the Western entrance to the village [Border Police officer Gabriel Dahan] met five people on the way back from the field: Ismail Badeer and his eight-year-old daughter were sitting on a two-wheeled cart behind a mule. Behind the cart walked Muhammad Aatzi of Kafr Bara and Gazi Issa, together with 14–year-old Abdulrahim Issa. Dahan put the two children on the cart and told them to drive off. The girl was crying, and Ibrahim, noticing the bodies of the cyclists, turned to Dahan and asked him, "Why do you want to shoot us?" Dahan answered, "shut up," and shot him and the other two men, killing them on the spot.[58]

"The hand on the clock in Kafr Qasim stopped at the moment of the massacre," village resident and MK Ibrahim

Sarsur wrote later. Before the day was done, 49 Palestinian civilians were dead. But the Jewish public in Israel denied the massacre. Uri Avnery wrote in *Ha'olam Hazel*: Why were the journalists silent? Why the professors? Why the judges? Why the doctors? Why the rabbis?[59] The silence of the liberal public is an inseparable part of the distorted model created in 1948. The massacre was perceived by the liberal public as an unfortunate isolated case, with help from a moral outlook attributing the event to certain individuals, not the political model of Jewish sovereignty.

Contrary to the accepted narrative, the first years of the state saw acts of resistance by Palestinians, including tumultuous demonstrations, struggles over land and setting up of underground cells and organizations. In 1959, the movement of Al-Ard (The Land) was set up, seeking to transform Israel into a bi-national state and society. The military regime tried to suppress these through intimidation[60]; in the words of Karkur police commander Zeev Steinberg, "We should foster the feeling of fear in the Arab population. If we'd come to them forcefully, it would have been easier for them to adapt as well."[61] This rule of fear was duly put in place, and it still exists in present-day Israel.[62]

While efforts to force upon the Palestinians Zionist history through the education system have failed, the state still prevailed in the struggle over land. About half of the lands of Palestinian villages in Israel became state property, through a variety of methods. Most of the effort was concentrated on locating and expropriating, one way or the other, refugee property. In 1949, only 2 percent of the Galilee population were Jewish, and the state launched the ethno-racial project of judaizing the Galilee. Following the infamous Kennig Report, composed in the 1970s by the Interior Ministry and referring to Arabs as a "cancer" in the body of the Jewish nation, huge swathes of Arab land were expropriated throughout the Galilee; some were used to build the cities of Carmiel and Upper Nazareth as ethnic segregation projects. About 100 Palestinian villages, by contrast, were announced as "unrecognized" by the state. The Israeli liberal left accepts these projects as legitimate, while focusing only on the settlements which were built beyond the Green Line, after 1967. But the Palestinians in Israel have voiced their objections.

The first Land Day, on March 30, 1976, began with protests against land expropriation. This marked the high point of a process that began with the Present Absentees Law, which allowed the state to confiscate some 40 percent of the Palestinian lands. Palestinians who stayed on their lands found it difficult to work them after the state began rationing their water and electricity, a rationing that didn't apply to neighboring Jewish villages and kibbutzim. The main clash in 1976 took place in the Sachnin Valley, where a large protest was held against the expansion of Carmiel at the expense of Arab properties; other protests were staged in Rama, Majd al-Krum, Araba, Kafr Kana, Nazareth, Umm al-Fahm and Taybe.

Oren Yiftachel believes that Land Day 1976 was the watershed from which a new Palestinian collective identity came into being, one that existing laws attempted to block. The land demands of the Palestinian collective were reflective of the racist policies of Israel, which preferred imagining itself and having the world imagine it as a liberal, democratic, Western state.[63] The demands prove that the false promise of the Independence Declaration, assuring "complete equality of social and political rights to all its inhabitants irrespective of religion, race or sex," could never be fulfilled under the model of the "Jewish" – even if it claims to be a "democratic" – state. This is why Yiftachel prefers to describe Israel as "an ethnocracy," rather than "a democracy," and Lev Grinberg called it "an imagined democracy," which constructs the internal conflict – and the state emergency regulations – as external to itself.[64]

The Israeli land policy has several integrated components. On the one hand, it acquires and deals out lands through supranational Jewish organizations that are committed to neither political justice in Israel nor human rights; and, on the other, it legally prohibits selling state land. Trade in land in the Arab sector is, therefore, one-sided: from (private) Arab ownership to public (Jewish) ownership. In 1991, the Committee of the Internally Displaced in Israel was set up, out of fear of the PLO compromising too much on the refugee issue and the organization's agreement to the two-states principle. This fact is important. It means that not all Arabs of 1948 feel represented by the Palestinian authority, and that the two-state solution denies their rights. Every year, on Nakba Day, the committee stages mass processions to the remains of the communities sacked in 1948. Discussion of Palestinian refugees is steadily on the rise among the Arabs of 1948, especially after the failure of the Camp David summit in 2000.

In October 2000, Israeli Palestinians took part in the Al Aqsa Intifada, known as "the second uprising"; thirteen youngsters were shot dead by the Israeli police. Their protests have shown once again that many of them did not necessarily share the positions of the "Israeli left," which saw the Green Line as a kind of a moral anchor and hesitated and mumbled when Israeli police shot and killed Israeli Palestinian protesters. The liberal Israeli media filled up with statements and allegations of the "betrayal" of the Palestinians in "Israel proper." The Jewish government of Israel, by contrast, was quite unhesitant, and reacted to the protests by shooting and killing the 13 protesters, in Umm al-Fahm, Ilabun, Sachnin and Nazareth. The state never once used this kind of live fire against Jewish citizens – even in situations of greater violence. The contradiction between a Jewish state and a democratic one is revealed time and again.

In response to the Palestinian protests in Israel in October and November 2000, the state began planning a massive expansion of Jewish communities in the Galilee, in the spirit of the racist Goenig Report. The Prime Minister's office prepared a plan to double the number of Jewish residents in central Galilee within five years. It was reported to be just "one of a series of steps being prepared by various ministries following the participation of Israeli Arabs in violent demonstrations."[65] The Defense Ministry meanwhile planned to accelerate the setting-up of para-military settlements in Wadi Ara, in a bid to "increase the residents' sense of security." Defense sources told journalists that they were "aware of the opposition the plan might provoke among the Arabs of Wadi Ara," but "these are state lands, the State of Israel needs these settlements, and the state doesn't need to ask anyone what to do with its own lands."[66]

And so, while the Zionist liberal left is busying itself with individual human rights, the state marked out the true arena of the struggle: the fight for the land, the fight over the future of the territories – including the ones within the boundaries of the Green Line, the ones whose occupation has been blurred in the liberal discourse. Legal practice within the Green Line has also proved that the issue of lands and settlement there is no matter for courts tasked with individual rights (see, for example, the Ka'adan verdict on the Jewish settlement of Katzir within the Green Line).[67] Supreme Court rulings can be defined as individualist and liberal, blind to the history and the rights of Palestinian citizens of Israel who became overnight a minority group.

In other words, Israeli liberalism can describe itself as

left-wing as long as there is at least an appearance of separation between "the territories in the West Bank" and "Israel"; as long as there's a separation between democracy and the Occupation; as long as Palestinians foreswear their homes in Talbiyeh, Jaffa, Azur, Ein Hud and 400 other villages, towns and cities; and as long as the state remains Jewish and "democratic," while the Palestinians known as "Israeli Arabs" remain present absentees in the political arena.

The political model of separation is rationalized and justified by the applied science of demography. One of the more prominent demographers, Arnon Sofer, has warned:

> In 2002, the percentage of Jews within Israel (inside the Green Line, including East Jerusalem and the Golan Heights) was 77.4 percent of all citizens. If we add to the Jews the Russian non-Jewish population (assuming many of them will eventually convert), the ratio will rise to 80.9 percent. If we take the [non-Jewish] East Jerusalem out of the equation, the ratio will rise up to 84 percent of all citizens. But, if we look at not only the citizens but the entire population living in Israel in 2002, including legal and illegal aliens – Arabs illegally staying in Israel and legal and illegal migrant workers, who are likely to remain here for many years to come, as they do in other countries in the Western world – then, we will find that the ratio of Jews in the population of Israel is as low as 71.8 percent, which is already disconcerting, because it makes Israel appear as a binational or multinational state.[68]

But Sofer doesn't stop here. His prediction for 2020 is that the ratio of Jews in the population will drop to 70.8 percent, and, if the Green Line should collapse, the demographic balance will be distorted even further: "If we discuss the entire Western land of Israel, we'll need to add also the Palestinians living in Gaza and in Judea and Samaria. If we should use the Palestinian census of 1997, according to which Palestinians numbered 5.3 million people in 2002, we will find that the number of Jews in all of Israel was 49 percent in 2007, and will drop to some 40 percent by 2020."[69] This is the politics of the Green Line, and this is its terminology. First, fear of "racial mixture," which could blur the Jewish character of Israel (including, it would seem, the illegally annexed East Jerusalem and Golan Heights). Second, the unfounded assumption that Israel is a progressive Western democracy that may not only lose its Jewish majority but sink into a "Third World" reality. Third, seeing religion as the biological definer of nationality, as if, as long as the non-Jewish immigrants from the former Soviet Union don't convert, their national identity will not be complete. The conclusion is teleological and somewhat confusing: Sofer defines the Palestinians in Israel as a demographic threat, yet insists on the Green Line, which preserves their status as a demographic threat.

The Israel Council for Demography began working in 1967. It consists of 40 members, mostly from the centrist mainstream of Zionism, who seek to resolve the conflict through the 1967 paradigm, to preserve a Jewish majority. The council was charged with "outlining a demographic policy that will guarantee the preservation of Israel's character as the state of the Jewish people, while, obviously, avoiding discriminating other sectors [of society]."[70] Among its members were the demography professor Sergio Della Pergola, of the Hebrew University, gynecologist Shlomo Mashiach, head of the Israeli Family Planning Association Ilana Zigler and former Health Minister Shoshana Arbeli Almozlino.[71]

The fetishist use of demographic instruments and stirring moral panic around the demographic issue sometimes provide reasons for the use of emergency regulations. In 2003, retired General Shlomo Gazit said that one could think of several scenarios in which democracy would need to be suspended in order to achieve demographic purposes. In May 2009, a bill ensuring imprisonment for anyone denying Israel's character as "Jewish and democratic" passed the preliminary reading.[72] That same month, the Ministerial Committee for Legislation endorsed another bill, calling for prison terms for anyone who organized a memorial day for the Nakba.

Palestinians living in Israel also played their part in gradually blurring out the Green Line – blurring that resulted in them being included in the externalized conflict.[73]Azmi Bishara contends that in 1967 the history of the Palestinians in Israel was created anew, because "the encounter with the West Bank and the Strip . . . accelerated the self-discovery . . . and the common . . . soon links were made with the national movement in the territories."[74] The fact that Jews living beyond the Green Line enjoy a system of state-sponsored privileges, including the protection of the Israeli law, has effectively turned the Green Line into a line separating Palestinians with citizenship and Palestinians without. The de-facto erasure of the Green Line makes the Palestinians of Israel the clearest indicator of the pre-1967 borders.

Palestinian nationalism within the Green Line recently came to the fore in a series of documents prepared by the local leadership, in early 2006. These included the "Democratic Constitution" published by Adalah, the "Haifa Declaration" released by the Mada al-Carmel research institute, and the "Vision for a Future" released by the national committee of Arab local councils in Israel.[75] The documents, which formulated a demand for national representation of Palestinians in Israel, brought vociferous and harsh responses from Jewish Israelis, including many who openly and unequivocally describe themselves as left-wing.[76]

We should note, however, that those described as Arabs of 1948 don't have a single consolidated position.[77] Here, for instance, is Nazir Majali, who supports "Israelization": "If we shake off our Israeliness day and night, if we deny it and abuse it, we'll fail. It will peek from every word we say, from every opinion we state; from the speech, the way of thinking, ways of life and conduct, opinions and costumes. Even our mentality is different . . . [it's] not the typical Arab mentality."[78]

The linkage between the Arabs of 1948 and the refugees of 1948 is a development profoundly frightening for the Israeli public; Arnon Sofer, for instance, describes it as "the risk of the lethal link between the Arabs of Israel and the Arabs of the territories."[79] Some of the Palestinians in Israel, by contrast, see the link as a challenge to the Green Line. We should note that, in the 2009 elections, Arab votes for Zionist parties collapsed to 18 percent; and we should also note half of Israel's Palestinians did not take part in the elections at all. This absconding (10 percent greater than in the entire electorate) is symptomatic, and may well express the Arab public's lack of faith in the Knesset, and the very limited ability of Arab MKs to shape political processes in the Jewish parliament. One possible future step would be a collective resignation of the Palestinian MKs and the establishment of an alternative parliament to represent the Palestinian minority vis-à-vis the Jewish majority. Such a resignation would underline the fact the Knesset is mono-ethnic and mono-national, and would throw the "Israeli democracy" into an international crisis.

The ones who have so far called out this "threat" are Avigdor Lieberman and his political party, Yisrael Beitenu (Israel is our homeland), who ran their campaign under the banner of "no loyalty – no citizenship." Lieberman is denounced as racist by many Zionist Jews (and rightly so), but this criticism is self-righteous, because the model of the

Jewish and democratic state leads to Lieberman's positions – which are based on the racial distinction between friends (Jews) and foes (Palestinians). For Lieberman, a Palestinian is a Palestinian, and he is forever a suspect. Lieberman produces an identity politics that brings out the inherent racism embedded in the idea of the Green Line, and reveals the pretense of Israeli liberalism.[80] Foreign Minister of Israel since 2009, Lieberman also challenges the 1967 paradigm of the Israeli liberals:

> We've already given up half of Judea and Samaria and all of Gaza. We've uprooted thousands of Jews and invested billions of shekels into Palestinian territories. And yet the peace process remains stuck. Earlier solutions don't help any more. It was a mistake to think the Occupation and the settlements are the cause of the conflict between Israel and the Palestinians. Looking back, there was no peace before 1967, only bloodshed and terrorism. The Palestinians had a good opportunity to set up a state between 1948 and 1967, but they didn't use it.[81]

Lieberman reveals the problems of the 1967 paradigm, which the liberal left tries hard to conceal. But the liberal left's stubborn insistence on that paradigm is rooted in more than just conceptual blindness and racism. As I hope to convince the readers below, it's also rooted in deep-seated economical and political interests.

THE JEWISH SETTLERS

The political thought on the right is far from unitary. The "pragmatist" wing endorsed separation in the shape of the so called "stars" program, initiated by Ariel Sharon in the 1970s and declared as Israel's official policy in 1991. The plan, which aimed at – and succeeded in – scattering Israeli settlements along the "borderline" and erasing the Green Line, saw a surge of settlements in various shapes and sizes established on and just beyond the Green Line over a period of ten years. The plan, widely supported by the "pragmatist" right and by much of the Likud Party, looks remarkably similar to Kadima's "disengagement" plan, to Kadima leader Tzipi Livni's diplomatic plan, and to the liberal left's Geneva Initiative.[82] The differences are minimal, and all are based on the Green Line and on separation, an idea so consensual that it is seen as apolitical.

The Oslo Accords advanced the principle of segregation along the Green Line paradigm, and presented it as a tactical–procedural idea preceding the discussion of the historical depth questions (the "core issues"), to establish a firm base for negotiations. The idea of "A New Middle East," as envisaged by President of Israel Shimon Peres and others, is also not one of shared existence but of a colonial relationship that uses separation as a leverage for exploiting the cheap labor available beyond the Green Line. Israeli Palestinians, in this worldview, are reluctantly adopted into a forced Israeliness that offers them, as individuals, civic equality that is never actually implemented because of the suppression of their rights as a national collective.

But over the years, the Zionist liberal thought became more and more colonial, and it is no longer clear what its demand for the end of Occupation actually entails.[83] It seems that, despite the principled position against settlements, the left has in fact accepted the existence of most settlements, and it accepts the distinctions between various kinds of settlements, which would allow some to be legitimized while the eviction from others serves as a fig leaf for continued occupation. Hava Pinhas Cohen, a settler in Anatot in the Binyamin area of the West Bank, writes:

> Let us suppose the people of Israel agree, as of tomorrow morning, with the slogan "Give back the territories – come back to our senses," and begins pulling out from Judea and Samaria. What will happen with the people? Will they evaporate? What will happen to their homes? . . . and where will the Green Line pass? Is Gush Etzion inside or outside? And Ma'ale Edumim? And Ariel?[84]

For the liberal left, the demand to evict settlers has become a penance sacrifice of sorts for the sin of the Nakba of 1948 – a near-metaphysical demand. Palestinians on different sides of the Green Line are offered different solutions; residents of the occupied territories are offered a porous political sovereignty over part of the land in exchange for irreversibly parting with the lands on the Israeli side of the line, while the Palestinian citizens of Israel are offered Israelization and accepting Israel as a mono-national ethnic state. The Oslo Accords like the two-states solution split the Palestinian people apart, politically, nationally, culturally and geographically; this was why Edward Said was so adamantly opposed to them.[85]

Another wing of the right, a more messianic one, supports the establishment of a single state across the entire area – a Jewish racial state. The idea of Greater Israel and the integration between theology and Zionist practices were phrased by Rabbi Tzvi Yehuda Kook, some 30 years prior to the establishment of the state.

Kook spoke of the State of Israel as the political incarnation of Knesset Yisrael, which is predestined to be revealed as a kind of a ladder planted in the ground and rising up to the heavens. The major eruption of Kook's thought from the margins to the mainstream took place after 1967, drawing on the ideas of his father, Rabbi Abraham Isaac Kook, who demolished the dichotomy between "complete exile" and "messianic salvation," offering an intermediary model.[86] The curious theological question posed by Kook Sr. was: how does belief in historical and theological inevitability co-exist with political activism – should a believer do nothing but sit and wait? Kook Sr. replies in the negative. His notion of determinism states that, even if the results are known ahead of their time, we should still act to realize them. His son went on to explain that the conquest of the land and settling it were part of salvation – salvation which is predetermined by divine politics that cannot be challenged by any kind of earthly ones.[87] This didn't stop him from binding together the eternity of the people of Israel and its metaphysical strength with the political and military strength of the State of Israel: "The State of Israel is a divine matter . . . and not only is there no withdrawal from kilometers of the land of Israel – heaven forbid – but on the contrary, we'll add more conquests and liberations, not least in the spiritual sense."[88]

A few weeks after the Six Day War, a select group of religious Zionists arrived to strengthen the resolve of the religious ministers in the government ahead of the struggle against withdrawal or territorial compromise. One of them, Rabbi Yaakov Filber – who was to become head of Kook Sr.'s Merkaz Harav Yeshiva (the Yeshiva Rabbis' Center) – said: "The integrity of the land of Israel is not in the purview of the government of Israel." Later, pre-eminent settlers' leader Hannan Porat told a meeting of the Gush Emunim secretariat: "We must educate ourselves: There's no such a thing as withdrawal, just like there aren't demons in the world."[89] Rabbi Baruch Lior wrote in the settlers' monthly *Nekuda*: "If the leaders of the state decide to secede us from the state of Israel, and set up an alternative state in the strip of the Philistines [the Green Line borders], we will deny their right to use the term 'State of Israel.'"[90]

Deputy Editor of the settlers' daily *Makor Rishon*, Uri

Elitzur, has stated that the land of Israel matters more to him than the State of Israel, and that opening the space to all Jews was more important than state sovereignty.[91] Columnist Haggai Segal claimed that the wall was being built with the participation of the liberal left, including Geneva Initiative members, in the hope of bringing Israel back to the Green Line. "The left hoped all these years that the fence would revive the Green Line and would force the settlers left stranded beyond it to come 'home' into sovereign Israel," he wrote; "This is why they petitioned to the Supreme Court time and again to stop the military establishment from push-ing the fence away from the line."[92] The brief history of the separation wall leaves no doubt – for unequivocal rightists like Segal – that the wall "succeeded" in "preventing terrorism" only because Israel retains military presence on both sides of the wall, not because of the wall itself: "The defense establish-ment did not build the fence and close the gate behind it, as it did in Gaza or in Lebanon, but retained military and intelli-gence presence in the Arab population in Judea and Samaria. There's hardly a night in which IDF soldiers don't knock on the doors of the Arabs of Judea and Samaria."[93] Segal also decries the misery of the Jews "stuck at checkpoints":

> the situation at the terminals is borderline nightmarish. The media weeps and moans about the fate of the Arabs stuck at checkpoints and completely ignores the suffering of the Jewish drivers. Every morning and afternoon long lines of cars stretch to the main terminals. The prolonged delay there undermines the daily life of hundreds of thou-sands of Jews in Judea and Samaria ... it takes about 40 minutes to get checked through the Hizme terminal in north Jerusalem, for instance ... many settlers suspect this bottleneck was meant to make life unbearable for them and get them to leave.[94]

More complex positions on separation have also been voiced. Eliakim Haetzni, for instance, praises demographic segregation offered by the fence, which, he says, "helps block a massive influx of Palestinians across the Green Line; the Jewish core in our sovereign territory is already melting away. There are today more Arabs from Judea and Samaria who have settled within the Green Line than there are settlers in Judea and Samaria."[95] In other words, even supporters of the separation wall on this side of the right wing don't see it as a border, but as a maneuver of the liberal strata designed to go back to the Green Line. Which means, in turn, that the political discourse that identifies the entire settler enterprise with the Gush Emunim faction alone offers only a reduced and denying version of the settlement project.[96] It's true that Gush Emunim launched the process, but it had many partners outside the movement, as we see below.[97]

We should also note another fact: in May, 2009, MK Tzipi Hotobeli of the Likud Party staged a conference calling for an alternative to the two-state solution. The conference was attended not only by the messianic right, but also by the more pragmatist right-wingers. Minister for Strategic Affairs Moshe Ya'alon claimed at the conference that, for Palestinians, the conquest of 1967 was not a unique event: "The occupation started in 1948, in all of Israel, from the river to the sea. Thus we can understand why Arafat went to war against Israel in September 2000, to duck the idea of two states for two people, even though they were very close to getting a state."[98]

In June, 2009, Prime Minsiter Benjamin Netanyahu declared at Bar Ilan University that he was willing to recognize a Palestinian state, as long as it was demilitarized, had no control of its airspace, did not get Jerusalem as a capital, agreed to cede the settlement "blocs" to be included in

Israel, and recognize Israel as the Jewish homeland.[99] It's not for nothing that the radical right endorsed Netanyahu's vision. The outline he offers leave the Palestinian state as little more than a farce. It's a colonial model of maintaining Israeli control over the already-perforated Palestinian territories. To be sovereign, a state must be able to protect itself from within and from without. A monopoly on the means of violence is a prerequisite of statehood. It's not for nothing Ya'alon shrugged off Netanyahu's speech, observing that the argument about "two states for two peoples" was obsolete, since it was merely a semantic pretence: "If the Palestinian political entity will be demilitarized, with international guarantees of demilitarization, and if there's no return of refugees into Israel and if they recognize Israel as a Jewish state – they can call it [the entity] whatever they like."[100] Ya'alon understands it's impossible to establish a Palestinian state under these conditions. He even demands that the "liberal," "leftie" prosecution service get rid of the term "illegal outposts," which has become part of the public discourse. To Ya'alon, this term – the product of legalist logic – signals an ideological stance supportive of the two-state solution.[101]

A third section of the right, more interesting for the purposes of this essay, even if it's relatively small, is that of democratic settlers who seek to open up the space between the river and the sea and establish there, with varying degrees of equality and justice, a bi-national society – for some, based on interfaith agreements. The rabbi of the Tekoa settlement, Menachem Fruman, maintains that the conflict will not be solved by secular politicians from both nations through mechanical separation and closing-up of space, but by theologies from both sides of the conflict. He described the settlers as "post-Zionists . . . Jews who prefer the Land of Israel over the State of Israel."[102] Fruman's proposal is one of an open space that allows for legitimate Jewish self-determination and sovereignty that do not lean on the model of a "Jewish and democratic" state within the Green Line.

To Sarah Eliash, member of the settler Yesha council and head of the girls' seminary in Kdumim, who opposed the Oslo Accords, the peace agreements in their current form are downright immoral. She calls upon the settlers to consider the oppression experienced by Palestinians. Eliash describes the wrongs forced upon the Palestinians in the territories as "Sabra and Shatila times a million," and calls for a new regime that would take Palestinian rights into considerations throughout the space: "The settlers and Gush Emunim never thought in that direction. What about civil rights, justice? Isn't this ours? Are these not also our values? We didn't refer to that. It's not a question of compassion, it's an issue that can no longer be dusted away. There have been comments, but not enough."[103] Writing in the *Nekuda* settler monthly, Vered Noam attacked the separation policy enforced by Israel through closure since the 1990s: "I never understood how the Green Line – an arbitrary line – became a moral indicator," she wrote. Noam describes the closure on Palestinian villages and towns as immoral and as a cultural-political construct concocted by the secular left: "The closure is quickly becoming permanent . . . the closure is a unique phenomenon . . . every decision made by the cabinet here is immediately labeled 'left-wing' or 'right-wing' . . . not so with the closure. Most of the Jewish public instantly gowns itself in a complacent mood . . . 85 percent of the population . . . support it. A wide cross-section of leftist and rightist voters alike."[104]

Noam explains that the closure policy is an expression of the Zionist left's age-old desire to separate from the Arabs, and at the same time unmasks the fascist right:

After five years of Intifada, after the knifing, the desire "to get rid of them" trickled deep into the consciousness of most Jewish citizens, including those defined as right-wing ... [a rightist] also yearns for a Jewish street and for Hebrew [only] labor, the writers and readers of this newspaper also benefit from the situation. We console ourselves by saying the closure is unilateral. We, after all, can travel to Ofra and Hebron. It's only "them," after all, who evaporated from our roads and cities. For the rightists, closure is the poor man's transfer. A Greater Israel without the Arabs. The goods without their price. We all understand the joy over divorce from the Arab of Hebron does not sit well with the marriage to Kiryat Arba.[105]

Noam also hints that crossing the Green Line cannot remain a privilege reserved for Jews alone.

[I never] saw any principal difference between Hanita [a veteran kibbutz within the Green Line] and Kiryat Arba, and between an Arab from Nazareth and an Arab from Bethlehem. I never understood how the Green Line – an arbitrary line – became a moral indicator. But I have to agree with those in the round glasses on one thing: We succeeded in Hanita and in Nazareth. In Nablus and Kiryat Arba we failed. Maybe because we wanted to fail.[106]

Rabbi Avi Gisser, of the settlement of Ofra, also doesn't see separation for separation's sake as a solution, and argues for taking into consideration the Palestinian right of self-determination and the predicament of the Palestinian refugees:

It may well be it's possible to see in the vision of our prophets a situation in which we exist as a sovereign state alongside another sovereign people. This possibility commits us to creative religious thinking. We don't have a clear set of rules, based on the Torah and the Halacha,

for implementing sovereignty. Some of the most serious
questions – of the character of the regime in the state and
on our approach to our neighbors, to the Palestinians, as
individuals with full political rights or as a group with a
right to self-determination – have never been properly discussed in the framework of halachic law.

He also says: "None of the agreements so far – from Oslo to
the retreat from Gush Katif – considered the problem of the
[Palestinian] refugees. They postpone it, hoping it evapo-
rates or resolves itself."[107]

Eliaz Cohen, a poet and a resident of the settlement of
Kfar Etzion, sees the Hamas movement as a partner for the
settlers, in terms of both sides' theological demands, and
sees a future in which settlers will live under Palestinian
sovereignty. During the "disengagement" from Gaza,
Cohen urged settler leaders to join hands with left-wing and
Palestinian activists to bring down Israel's separation wall.
He says Israel would be better off integrating into the region
and into Islam than remaining the spearhead of the Crusader
West. Of Porat, his neighbor in Kfar Etzion, Cohen says
that "Hanan Porat is unaware that his return to Kfar Etzion
is the beginning of the right of return, that it reinforces
the right of the Palestinians to go back to Jaffa or Acre."[108]
Cohen also calls the bluff of the 1967 paradigm – its best-
kept secret about the Palestinian refugees: "I'm driven mad
by the thought we should bear the brunt of the Nakba, that
our eviction would somehow whitewash the sins of 1948."[109]

A similar idea is being voiced by author Eyal Meged, who
went from the liberal left to the right wing:

We can tell the settlers today: You've played a great historical role for the left – you were the cleaners of its conscience.
You were forced to clean up the conscience of those sitting

in Arab homes and in Arab lands in Katamon and Talbieh, in Baka and in Abu Tor, in Biram and in Yad Mordechai and in Sheikh Munis.[110]

Gisser said, in a similar vein, that there's a kibbutz sitting atop every ruined Palestinian village, but the settlements were more moral because they replaced no villages.[111]
Rabbi Micha Odenheimer suggests:

> There is a striking, if obviously very partial, resemblance between the kibbutz movement in the years before the foundation of the state and in the first two decades of independence, on the one hand, and the settlers of the 1980s and 1990s, on the other. Like the kibbutz movement in its ideological heyday, the settlers are a small group, their ideological core even smaller, but their political clout is much greater than their numbers.[112]

Liberal Jews deny this continuity, and insist on a binary juxtaposition of the secular and the messianic, which allows it to whitewash the Labor movement and the liberal left from their ingrained messianism and the colonialism they practiced before 1967. This is what Gadi Taub writes of the settlers: "Zionism's perception of sovereignty emerged from a democratic worldview ... this is why, within the sovereign state, the Arab residents are citizens."[113] Yishai Rosen-Zvi highlights Taub's whitewashing maneuver: "Taub takes this popular thesis and radicalizes it down to a simplistic dichotomy between fantastical messianic Zionism and rational secular Zionism ... the result is a caricature of settlers, which is used more as the mirror image of good, secular Zionism than for its own sake."[114] Considering this definition, it's hardly surprising Taub makes no mention of the military regime, the land expropriations, the budgetary discrimination, the unrecognized villages and the emergency regulations – still in force to this day. The 2005 amendment to the Citizenship Law, meant exclusively for Palestinians, is also not mentioned in Taub's book. It would appear it's too difficult to blame all that on the settlers alone.[115]

Rosen Zvi concludes: "Attributing the Occupation to the settlers alone requires disregarding reality and focusing on methaphysics . . . forty years is a bit too much for [innocent] mistakes [by the secular state]. Such a time period requires us at least to consider the patterns behind the many accidents." "The many accidents," in fact, indicate the regularity of cooperation between the liberal state and its settlers. Eliakim Haetzni, one of the settlers' leaders, once remarked that "it's not the right wing that punished them [the Arabs of Judea and Samaria], but the Left. The Left expelled them in 1948 and built them a wall in 2004."[116]

Moreover, the secular Zionist movement is taking an active part in the current "messianic" settlement enterprise. As much as 84 percent of the settlements in the Jordan Valley and 74 percent of the settlements on the Golan Heights were initiated by so called "secular settling organizations" – which is to say, parts of the Labor settlement movement.[117]

Just as the Israeli left is more nationalist than it would seem, so is the right closer than it seems to mainstream Zionism. Shlomo Fischer demonstrates that religious Zionism is a modern movement that endorsed the modern aspects of Zionism, and not, as it's stereotypically portrayed, an offshoot of classical Zionism.[118]

Liberal thought based on the Green Line has legitimized the racial realities of the Jewish and democratic state; denied the role of the secular state and the liberal elites in the project of ethnic cleansing; and decided on the settlers as the scapegoat to be sacrificed so that the elites can acquire moral standing. Resistance to settlements and occupation stems, at least in part, from a desire for separation from the Palestinians and to preserve the model of the Green Line, a model which excludes the possibility of a moral appreciation of the wrongs done by the Jewish state to the Palestinians.

At the same time, liberal thought never once considered the moral implications of evicting settlers. I would argue that, if the space were to be opened up and political justice between Palestinians and Jews achieved (including the right of return for the Palestinian refugees and economic redistribution of natural resources), most settlements could be left where they are. Unlike the left, the right is already discussing the moral aspect of the eviction. Vered Noam writes: "Can the government be allowed to shirk its responsibility for 120,000 of its citizens, to uproot their life's work and the very point of their lives? . . . it's strange that the left, sensitive as it is to moral matters, has never grappled with this grave moral dilemma."[119] And Rabbi Odenheimer adds:

> The left must stand by the right and guarantee Jews access to the holy places in Judea and Samaria, even if these areas are moved to Palestinian control, and ensure that the Muslim world acknowledges the Jewish roots in the land. We can separate historical and religious ties from political sovereignty and military control, but they cannot be erased, denied or broken. It may well be that to achieve Palestinian cooperation on recognizing and protecting Jewish sites, Israel would need to recognize the Palestinian villages that fell victim to the Independence war and commemorate them. And so, in a strange and circumventory manner, the settlers may yet play a role in committing each side to retaining the dreams and memories of the other.[120]

The proposal for freedom of movement across the space has been aptly phrased by Hillel Cohen, a co-founder of the

"Sons of Abraham" group in Hebron, who had called for "an arrangement that will guarantee the right of settlement across the land and the right of immigration for both people, allowing each of them their appropriate political representation."[121] The option proposed by Cohen is based on his own personal political practice, which for a long time has been blurring the traditional distinction between left and right.

All these are mere statements, and the distance between statements and actions is huge, but I see here possibilities that cry out to be explored. The fact that the voices I quoted are a minority in their community should not be of significance at this stage; historical options need not necessarily be verified by jam-packed conference halls. Such options are also put forward by individuals who think them out, write them down and use them to shape public opinion.

One of the key points I outlined in the first chapter was the need to breach the Gordian knot between "Occupation" and "settlement," or, at least, to stop seeing them as synonymous. The Occupation of Gaza, for instance, is alive and well even without Jewish settlers and settlements in Gush Katif. The distinction between the "settlers" (*mityashvim*) within the Green Line and the settlers (*mitnachlim*) in the territories is artificial. I would like to offer two points as a substitute: first, the Israeli left must consider the moral implications of clearing settlements and include them in a more coherent political position; second, I would suggest paying more attention to the democratic voices among the settlers. I can envisage a productive coalition that will see leftist activists, Palestinians and democratic settlers united on one front, which will seek to find a solution more just than the violence and arbitrariness of the Green Line. In the wake of the publication of this essay in Hebrew, there is already one movement which drives in this direction. The corner-stone of this realignment of the new left may well be provided by the minorities coalition of the Third Israel.

THE THIRD ISRAEL AND ITS POLITICAL ECONOMY

1

The territories Israel occupied in 1967 served as land for building an exclusive welfare state, for Jews only; immigrants to this state included Mizrachi Jews, ultra-Orthodox and immigrants from the former Soviet Union.[122] According to journalist Dmitry Slivniak,

> In secular Ariel every third resident spoke Russian even before the great wave of immigration [in the 1990s]. But even the supposedly religious Kiryat Arba manifestly changed over the past decade. If you board the no. 160 traveling to Kiryat Arba from Jerusalem, you'll find not only "stereotypical" settlers, but quite a few men and women of all ages with a completely secular appearance.[123]

One of the facts most obfuscated in the public discourse is that today there's a near parity between the numbers of Ashkenazi and Mizrachi Jews in the settlements.[124] The settler population can be divided into three sociological categories: 36 percent Ashkenazi Jews, 30 percent Mizrachi Jews, and 34 percent Jews born in Israel whose origins cannot be determined as the Central Bureau of Statistics does not provide sufficient data on their grandparents' generation.

The Third Israel consists of Mizrachi Jews, ultra-Orthodox and Russian immigrants who relocated to the settlements in a bid to improve their socio-economic standing. Nevertheless, the ethnic structure of the settlements is as exclusionary as the society within "Israel proper." The men and women of the Third Israel reside in the social periphery of the settlements and are excluded from the project's leadership. Rafi Vaaknin, of the settlement of Psagot over Ramallah, explains how the settlements became exclusionary:

> The vetting and selection processes of the selective communities prevented the acceptance of many into our community. Many candidates were disliked by the admissions committees, and hundreds, if not thousands, of families were rejected. Rumors and information on the selective admission soon got around and who knows how many families didn't apply in the first place, knowing they would have poor chances of withstanding any kind of selection or social and personal vetting. I mean mostly families of Mizrachi origins, from the [slum] neighborhoods ... the roots of these abominable selections go down to the method of the new settlement process ... the community village model ... copied from the kibbutz movement, communities based on selected populations that accept or reject potential residents.[125]

The liberal left narrative – of messianic settlers versus liberals who supposedly have nothing to do with the Occupation – overlooks the political-economic reasoning behind the settlement project. Glaring in its absence from the narrative is the fact that the Occupation behind the Green Line is maintained and sustained also by the Third Israel, invisible to the liberal left, thanks to its blindness to questions of ethnicity and class. It also ignores the fact the settlement enterprise is run not only by the military, but also by Israeli liberal capitalism, which combines real estate, industry and cheap labor,[126] thanks to the enduring links built between the Israeli and the Palestinian economies. In fact, it's no longer clear whether we may speak of two separate economies; recent studies have shown that, despite the gaps in quality of life, income and freedom of movement, all the major economic trends occur on both sides simultaneously.[127]

The economic activity on the crossings between Israel and the Gaza Strip is a particularly fine example. Under the siege policy of the Israeli government, the Defense Ministry gets to decide what goods go into the Strip; very often, the consumer choice of the Gaza civilian is offered according to the interests of private companies and producers. The fruit growers' lobby, for example, successfully pressured the Defense Ministry to increase the number of fruits going into Gaza, at the expense of other products; the Israeli Cattle Breeders' Association launched a lobbying campaign in 2009 to similarly increase the quota of beef going into Gaza. One fruit grower explained: "The Gaza market ... serves as an indicator of the Israeli market and defines the income of [Israeli] farmers. Although the Gaza market is small ... it has considerable influence on prices inside Israel."[128]

Considering this, it's little wonder the Defense Ministry is refusing to release the full list of products entering the Strip. The refusal is meant to create uncertainty among the Hamas leadership, but it also allows for flexibility and responsiveness to the needs of the Israeli market. Israeli capitalism thus benefits from the Gaza market and controls it via the siege. This is, of course, true for the West Bank as well.

2

It is impossible to discuss land in the political sense, as a basis for sovereignty, without considering it as a means of production and a capital asset. Any analysis failing to entwine these two aspects of the land will be sorely lacking. Israeli social democracy is selective because it insists on separating the two.

Since the early 1990s, the state has been allowing Jewish farmers – especially in kibbutzim and state-owned farming land – to unfreeze land, making real-estate use of the land once reserved for agricultural needs. The explanation for the new policy was ostensibly the lack of housing for the newly arrived immigrants from the former Soviet Unions. The agricultural elite fought to cement this change in laws and regulations that would turn the Jewish farmers into land-owners. This includes a bill entitled "Cementing Farmers' Land Rights," which applies to 1 million acres out of the 4 million within the Green Line. Allocating most of the land reserves within the Green Line to a small group of Zionist farmers has no social, moral or economic justification. It reduces even further the chances of returning some of the lands expropriated from Palestinian owners or allowing the owners to return, and increases even more the inequality between land-owning Jews – a mostly Ashkenazi agrarian aristocracy – and Israel's Palestinians, as well as the gaps between the landowners and the Second and Third Israel.

The privileges regime runs Israeli space through the system of regional councils, which operate on policy developed in settlers' societies. Not a single new Palestinian community has been built in Israel since 1948 (excluding the Beduine towns), and over 100 existing communities were declared "unrecognized." Between 1995 and 2001, only 0.25 percent of the land was made available for Arab use, while only 2.5 to 3.5 percent is owned by Arabs, despite the latter being some 17 percent of the population.[129] Palestinian citizens of Israel have no access to the land, to the planning departments, to the Israel Land Administration, or to the supra-national organizations managing the lands, like the JNF and the Jewish Agency. The division of land in the Galilee discloses not only disproportionate distortions between Arabs and Jews, but also between Jews and Jews, based on ethnicity and class. In the Galilee, 63 percent of the lands are in the jurisdiction of regional councils with a Jewish Ashkenazi majority, and are populated by a meager 6 percent of the area's population. Only 21 percent of the land is in the jurisdiction of local councils with a Mizrachi majority. The situation of the Arab population there is considerably worse: Arab local councils control 16 percent of the land, while Arabs form 72 percent of the population.[130]

Segregation within the Green Line is no less than the segregation across it. In fact, the more complex and ambiguous the "exterior" border becomes ("fence," "wall," "disengagement," "retreat," "reinforcement"), the tougher and clearer are the internal borders between ethnic and economic groups. The book *Separation*, edited by Chaim Yaakobi and Shelly Cohen, describes the architecture of Israeli space as an enfilade of separations: The wall between the Palestinian Juarish and Jewish Ganei Dan neighborhoods in Ramle; the earthen mound raised by Caesarea Jewish residents between themselves and Palestinian village Jisser al-Zarqa; the wall planned to be built between the Arab neighborhood of Pardes Schnir in Lod and the moshav of Nir Tzvi. Yaakobi and Cohen point out a rise in the numbers of gated communities like Andromeda Hill in Jaffa, and border conflicts between communities – Modiin, Reut and Maccabim – which blur the Green Line and create new racial, class and national separations.[131]

The border conflicts within the Green Line are, in effect, political conflicts over land resources symptomatic of the great distortion at the basis of Zionist settler ideology. This is an expansionist ideology, operating by appointing its clear delegates (in this case, regional councils) to safeguard assets and preventing the expansion of the "others": mostly

Palestinians but also Mizrachi Jews, which is plainly obvious in the demographic profile of the so-called "community villages." These communities have no Arab residents at all, and the ratio of Mizrachi residents is blatantly smaller than their ratio in the general population. More than one petition to the Supreme Court has been filed against discrimination; all were rejected. In one of them, organization for legal justice Adalah claimed, through its attorney Suad Bishara, that the criteria of "social compatibility" employed by such communities "has no basis in law, is unclear, ambiguous and non-specific, which allows considerable space of judgment for a small group of citizens to determine the residence and fate of many candidates . . . the criteria bars Arab families, Ethiopian or Mizrachi Jews, single-parent families, bachelors and many others."[132] But the Supreme Court, operating as it does in accordance with the concept of "A Jewish and democratic state" and on the basis of a liberal "constitution" drawn up by long-time President of the Court Aharon Barak, did not manage to deal with the petitions as petitions presented by a national minority, and instead opposed them as individual petitions, on a case-by-case basis. In 2011 the Knesset of Israel institutionalized this practice in the law for communities smaller than 400 residents.

Regional councils hold almost complete sway over Israel's land reserves and potentially highly taxable areas; although nearly 70 percent of Israel's population live in cities, regional councils control nearly 80 percent of the land. This includes not only agricultural land, but highly taxable industrial areas.[133] In the Tamar regional council in the Negev, land reserves per person are 1,000 times larger than in nearby impoverished city of Dimona. Read this again: for every square kilometer of land per Dimona resident, there are 1,000 square kilometers of land per resident of Tamar. Moreover, nearly every highly taxable asset falls under Tamar's jurisdiction: the Dead Sea industries, the Dead Sea hotels, the gas stations and even, until about four years ago, the (infamous) Dimona nuclear plant. If some of these assets were to be transferred to Dimona's jurisdiction, perhaps the city would become economically independent.

This spatial control, exercised through political, cultural and economic mechanisms, chimes in remarkably with the inner logic of the Zionist border regime. It is sustained through cultural texts about "pioneering," about drying swamps, about the elements of natures, and about wars, but in fact it's a cultural system justifying internal colonization of the land through ethnic and national separation. Perhaps this is why settlers evicted from Gaza wanted to create their own regional council: regional councils are the code for the territorial realization of Zionist nationalism.

This ethno-racial separation lies at the very core of the Jewish social-democratic worldview, which denies the Palestinians of Israel their collective rights. Labor leader and chief spokeswoman for Israel's social democrats Shelly Yachimovich candidly admits to this limitation:

> To my mind, Zionism is, among other things, the strongest and most effective unifying mechanism of the Israeli society, and part of this society's crumbling and shunning its responsibilities towards its citizen stems from the weakening of the Zionist vision. This is also one of the reasons for the death of class solidarity and the abandonment of workers to their fate, each to his own. Because when there's no more "us" there's only a weakened, dehumanized "me." My parliamentary work . . . which focuses on workers, on combatting the privatization of the state and so on – rests upon Zionist and socialist values.[134]

While Yachimovich believes Zionism can advance social-ist values, even Zionist historians like Anita Shapira and Zeev Sternhell agree that identification with Zionist values was one of the main reasons for the divisions between rich and poor on a class, gender and ethnic basis.[135] Separation between Jews and Arabs in the labor market is also the product of a political regime, although it is reinforced by other processes, such as the intense privatization Israel has undergone since the mid 1980s.

When Yachimovich speaks of her opposition to racism, she speaks of opposing it on the individual level – not the national or institutional one. Why doesn't Yachimovich – and her "social democratic" comrades, for that matter – take up the fight against the land aristocracy?[136] Why don't they demand a reform to the policies of the Israel Land Administration, especially its blatantly racial regulations? Israeli social democracy in its current form will never be able to cope with this kind of criticism, because its class and identity understanding is limited by Zionist racial thinking. It's an airtight paradigm that misses the causes and effects of Israel's stratified structure, with the support of a flourishing intellectual, educational and cultural practice that can be termed "the justification regime." Speaking through the veil of this regime allows for simulating a social democracy – mostly for Jews alone.

Such a social democracy creates an insufferable rift between the conflict with the Palestinians and the inequality in Israel, while accepting the separation enforced by Israeli capitalism between "security issues" and "social justice." It obfuscates the fact that Israeli capitalism profits from the conflict in its current form and actively contributes to the erasure of the Green Line.[137] It also blurs the fact that the landscape of conflict has shaped the social structure of the Third Israel – Mizrachi Jews, ultra-Orthodox and immigrants from the former Soviet Union – living in the settlements.[138] If Second Israel was shaped in the years before 1967 by spreading immigrants along the borders of the Green Line, Third Israel was shaped from the 1980s onwards, with help from the neo-liberal project – which increased inequality in Israel – and through the settler project – which opened some of its gates to the victims of the neo-liberal economy. Third Israel merged with the settlement project, finding there social and economic prospects for upward mobility.[139]

To understand how Third Israel has become such a crucial element of the settlement project, I would suggest using the term "social imperialism": an attempt by the imperial system to obtain the support of the masses, including the working class, through a variety of pacifiers and temptations.[140] In Britain, social imperialists shaped a policy recruiting members of all classes into defending the wealth accumulated by the empire. Here, Israel developed in the territories a progressive, generous welfare state for Jews only.

Here is where the limitations of the Green Line social democracy are revealed: It ignores the threat that its peace discourse poses for members of the Third Israel. It also obfuscates the fact that many of the Occupation's most noticeable mechanisms – land control and separation walls – exist also within the Green Line and are responsible for the creation of a Third Israel in the first place.[141] It is also impossible to ignore the social-democratic position on Israel's Palestinians, which is partial and lacking, based on a perception of Israeli citizenship in its liberal form and expecting the Palestinians to make do with (inferior) civil rights and give up their national rights – which are, after all, social and economic rights as well. These anomalies are unsolvable within the 1967 paradigm. They require re-thinking about 1948 as a starting point.

Admittedly, 1948 is an arbitrary "beginning." Yet it is the

first time in the history of the conflict that Israel practiced an independent sovereign power. This resulted in an ethnic cleansing of hundreds of thousands of Palestinian refugees, not least by preventing them from returning to their homes and lands.

4

1948 AND THE RETURN TO THE
RIGHTS OF THE PALESTINIANS

On the noon of 30 June 1967, a grey Fiat with white
Jordanian license plates was ploughing steadily north,
through the valley known twenty years earlier as Marj Ibn
Amer ["Jezreel Valley"], and climbing up the coastal high-
way to the southern entrance to Haifa.[1]

Thus does Palestinian novelist Ghassan Kanafani describe
the return of Said, the protagonist of the *Return to Haifa*, to
his native city. *Return to Haifa* was written from a perspective
of time and space diametrically opposite to that of the Green
Line paradigm. Here, 1967 is not only a time of conquest,
but also a time of reopening of the space, which allows Said
to return, if only momentarily, to visit his home, and even to
meet his son, with whom he had to part for 19 years because
of the time and the wall of the Green Line. Here is how the
opening pages of the book describe the emotional structure
of that dramatic, mythologized moment of return:

On the outskirts of Haifa, where he arrived in his car by way of Jerusalem, Said S. felt that something was tying up his tongue. He sank into silence and felt his sorrow climbing up from within. For a moment he nearly relented and turned back. Without looking at her once, he knew she was weeping softly, and suddenly the voice of the sea rolled in, exactly as it did back then.[2]

This symbolic moment teaches us about both the liberation and the violence embedded in the Green Line as a borderline. The breaching of that border was a moment of liberation for the Palestinians who stole across it for many years to meet their families in Gaza and the West Bank. It was a moment of liberation for communities like the village of Bartaa, near Wadi Ara. In 1949, the Green Line split the village in half, tearing apart families, friends and landmarks. The 1967 war was, for that village, a moment of reunification and escape from the separation model. That moment of occupation, which was also a moment of "relief," points to the importance of 1948 in understanding the current state of the conflict. I would like to offer a reading of 1948 not as an end predestined to happen, but as a historic opportunity missed. I start with the history of the Nakba, the Palestinian disaster, although I discussed part of it earlier in relation to the Palestinian refugees and the Arabs of 1948. I argue that Israeli Jews will have to come out of the closet, so to speak, and acknowledge their responsibility for the Nakba.

THE NAKBA

When the UN accepted the Partition Plan, most of the Zionist movement was in consensus: a Jewish mono-national state should be established. To the opponents, however, Jews and Arabs alike, a Jewish state was anything but self-evident.

Even Zionists doubted the necessity of a Jewish state (e.g. intellectuals like Shlomo Zemach and Robert Weltsch, who saw the Jewish state as a fetish). Author Moshe Smilansky, who combined Ahad-Ha'am-style Zionism with the political interests of the old, non-socialist farming communities, was opposed to state sovereignty as late as summer 1947.[3] But the main challenge to nationalist statehood from within the Zionist camp came from movements like Brit Shalom, Ichud and Kedma-Mizracha. The main spokesmen of these groups and their affiliates, including Judah Magnes, Martin Buber and Ernst Simon, adhered to the idea of the bi-national option.

This was rooted in the historical period of the time. Nearly all of them rejected "exaggerated nationalism," in Buber's words, and opposed the establishment of a Jewish state pre-destined to be locked in permanent war with the Arab world. They argued that transitioning from the model of a Jewish national home to the model of a Jewish nation-state would lead to a prolonged war with the Palestinians and with the rest of the Middle East, and, at the end of the day, to a moral and political defeat.[4]

In the late 1920s, Ghersom Scholem believed that the Zionist movement's close links with imperialism might make it into a passing episode in the history of the Jewish people, sure "to be consumed in the revolutionary flames of the awakening East."[5] Zionism's cooperation with imperial-ism was nowhere more manifest than in the 1917 Balfour Declaration. The Declaration was an odd document, which saw one empire (Britain) granting rights over territory to one national group (Jews) at the expense of another national group (Palestinians), while the territory itself was still con-trolled by a different empire (the Ottomans). The fact the Palestinians are described in the original Declaration as "non-Jewish communities" still gives one pause even nearly a century later, considering the Jews were a mere 7 percent of the country's population at the time.[6] This formulation reflected the British perception of the Palestinians as devoid of national identity, while Jewish national identity was real and undeniable.[7] In 1912, Gershon Scholem wrote: "Zionism won in the field it never intended to fight in, and victory cost it the very marrow of its life."[8] Martin Buber, who recognized the historical rights of Jewish people in the land of Israel, did not believe that military triumph was synonymous to a just verdict or final victory. On the contrary, for him a state with a Jewish majority, and an exclusive monopoly over territory, meant "a tiny state of Jews, completely militarized and unsustainable," which would maintain a policy of "the military might of an expansionist state."[9] He warned against Zionism turning into a crude, egocentric nationalism, imitative of the European nationalism of the time, in an attempt to be "a nation like all others."[10] At the same time, philosopher Shmuel Hugo Bergman also lashed out fiercely against the proclaimed need to achieve a Jewish majority in Palestine. A majority in Palestine, he warned, would not change the fact Jews were a minority in the Arab world. He believed that Jews were wrong to establish aggressive state nationalism while leaning on British power, instead of searching for an understanding with the Arabs.[11] In the aftermath of World War II, many members of these groups thought that the war would have weakened nationalist frameworks, and that the emerging world order would lean on supranational federative systems.[12] Their members tried interesting Palestinian leaders in this prospect, but to no avail.[13]

In the late summer of 1947, the political clout of opponents to the establishment of a mono-national Jewish state along the lines of the Biltmore plan was shrinking fast. The political Zionists, led by Ben Gurion, had no doubt the initial sovereign authority must be established through force of arms. The violence of the civil war was superseded by the establishment of the regime. The violence through which the regime could be altered was now illegal, while the violence through which the regime and the state were established was retroactively legitimized in the Israeli state law. The statist approach advanced by Ben Gurion created the social, economic, ethnic and political basis of the new situation on the ground. It was based on the ideology of the melting pot, in a relentless attempt to define Israeli society as European. It was the establishment of a cultural and political hegemony that presents the state as universalistic, equitable and modern, and the state's actions as neutral and representative of society as a whole. This violent enforcement was accompanied by the creation of myths and national narratives that served to establish the supremacy of the Jewish rule of law and the creation of a new historiography.

The Palestinians described the establishment of Israel as al-Nakba (The Catastrophe), a term that appeared first in a book by Constantin Zureiq, published in Beirut in August 1948, and soon became the accepted term for describing the trauma of 1948,[14] a time which was also described by writer Salman Natour as "the time of chaos." As mentioned earlier, the number of Palestinians who became refugees varies between 520,000–650,000 according to Jewish sources, 800,000 according to Palestinian sources, and 710,000 according to the British. Today, their numbers are variously described as between 5.4 and 6 million, depending on the source. These refugees were uprooted from some 400 cities, towns, neighborhoods and villages, most of these demolished and erased from the map and the others populated by Jewish immigrants.[15] In addition to the refugees who form the external diaspora, some 15 percent of refugees are internally displaced, mostly from their Galilee communities.[16] The property of the refugees, including the internal refugees, was confiscated by the Custodian of Absentee Properties. There are many testimonies of massacres and forced expulsions in 1948. One of the more infamous ones is Haganah's (the pre-state Jewish military units') Plan D, prepared in March 1948 and aimed at evicting "hostile forces" and establishing a territorial continuity between large concentrations of Jewish population. Historian Aadel Manaa lists additional massacres in Biana, Dir al-Assad, Nahf, Rameh and Illaboun.[17]

The Palestinians' fear of the Jewish forces cannot be understood outside the context of the massacre in the village of Dir Yassin, carried out by Jewish Leehi and Irgun forces (the pre-state revisionist Jewish millitary fractions), with the assistance of a Hagannah mortars unit. The Jewish para-militaries took revenge for their losses by going into the village and killing men, women and children. The numbers here also vary between sources – Jewish sources maintain the number of victims was about 120, while Palestinians insist on 250. The Jewish forces raped Palestinian women in the village and brutally abused survivors, who were then paraded through Jerusalem. The Dir Yassin massacre, although not the only one of the war – there were many others, including Tantura and Tiberias – was etched into Palestinian consciousness as proof of the Jews' immorality and cruelty.[18] Khawla Abu-Bakr recalls the fear spreading through the Palestinian population and the circumstances that turned Palestinian families into what Israel later dubbed "present absentees":

> Stories of the massacres carried out by Hagannah and Irgun forces in Palestinian villages began to arrive. Rumors said the Jews would plant false information on an impending attack on a certain area to get the men to rush to the assistance of the attacked force and leave their own homes exposed . . . many left their villages in the Haifa area and searched for protection in safer places.[19]

Benny Morris does not use the term "ethnic cleansing" to describe the Jewish conquest of the land. He indicates cases of massacres and transfer through which the space was cleansed, but maintains these did not come as a result of orderly instructions from above. He notes the differences, for instance, between commander of the Southern front Yigal Alon, who organized systematic expulsions, and the commander of the Northern front, Moshe Carmel, who carried out selective expulsions only – usually only of Muslims, not Druze or Christians, as in the village of Mi'ilia. [20] Historians Walid Khalidi and Ilan Pappe disagree: they argue that, even if there hadn't been a clear order from above, Zionism was imbibed with transfer ideology that was realized in that war. The 1956 Kafr Qasim massacre shows that many atrocities are not the results of clear orders to commit them but of a consciousness and discourse that allow them. Expulsions continued after 1948, such as the expulsion of the residents of al-Majdal (present-day Ashkelon) in 1950, and the expulsions in the aftermath of the 1967 war. The state of being a refugee has become the key symbol of the Nakba. The Nakba is unfortunately denied in the Israeli discourse, and the Israeli legal system withholds funding from civil organizations that acknowledge the Nakba.

ERADICATION AND DENIAL

Walid Khalidi has meticulously documented the Arab neighborhoods, cities, towns and villages eradicated in the 1948 war; his work is nowhere to be found in history schoolbooks in Israel. Esther Yogev and Eyal Naveh show how history books serve as an instrument of the Jewish regime for the enshrining of the existing political order. A textbook for the matriculation exam in history, for example, states: "During the Liberation War, masses of Arabs escaped Eretz Israel to nearby Arab countries. The Arab leaders encouraged that escape: they saw the refugees as an excellent bargaining chip with the Jews [*sic*], something that could be used to significantly pressure world opinion."[21] And another textbook claims: "The local Arab leadership had no faith in victory. This feeling spread to the rest of the Arab population. It was the leadership who called on the Arabs to abandon any location conquered by the Jews. It is responsible for the wave of Arab refugees and this distressing problem that exists until today."[22] It's enough for the word "Nakba" to be mentioned once in a schoolbook to provoke a firestorm in the Israeli parliament (Knesset). [23] Such a book by Esther Yogev and Eyal Naveh was dropped from the curriculum, despite not making any radical claims about the model of the "Jewish and the democratic" state. [24] Boaz Vanetik, a teacher at the Amal high school in the southern town of Ofakim, explains:

> These are highly charged materials, politically. Most of the history teachers try to be very careful in these classes, if they ever even get to them. When I just started teaching I decided that if a student of mine completes 12 years of school with a good grade, but without knowing Israel had a part in creating the refugee problem, I failed as a teacher. There's no clear ban on dealing with "sensitive" material, but on educational days and courses we're clearly told to be very cautious on these matters. I don't want my student to take up my opinion as his own, but I want him to understand there is no single discourse about history, and that the attempt to present and teach a single truth is wrong.[25]

Social sciences in Israel have also created a structure of denial around the history of 1948 through the myth of the Green Line.[26] Canonical sociology, for example, described the War of 1948 as the "establishment of the state of Israel," and the relationship between Jews and Palestinians in Israel as "a rift": "The establishment of the State of Israel did not reduce the societal rift that splintered the Jewish yishuv in Eretz Israel. On the contrary, the shift from Jewish pre-state (yishuv) to statehood created another internal rift that was external to the Jewish settlement: the Jewish–Arab rift." [27] The dismembering of the Palestinians across and beyond the space, the oppressive military regime, the destruction of their families and the very fabric of their political and urban lives have become diminished to "another rift in Israeli society." But this "other rift" is the very basis of Israeli democracy (or lack thereof), based upon racial laws and regulations, as well as on police and military violence. These mechanisms of violence include a relentless state of emergency, land expropriations and demographic manipulations, using a selective Citizenship Law and introducing amendments into that Law based on racialized policy.

Another interesting point is that Jewish leaders themselves were uncertain back then of the stability of the political model and the population that would form in Israel. With the foundation of the state, the cultural system rallied to legitimize the model. As Hannan Hever observed: "Almost overnight, literature written in Eretz Israel was requested to change its identity from Hebrew literature . . . to Israeli literature, measured, estimated and demanded to fill various roles in its new Israeli state." Hever quotes Avraham Kariv at the conference of the Union of Hebrew Writers, a year and a half after the establishment of the state: "Our state gave us an identity card," he said. The group of authors known as the 1948 generation was the main cultural carrier of the Jewish (and "democratic") state, and sustained the violence, both national and racial, intrinsic to the state.[28]

The Palestinian literature within the Israel of the Green Line was forced to speak in a code concealing the violence and the trauma of the ethnic cleansing carried out by Israel.[29] In his book *The Pessoptimist*, Emile Habibi used vague and convoluted language to describe what happened to the Palestinian residents of the village of Tantoura:

> And then I showered fishing rods and nylon threads on the boy who would acquiesce to my request and would go down to the water to untangle my fishing rod from one of the rocks. And I asked him: "What is it with you and that girl that wouldn't let her take part in your fishing and games?" And he answered "The Tantouri?" and told me what he knew about her.
>
> They did not know her name and called her the Tantouri, because she came from [the village] Tantoura. And he said she was on a visit in Jisr al-Zarka when Tantoura was taken and its residents migrated, and therefore she stayed in Jisr al-Zarka. The events of that autumn evening on the empty Tantoura beach have remained a deep secret among state secrets until this very day. But I can't imagine they will prevent you from exposing it now, after what happened in June. And neither do I know what they wrote in their closely guarded notebooks on what happened that evening. And what I have learned and will never forget, it is now before you, to the very last detail.[30]

Habibi's condensed literary language seeks to recreate what many sought to blur and eliminate: the "state secrets" on "that autumn evening." By doing so, Habibi undermines the foundations of the political discourse in Israel, and tries to recreate, in retrospect, a different discourse of the 1948 war. Habibi doesn't only describe the events of those days, he also directs our gaze towards the coding of the ethnic cleansing of Palestine in 1948.[31]

Another story by Habibi, "Rubabika" (the Arab word for a

junk pedlar), part of his first late 1960's Arabic collection of stories *The Six Day Sextet*, presents a critical look at the time of the Green Line, describing the refugees of 1948 as "faded shadows." In many ways, *Rubabika* is a complementary story to *Return to Haifa*, from which I quoted at the opening of this chapter. That story, by Ghassan Kanafani – himself exiled as a child from Haifa to Lebanon, later a spokesman for the PLO and the victim of a car-bomb assassination, probably by Israel – tells the tale of a visit to Haifa by Safia and Said, a Palestinian couple who lived in the city in 1948 with a five-month-old baby named Khaldun.

On one hurried day in April 1948, Said leaves his home and doesn't manage to get back to it. He is carried along by a crowd running towards the border (some 60–70,000 Palestinians left Haifa or were deported[32]). Safia, who goes out to search for her husband, also gets lost, and together they are pushed onto a boat, leaving the baby behind. After the War of 1967, when the space reopens, the parents return to Haifa, to look for their home and try to find out what became of their child. But the house is occupied by a couple of Holocaust survivors who, it transpires, took in baby Khaldun. The name of Said's son is now Dov, and he serves as a soldier in the IDF. Said is forced to see his son as a "Zionist occupier," contrasted with his second son, Khaled, who wants to join the Fedain and fight for his country.

Through this allegory – in which the baby represents Palestine – Kanafani poses moral and political questions on the abandoning of Palestine by the Palestinians. He shows that, while the Palestinians made do with the memories, the Jews were the ones who actually raised the child. Dov, the Zionist soldier born as Khaldun, asks his father: "What did you do in these 20 years to get back your son?", adding that, in his place, he would have used a gun.

The question of the Zionist soldier is the question

confronting Palestinian consciousness. As Faisal Daraj[33] demonstrates, Kanafani weaves into his novel two complex theses. One is that the Zionist is worthy of Palestine, because he fought for it. The other is that the Palestinian will be worthy of Palestine only when he fights for it. The paradox is that such a struggle will effectively have to equate itself to Zionist warfare. The child Khaldun/Dov, left behind, is the symbol of the Siamese bond between the two nations that would not let them be separated.[34]

While Kanafani seeks to establish a nationalist litera-ture of struggle, and sees 1967 as a point of liberation that creates a national culture of resistance, contrary to the eradication and suppression of the Nakba in the Israeli and earlier Palestinian discourse, Habibi, in a complementary move, underlines the broken story of Palestinian nation-hood. For Habibi, the broken story will never be complete, because the renewed encounter of 1967 cannot heal the fractures and tears of 1948. This is a "torn, wild, shred-ded, incomplete and unclosed" narrative, a partial one,[35] as exemplified in an allegorical anecdote about a grandmother: "She would always fall asleep before the end of the story, and so we never knew the beginning or the end of the story about 'naughty Hassan.' When we grew up, we began recall-ing our grandmother and the story we called 'the broken story.'"[36]

A broken biography is also the subject of the book *Arabesques*, published by Anton Shammas in 1986. Shammas is a Palestinian Arab, a native of the village of Fassuta, who today lives in Michigan. The novel, a semi-autobiographical work on the history of the Shammas family from the early nineteenth century, was published in Hebrew.[37] When the book was released, the writer Amos Oz was asked in an interview: "The new book of Anton Shammas, *Arabesques*, has received much attention from critics. Does the very existence of this novel, written in Hebrew by an Arab, constitute to you a turning point in Israeli society?"[38] And Oz replied: "I think, indeed, that this is a victory. Not necessarily a victory for Israeli society, but a victory for the Hebrew language. If the Hebrew language was attractive enough for a non-Jewish Israeli to write in it, it seems we've achieved our goal."[39]

Hannan Hever argues that in his comment, Oz exposed doubts about the true force of the Hebrew language. He presents Hebrew as both the language of the dominant majority and the language of a minority struggling for recognition and cultural hegemony. This duplicity, Hever says, creates a flexible discourse that allows Israeli authors to move from majority to minority language, as in the expressions "nation under siege," "a second Holocaust," "the Arabs want to throw us into the sea." The Israeli discourse thus camouflages the power of the dominant majority, a national majority, through linguistic gestures and the psychological consciousness of a minority. Such a move, Hever says, makes perfect sense because of the contradiction between Israel's image as a small democratic state fighting for its existence, and the great Israel oppressing another nation. However, the contradiction also simultaneously undermines the moral boundaries of the national culture and the traditional overlap between the ethnic identity of an author and the language in which he writes. Shammas's writing reveals the duplicity: while a national minority writes in the language of the majority, the majority behaves like a national minority. By writing in Hebrew, Shamas seeks perhaps to suggest the state of the Jews takes up the political program of the State of Israelis, a state of all its citizens. By doing so, he exposes the pretenses of the Israeli liberal left regarding the Arabs.

Arabesques tells the story of a debate between narrator Shamas and the Jewish-Israeli author Joshua Braun (A. B.

Yehoshua) during a trip to the creative writing center in Iowa City. Shammas presents Yehoshua as a racist, and Yehoshua, in turn, says in an interview that, once a Palestinian state is established in the occupied territories, Shammas may pack his things and cross the Green Line to live there. Shammas replied to Yehoshua, again via the media, that his proposal was not very far from Rabbi Meir Kahane's idea of resolving the issue of the state's Jewishness through the expulsion of the Arabs. As in many other cases, the line between liberalism and racism among Jewish liberals in Israel is very thin indeed.[40] After all, the Jewish liberal project in Israel rests on the destruction of 400 Palestinian villages and the expulsion of Arab – or simply all – residents from 11 more cities. Walid Khalidi traced 418 villages within the Green Line, including some whose inhabitants were expelled after 1967, on the sites of which hundreds of Jewish communities were established.[41] Khalidi used archives in the United Kingdom, in the West Bank and in the United States, and his database is used by researchers all over the world – except in Israel.

The history of 1948 was erased not only from the writing culture, but also from the maps of the Israel Mapping Center, the JNF, the Nature and Parks Authority and the Names Committee. As revealed by geographer Meron Benvenisti, on July 18, 1949, nine well-known specialists in cartography, archeology, geography and history met in the Prime Minister's office in Tel Aviv. They were all members of an institution called "The Hebrew Society for the Study of the Land of Israel and its Antiquities." The goal of the Hebrew Society was "to provide real documents of the continuity of the historic thread, which has never been broken, from . . . [biblical time] to the days of the conquerors of the Negev in our own time."[42]

Ben Gurion appointed the scholars to a Committee for

Names in the Area of the Negev, charging the committee with "determining Hebrew names for all the places, mountains, valleys, water springs and roads in the Negev." This was the beginning of the temporal and geographical perception that erased the memory of 1948. A map is a powerful instrument that acquires the status of truth. The committee's departure point was that Arab names should not be fully erased, for this would bring about "a scientific disaster." Professor Shmuel Yevin observed: "There's no argument regarding the actual need to Hebraize, but the Arab names should not be erased from the map. Otherwise we'll block the path for the scholar and the scientist, and we should leave an opening for those who will come after us. The Arab names should not be erased from the map."[43] The compromise came in the shape of a glossary for converting the old names into the new. This was the last time the state used Arab names. Generations of Israelis used the new names in the Negev, without ever knowing all were derived from Arab names: Wadi Ruman became Rimonim Stream; Manaya became Timna; to the committee, the Arab names were distorted Hebrew names, not the other way around. The old names were replaced with names with a biblical ring to them, all of them referenced in the Jewish canonical writings. The state bureaucracy proved strong enough to force Hebrew names even upon the Bedouin; the name of the township of Rahat, for instance, is entirely the fancy of the names committee. The arguments for erasing the history and geography were fascinating: "The names we found are not only foreign to our ear, but broken in their own right . . . their meaning is blurry and many of them are chanced private names or names carrying negative, even derogatory meaning . . . many names are repugnant in their gloomy, bleak meaning."[44] This evasive and hypocritical explanation reveals the racial morality underneath the project.

THE PRESENT TIME OF THE PALESTINIAN NAKBA

The events of 1948 were, and are still, a trauma for the Palestinians of 1948 and their descendants. This trauma must be incorporated in the history of Israeli society so that we may deal with it through taking responsibility. Incorporating the Palestinian trauma, and its consequences, will also expose the Jewish trauma of 1948, which is manifest in the fact the 1948 war has never really ended.[45]

Sexual trauma expert Effi Ziv seeks to redefine the psycho-analytical concept of trauma so as to include not only past events but also what she describes as "insidious trauma" – a trauma with social or political roots that continues into the present. She argues that the currently dominant approach to trauma cannot cope with its extension into the present:

> In this [clinical] formulation, "trauma" does not refer only to a manifest event whose boundaries are marked by their exclusivity (such as natural disasters, traffic accidents or wars). This definition demands the visibility of continuing traumatic experiences that are by their very nature often invisible or denied . . . this is the main reason I would like to define trauma as a social and cultural category . . . as insidious traumas, to underline the uncompromising recurrence of traumas of social origins.[46]

Ziv's perception of insidious trauma, different from post-trauma, would seem to chime in with the fact Palestinians don't refer only to the extreme trauma of 1948, but to the cementing of that trauma through insidious repetition, because the reality of that war never ended for them. Palestinian women from Lod and Ramla interviewed in recent years by Fatma Qassem describe the implementation of "Plan D," a transfer

plan which was carried out against the Palestinian inhabitants of these cities in 1948, without distinguishing "Israelis"
from "Jews" and "past" from "present": "The Jews came
in," "The Jews took us," and so on. They immortalize the
dramatic moment through the verb "we migrated," describing the period of what Qassem calls "the time of migration"
through the expressions "we were expelled," "we migrated,"
"they migrated," "we left."[47] These are not only descriptions
of the "past" but, first and foremost, description of the past
mediated by the present. They mark the fact that this is an
insidious trauma that cannot be treated as a matter of the past
alone. This experience is re-enacted time and again in the
present, in different forms.

The time of the Green Line allows us to contain neither
the histories of the Nakba nor the trauma's repetitiveness in
the present. But the continuity between 1948 and 1967 is the
very cornerstone of Palestinian national consciousness. Here
is how it appears in the moving testimony of Khwala Abu-
Bakr, which captures what happened to her family (within
the Green Line) on the day the war broke out in 1967.
Using Ziv's definition, we can say the testimony unveils an
"insidious trauma," which sees 1967 as part of a recurrence,
a continuity, not a watershed:

> When the war broke out, Mahmoud and Nada Abu-Bakr
> gathered their five children for a briefing . . . both were
> heartbroken, having lost their youngest child, Bachr, in a
> playground accident at their neighbors' . . . the children –
> Scheherazade, the eldest at 14, Khawla herself, then 12,
> 9–year-old Ahmed and 7–year-old twins Asma and Basma
> – were commanded to memorize their full names: Their
> own first names, then the names of the fathers of the family,
> six generations back, then the last name, and, finally, the
> address of their home in Acre.[48]

She describes this terrifying moment by speaking of herself in the third person: "Khawla clearly remembers how she memorized: *Ana bin't arab* (I am an Arab). *Ismi Khaula Muhammad Ahmed Daud Taha Yassin Abu-Bakr. Beti b'harat al-yahud talata'ash, Akka* (my home is in the Alley of the Jews 13, Acre)."[49] Her parents, Nada and Mahmoud, took no chances: "They wanted to make sure that each of their children would be able to present themselves in the manner appropriate to Arab countries. If, during or after the war, they should be expelled or simply lost, they would be able to seek the assistance of nearby adults."[50] This trauma of the expulsion of 1948, recreating itself, not only happened in the past, but also is an insidious trauma in the present.[51]

Zochrot (We [fem.] remember) is the main Jewish organization clearly and methodically dealing with the questions of the history and trauma of 1948, both as a post-trauma and as an insidious trauma, "aiming to raise awareness of the Nakba in the Israeli public, to bring about the recognition of the moral debt for the wrong caused by the state and state institutions to the Palestinian people, and to advance the realization of the right of return of Palestinian refugees."[52] One of the main targets for Zochrot's criticism is historical denial – for instance, as shown by Salim Tamari, the archeological museum in Jaffa fails to mention the modern Palestinian history of the city. The section of the museum dedicated to the twentieth century covers only four isolated events: the conquest of Jaffa by General Allenby in 1917, the great Palestinian revolt of the 1930s, the "liberation" of Jaffa in 1948 by the Jews and the unification of Tel Aviv and Jaffa in the 1950s. Zochrot conducts symbolic return processions to communities wiped off the map during and after the 1948 war, and has even prepared a detailed proposal for the inclusion of the history of the Nakba in the Jewish national school curriculum. Zochrot investigates existing

Palestinian structures, Palestinian villages integrated into Israeli cities, concealment of village ruins by foresting, and the editing of names. Most of Zochrot's information sources are Palestinian, and they make extensive use of the work of Walid Khalidi in Beirut.[53]

In parallel, Zochrot also documents the activities of the Jews. The organization's journal *Sedek* (Crack) carried a fascinating interview with Elazar Davidi, a kibbutz truck driver who took part in the demolition of the Palestinian village of Hunin for the constructions of moshav Margaliot and the Osishkin House of kibbutz Dan,[54] as well as an interview with Yitzhak Hadas, who was one of the demolishers of three Palestinian villages – Emmaus, Yalo and Bayt Nuba – on whose lands the JNF built Canada Park. There's also an interview with Shimon Yair, a member of the Israeli Demographic Council, who explains to the *Sedek* interviewers how a Jewish and "democratic" state actually works:

This is the thing we found it most difficult to discuss openly . . . the issue of encouraging the birthrate, when the hidden trend was, about the Arab population, whose average was nine births per woman and we, you know, had a maximum of three, something like that . . . in 67 . . . encouraging the birthrate . . . and in 86 as well . . . we always feared High Court petitions and I hope you don't quote me, because a family from [the Arab towns of] Taybeh and Umm El Fahm could petition the court.[55]

In March–April 2009, Zochrot hosted a photo exhibition curated by Ariella Azoulay, based mostly on state archive materials, through which Azoulay sought to revisit 1948 and create a new organizing narrative.[56] The real importance of the exhibition was that it opened up the question of 1948 in time and spaces and the fact that its continuous description did not cut the Palestinian community into shreds, but rather creates a continuity between 1948 and the character of the Israeli regime. The official state archive footage teaches us of the mechanisms employed to carry out the ethnic cleansing: classification, separation of population from land, separation of women from men, setting up prisoner-of-war camps and internment camps, cases of massacres and rapes, intimidation, eradication of villages and expulsions. Expulsion in particular is shown by the photographs to be a many-layered phenomenon. Ben Gurion's warning to the Palestinian population that "we are not responsible for the protection of those who remain" should be seen as a decision to expel even if it's not stated in so many words.

The exhibition presents the Kafkaesque process that saw some of the 1948 refugees become "prisoners of war" in their own country, and then be transferred at the end of the war to Jordan, as part of their "release." The construction of the Green Line turned them into eternal refugees. Some of the Palestinians who remained within the Green Line found themselves in "temporary spaces" that became, in time, "temporary camps"; some stayed in urban ghettos. Meanwhile, the JNF was whitewashing away some of these deeds by planting forests over the ruins. It is a common practice among American Jews to contribute to the JNF, proudly planting a tree in Israel, not knowing that plantation is partially a cover-up practice for Israel's crimes. Elsewhere, refugees were replaced with immigrants; in Jaffa alone, 70,000 Palestinians were expelled and their homes were filled up with 45,000 Jewish immigrants. The Jaffawites that remained in Jaffa were herded into the Ajami quarter and had to obtain a permit every time they wanted to leave. As Israeli citizens, the Palestinians could no longer resist their situation, because any such resistance would constitute a challenge to the very nature of the regime.

Noga Kadman's book *Erased from Space and Consciousness* is probably the most comprehensive Hebrew book on the ethnic cleansing that Israel drove through the culture and space of 1948.[57] Kadman shows how the judaization of physical space is also judaization of memory, and vice versa. She rightly observes that "The approach of the Israeli society to the villages emptied out in 1948 . . . can serve as an indicator for the readiness of that society to arrive at a sustainable solution to the conflict,"[58] because suppressing the Palestinians' history will reduce their clout in the conflict as the Israelis understand it, thus reducing the options they can choose.[59] This conclusion is important. The ignorance in Israel regarding history from the Nakba perspective is not just an educational failure, but a moral one. Moreover, a complete understanding of what happened in Israel in 1948 will advance the future of the Jews, not just the Palestinians. This is why it is crucially important to study the work carried out by Zochrot and other organizations like Bimkom and the Israeli Committee Against House Demolitions.[60]

The options the organizations introduce into discussion are not simple either/or choices, because there are many definitions of the concept of "return."[61] This is contrary to three (not mutually exclusive) approaches to denying the 1948 ethnic cleansing of Palestine, which dominate the Jewish discourse.

The first approach, that of the mainstream, denies any Israeli responsibility for the creation of the refugee problem. The canonical stream of Zionist historiography, which supports this position, attributes the mass movement of Palestinians out of Israel not to ethnic cleansing carried out by Jewish forces, but to the Arab leaders allegedly instructing the Palestinians to abandon their homes and villages. This argument, which still enjoys some prominence among Jewish-American groups, is unsubstantiated by historical facts.

The second approach rejects Israel's responsibility for turning the Palestinians into refugees, and brings up the argument of a "population exchange," according to which the Middle East experienced a de-facto transfer, which sometimes happens in wartime, through which the Palestinians "fled" Palestine while Jewish refugees "fled" from Arab countries. This approach is highly questionable both morally and politically – let alone logically. The political theory that led the Israeli government, and some voluntary organizations, to establish this supposed equation was based on moral and political distortions. Israel "nationalized" the property of the Arab Jews to use it, symbolically, rhetorically and legally, as Israel state property.[62] The government argued for offset between the property of Arab Jews and the property of the Palestinian refugees – nationalized in 1948 under the purview of the Custodian of Absentee Property – to shake off its responsibility for compensations. Estimates of the overall worth of Palestinian property vary: Palestinian sources believe it to be in the range of $5.2 billion, the UN Reconciliation Committee set it at $1 billion ($6 billion in today's money). The offset approach is applied, moreover, to the right of return, although there is no relation whatsoever between the Palestinian refugees and the Arab Jews.[63] This approach is used by Israel, and Jewish organizations, to avoid a true and direct solution to the Palestinian refugee problem. The idea of offsetting the return has been advanced, since the 1970s, mostly through propaganda organizations such as WOJAC (World Organization of Jews from Arab Countries). Israeli spokesmen for the organization went as far as claiming that the Jewish refugees from Arab countries spent the 1950s in refugee camps, just like their Palestinian counterparts.

Even Shlomo Ben-Ami – who chaired the Israeli committee for negotiation of the refugee problem and, as Foreign

Minister, was one of Israel's top negotiators in the failed Camp David talks in 2000 – admitted as early as 1993 that there was a fundamental problem in presenting the Arab Jews as refugees, "because they fought for the Zionist dream." The Israeli idea of offsetting the theft of Palestinian property in Palestine with the theft of Jewish property in Arab countries is, obviously, absurd. Wrongs caused by the Iraqi or Egyptian authorities to their Jewish subjects cannot be offset by the wrongs caused by Israel to the Palestinians under its control. It seems reasonable to assume that an international foundation will be set up at some point in the future to compensate the Palestinian refugees who will not get back to their houses and lands, whether by choice or not; and Israel needs to contribute its own generous share to such a foundation. The offset idea cannot be allowed to serve as a scarecrow to frighten off the moral claims of the Palestinians.

The third approach is that of the *Yellow Wind*, or the 1967 paradigm, which acknowledges Israel's moral and political responsibility for the refugee problem, but rejects the right of return on the assumption it would bring about the end of the Israeli state.

In contrast to the mainstream discussion, which is based on denial and rejection, Zochrot has this definition of the right:

> The right of return is the personal right of each and every refugee expelled from the country (including their descendants) to choose whether to return to the place they were expelled from, to receive compensation or to become citizens and rehabilitate themselves in a different country. The right of return is not necessarily physical, actual return, but the possibility of choice between actual return and its alternative. It is a personal right, and at the same time it is also

a collective right, the right of entire communities to return
to community life, and it is enshrined in international law.[64]

I agree with the definition in principle, notwithstanding several reservations I will offer further on – such as,
for instance, that there should be no collective return of
Palestinian communities if the sites of their communities
have already been settled with Jews, since we cannot amend
one historical wrongdoing by creating a new one.

Still, I argue that the Arabs of 1948 are currently the ultimate "impediment" to this regime, inasmuch as they serve
as a constant reminder of the skeleton it keeps in the closet:
the ethnic cleansing of Palestine in 1948 – the expulsion,
the expropriation of land, the obliteration of towns and villages, and the "inaccuracy" of the historiographic narrative
aimed at justifying all these actions. The fact that the cleansing of the Jewish sovereign territory – achieved by expelling
Palestinians, by frightening them and by forcing them to
flee – remains incomplete leaves the ongoing presence of
Palestinians in Israel as profound testimony to the undemocratic nature of Israeli sovereignty. A new Jewish political
theory must return to 1948 as an Archimedean point for
thinking about the conflict. Contrary to the peace discourse
that removed the Arabs of 1948 from the conflict equation, it
is necessary to return to negotiations that include the Arabs
of 1948, and also the Palestinian refugees as a whole (including those living in refugee camps in Lebanon and Syria),
in defining sovereignty in a new format. My basic assumption is that division of the land into two state units with a
wall separating them is not possible; it is also immoral and
destructive on political, geographic, economic, civic and
religious grounds. Rather than regarding sovereignty as an
exclusive monopoly over territory and over national identity
in the format of the Westphalia peace treaties of the mid

seventeenth century, I suggest considering a post-Westphalian sovereignty, a sovereignty that is, in essence, porous, non-continuous and multiple. It assumes the existence of cross and joint sovereignties organized in a complex manner in different spheres of a common spatial region.

A SHARED TIME

The problem of 1948 is still out there, and reality will force Israeli Jews to confront it, whether they choose to or not, when the trajectory of violence hits its highest point.[65] There exists today a fairly comprehensive documentation of what occurred in 1948. The historians debate not so much the facts, as their interpretation.[66] The question of whether the Palestinians fled or were expelled – once the focal point of the debate – is no longer at the center of the historiographic discussion. Contrary to the disagreement on the question of escape versus expulsion, both sides agree that Israel has prevented the return of the refugees while denying the question of 1948. This conclusion is shared by both the radical left and the radical right in Israel.[67]

The liberal stratum of the Israeli society will have to choose between sticking to the denial regime and getting the skeleton out of the closet, and this latter choice is going to be hard because – among other reasons – that stratum's privileges are fed directly by the time of the Green Line. Much to its chagrin, the liberal left might become a reactionary force. Going back to 1948 will, essentially, redraw Israel's political map from scratch. This will be based on the principle that borders do not necessarily need to be linear and continuous. It will create a bi-national regime, which does not necessarily mean a bi-national state. There are many creative options for such resolution. The change will include a "post-Zionist" camp consisting of members of the radical left and the democratic stream of the settlement movement. On such a political map, some of the Zionist left and center parties will be cast as the anti-reformist right.

There's no single model for a bi-national regime and a bi-national society.[68] Even those supporting the bi-national model refrain from making that model too concrete.[69] Tamar Hermann divides Palestinian bi-national thought into three categories.[70] The first believes, in the spirit of Edward Said, that a bi-national state is the guiding principle for the very long term, because the chances of its realization today are slim. This positing has support in international literature, such as the works of Noam Chomsky. Another group believes that bi-national discourse should be used to frighten the Jews into hurrying up the process of establishing the "two states for two peoples" solution. A third group sees the bi-national model as a technical instrument to guarantee Palestinian majority in the contested space, bringing us back, unfortunately, to the demographic discourse. And yet voices in support of a bi-national society are increasing among the Palestinians, including ones who formerly supported two states for two peoples.[71] Such voices also multiply in the international community: the British daily the *Guardian* asked why no one fights for equal rights in one bi-national state, especially as such a state existed, de facto, in the country before 1948. And British-American historian Tony Judt famously wrote: "The very idea of a 'Jewish state,' a state in which Jews and the Jewish religion have exclusive privileges from which non-Jewish citizens are forever excluded, is rooted in another time and place. Israel, in short, is an anachronism."[72]

I would like to pause for a moment on Judt's use of the term "anachronism." The term expresses a perception of time, in this case a particularist time perception out of sync with historical time. As I have argued earlier on, perceptions

of time express different political perceptions, and form a
basis for struggles between groups. The standardization of
time carried out in Europe and, later, in the United States,
in the nineteenth century, is one very clear example. The
British Post Office began using Greenwich Mean Time, and
by 1855 its usage spread to 98 percent of the European population. At the end of that same century, American railroad
companies began pushing for a standard American time,
after train accidents brought home the dangers of a lack of
a shared time perception between different communities.[73]
We should remember that a struggle was waged over time
standardization between different nations – such as France
and England – and within the nations themselves (such as
the conflict between the train corporations and religious
communities) that opposed human intervention into "natural" and "divine time."[74]

In the context of the Israeli–Palestinian conflict, we should
reconsider a time perception that would be shared by both
nations and would allow them to meet, in time as well as in
space; Emile Durkheim reflected once that, without a shared
perception of time, no shared social life can be sustained.[75]
Returning to 1948 will allow Jews and Palestinians to meet
by synchronizing their clocks and watches and shaping new
patterns of control – not the one-way patterns of control
shaped by the time of the Green Line.

The time of the Green Line is forever moving towards
a past, a selective past, not to a shared future in the region.
I seek here to endorse a term coined by Jacques-Alain
Miller, who called this dormant state "retrospective time":
"We observe two times: A time that progresses, a time that
goes towards the future, and retrospective time, that moves
towards the past. The latter time is the one that, in some
senses, conjures the illusion of eternity: Everything belong-
ing to the future has already been registered somehow in

the past."[76] In the consciousness of the time of the Green Line, frozen in the historic time of 1967, the possibility of giving back the occupied territories still exists. But the historical context of the conflict has changed completely. Palestinian nationalism became more assertive and more radical, the settlement enterprise became an inseparable part of the Israeli "democracy," and demands for an unpartitioned country became more and more common among the Jews, as did the demands for recognition of the refugee experience, which grew stronger through political decisions (like the ones made by the Arab League) and a methodical, historical documentation of the experience's scope and assets.[77]

We should assume that going back to the time of 1948 will be a process of many rounds, taking place in phases, over a prolonged period of time. It will need to begin with some degree of synchronization of historical perceptions held by the Arabs and the Jews. It doesn't necessitate forsaking national or theological time perceptions, but it does require creating a new time that would allow shared living, a time with spatial aspects. We should conceive of a time–space that would allow the integration of communities, sovereignties or municipalities, in accordance with religious links, with consideration of the settlement enterprise, recognition of the Arabs of 1948 as a national collective in areas where there is a territorially continuous Arab majority within Israel, a shared administration of holy sites, and military balancing with regional cooperation.

The year 1948 is an arbitrary date. We could have started the analysis with the Balfour Declaration, the 1929 riots, the Great Arab Rebellion, the Biltmore Plan or the Partition Plan of 1947. The year 1948 is, to me, a balanced starting point, because it allows the inclusion of the Palestinian history of the Nakba, even if not in its entirety, and, at the same time, recognizes the existence of the Jews as a national collective, including their achievements since 1948.

Returning to the moment of 1948 would also open a myriad of opportunities for the Jews: it would allow them to expand their vocabulary and include in it the Palestinian trauma and catastrophe, but also the suppressed trauma of the Jews themselves. I see here a just solution that allows the inclusion of what both nations, with all their tremendous complexities and differences, have suppressed. The stories of the Nakba would be included in schools curricula. It's a prerequisite although an insufficient one on its own – for the establishment of a democratic regime. I've already noted that democracy is more than the procedural mechanism of governance: Israeli democracy can never be complete unless it includes the history of 1948, which will serve as the basis for a shared constitution that will do justice to both nations in the contested space, and divide its resources fairly and equitably.

Yet such a democracy can still allow for national sovereignties in agreed locations, according to the historic and religious links of the place, including Jewish history in Israel since 1948. Places shared by more than one religion, as in Jerusalem, can be jointly administered under a shared religious sovereignty. The work of actually dividing the space can be based on creative new ideas, such as separating the spheres of military, religious and national sovereignties. The demand for an exclusive space with Jewish characteristics is legitimate, and therefore it will be answered, as will a similar demand on the Palestinian side. A constitutional court can rule on disputes, while maintaining the basic law that no wrong will be amended by the creation of another wrong. The risks in altering the current regime – as is the case with the alteration of any incumbent regime – are enormous, and might be accompanied by violence. But the current model could lead to Armageddon, and urgently demands creative change that will allow a wider, more honest discussion between the two peoples.

5

THE RETURN TO THE RIGHTS OF
THE JEWS

The years after 1967 were marked by a rapid radicaliza-
tion of the groups that rejected the Green Line model: the
Palestinian refugees, the Arabs of 1948, the settlers and
many of the offspring of the Third Israel. These groups see
the Green Line itself as an anomaly, a whim of the Jewish
white liberal elites – all the more so as the very mainstream
of society has also treated the line with contempt, going as
far as bloating it from a borderline into a substantial strip
of land. These processes grew into an established practice,
especially after 1977.

The fruits of these processes ripened through the 1980s.
This decade was a cocktail of identity struggles in Israel –
some of them bloody – and the appearance of suppressed
forces at the front of the stage. In 1982 Israel waged a
total war in Lebanon, which was a total war against the
Palestinians. But what the Lebanon War suppressed in the
Israeli memory re-emerged, to Israelis' surprise, in the first
Intifada in 1988.[1] The suppressed Mizrachi identity re-

emerged with the Sephardi Shas revolution in 1984. The election of Meir Kahane to the Knesset in that year brought to the fore a discourse on biological racism against the Palestinians.[2] During the same period, Gush Emunim grew stronger, the settlement project was boosted by the 1977 transfer of power to the Likud Party, and Mizrachi Jews, ultra-Orthodox and immigrants moved to the settlements, many to improve their economic standing. The coalition of the suppressed made everyday political practice in Israel both post-liberal and post-secular. This was not a sharp rift with the liberal worldview, but part and parcel of its hidden theology and its nationalist underpinnings. These changes within the society in Israel challenge this liberal white position, and require a more inclusive and comprehensive worldview.

For example, there is a wide agreement among researchers that we effectively live in a post-secular world, and that liberal secularism is a minority ideology. Although there's much discussion of what post-secularism actually means, there's no disagreement that there are more religious people living in the world as a whole and operating within its political system than ever before. The last decades have seen an exponential rise in church attendance in the United States and parts of Europe, an eruption of religious and fundamentalist movements in Islam, a revival of neo-evangelism throughout Latin America, a "return to religion" in Africa and Asia and messianic religious struggles that shape politics and culture in Iran, Sri Lanka, India, Pakistan, Saudi Arabia and, obviously, Israel.

Religion – which appears in new shapes and guises in the public sphere and in the civic politics of the state – testifies that modernization does not necessarily lead to secularization. Global politics are also becoming theologized, and the attack on the World Trade Center has accelerated the development of a global discourse phrased around the idea of an inter-religious struggle, mostly between the Judeo-Christian theology and Islam. This doesn't mean all religions appear similarly in the public sphere or that the relations between religion and society are the same in every society, but comparative data indicate a strong hybrid between religion and secularism in modern society, in the East and in the West alike.

This post-secular world does not allow for the existence of secularism as an independent category, in the utopian spirit of European Enlightenment. It would seem that, even as church attendance in Europe overall is dropping, the theological-political discourse on the continent increases; one of the most prominent comparative religions scholars, José Casanova, argues that the European Union rests on Christianity as its organizing category.[3]

In Israel, the introduction into the center of politics of social and political groups previously marginalized by the historic Labor movement has changed the conditions of the "deal" they had cut with the state and the conditions of the ostensible "secular" pact. Sociologist Yagil Levi argues that, since the 1980s, the hegemonic structures of the army have been changing remorselessly. Middle-class and elite male secular Ashkenazi Jews, once the very core of the combat units, have vacated that slot in favor of Mizrachi Jews, religious-Zionists, new immigrants (especially from the former USSR and from Ethiopia) and, slowly, to women. Levi describes these changes as amounting to "a new social architecture of the military."[4]

Most of the decision-making elites in this new political cosmology are opposed to the Green Line and its political imaginings, and have contributed their share towards its eradication. The new cosmology eroded the 1967 paradigm and exposed its political futility. A new, reformist, Israeli politics will be operated by a coalition of left- and right-wing democrats – Arabs and Jews – who believe in sharing a single space rather than in the futile two-state solution. This will require a new concept of sovereignty: one which is not based on one rigid, linear and continuous borderline. It is fragmented, scattered and not continuous.

POST-WESTPHALIAN SOVEREIGNTY

Sovereignty, described by Thomas Hobbes as Leviathan's life-breath, may be the most important concept of modern political theory that has yet to undergo a process of systematic theoretical critical deconstruction. Its definition in international law (at least since the end of the nineteenth century) as a monopoly over territory is anachronistic and limiting. As Isaiah Berlin noted pointedly in his essay on nationalism, it is a definition of sovereignty subordinated to the rapacious Moloch of legal and territorial necessity – and, we may add, the Moloch of the violent victor.

We should recall that sovereignty, grounded as it is in political theory and practice, is based on the European model of territorial exclusivity. This view originated in the political lessons of the Peace of Westphalia (1648) and culminated in the development of the concept of citizenship 200 years later. In the seventeenth century, space appeared as sovereign territory; in the nineteenth century, with the development of history as an academic discipline, space also became subordinated to temporality. Since the end of the nineteenth century, European political thought has been based on the holy trinity of sovereignty–territory–citizenship. This is the trinity that established the European nomos as a theology of territorial law and defended its achievements. This trinity finds support in the modernist discourse that subordinated the concept of sovereignty to territory, war to international law, society to state sovereignty, and civil rights to the nation-state. Foucault characterizes this chain of logic as an "over-determined discourse on sovereignty," regretting that Westphalian sovereignty became the starting point as well as the essence of political thought. This overdetermination has taken over political thought and prevents us from thinking about the concept of sovereignty as anything other than a fabrication of the Leviathan as "mortal god."

Critical perspective on sovereignty will enable us to present it as a multifaceted concept rather than a stable, unitary category. Sovereignty is a porous, discontinuous spatial and temporal practice covering vague regions. This is the nature of borders themselves. These features are not deviations from the "ideal model" of sovereignty, but the opposite: they reflect the anomalies on which the definition of territorial sovereignty was initially based. The responses to the wave of terrorism that began with 9/11 have exposed time and again that the use of "exceptions to the law" has become the accepted practice of Western democratic states, and that the exception is in fact an integral component of the preservation of sovereignty both "internally" and "externally." It is a mirror image – even if inexact, because of changes over time – of the violent means with which sovereignty was initially established. Exposing this violence teaches us that territorial sovereignty is not truly unitary and homogeneous, and that it is based on violence organized along racialized lines.[5]

Contemporary critical literature proposes, with varying degrees of success, a number of alternative concepts that could be called "post-Westphalian sovereignty": "liquid sovereignty," "sovereignty gaps," "pourous sovereignty," "multiple sovereignty," "crossed sovereignty," "shared sovereignty." These conceptualizations are based primarily on the global logic of massive migrant streams throughout the world and the shifting of boundaries between racial groups, so that they no longer easily correspond to existing territorial borders and territorial homogeneity. Many additional elements create various spheres of sovereignty that cross both territories and the logic of fixed national boundaries: corporations, international financial institutions, communication technologies, theologies and ecological networks. Today, states – including Israel – are likely to divide sovereignty: privatizing state institutions, for example, and transferring trusteeship to a third party.[6] The members of the European Union have also established joint sovereignty in certain areas. While the need for post-Westphalian sovereignty in these instances stems from globalization, these examples can provide inspiration for other cases as well.

The idea of joint and rhizomatic sovereignty has been proposed in the past in the context of the Zionist–Palestinian conflict, but has never been taken seriously because of paradigmatic blindness and fear. If we think about joint sovereignties of Jews and Palestinians, we must admit they will not be based on linear territorial continuity but on joint, intersecting spheres of sovereignty that will provide solutions to the national, cultural, religious, economic and political aspirations of diverse communities. Mathias Mossberg, a Swedish diplomat, suggests thinking about sovereignty as political authority delegated to a series of institutions such as parliaments or councils administered autonomously and subordinated to a non-linear sovereign structure.[7] Mossberg refers, for example, to the ideas of condominium and federation. A condominium permits joint sovereignty over a territory, with political authority assigned horizontally. A federation permits joint sovereignty over a territory, with political authority assigned vertically. Some sectors of society (most notable is Jerusalem) would be under the authority of international institutions, whose incorporation in the various sovereign spheres would permit considerable political flexibility. Lev Grinberg proposes a fascinating hybridization of two democratic nation-states and seven provinces (or federations) that are part, to some degree, of the nation-states. This division would be based on a distinction between sovereign authority that is divisible and sovereign authority that is indivisible.[8]

These ideas of joint sovereignty are also based on my view that the Jewish territorial sovereignty achieved in 1948 as the ultimate aim of Jewish emancipation and "re-entry into history" had paradoxical consequences: rather than synchronizing Jews with history, as promised, it imprisoned them in a mythic conception of time and space external to both world history and the history of the region. Perhaps this is what the late Tony Judt meant when he described Zionism as "anachronistic." The violent perception of Jewish territorial sovereignty led to the adoption of an insular, myopic approach. Jews and Judaism once again became "an autarkic diaspora economy" that had lost its sense of history and neglected the rights of the Jews themselves, while creating a sovereignty that preserved master–slave relations between Jews and Palestinians. Against this picture, post-Westphalian sovereignty would require Jews to forgo some of their privileges – as did Afrikaners in South Africa in 1994 and more. Such a structure differs from the 1967 paradigm adopted by Zionist liberalism, which proposes (at best) mutual recognition but preserves the master–slave domination structure. This is because the Arab of 1948 will never enjoy national rights, and the Palestinian state will be truncated, devoid of natural resources, and militarily weak.

An alternative view of sovereignty might treat the Arabs of 1948 as partners in negotiations (not only as a passive population excluded from them) and allow the Palestinian refugees to return. My argument is that any return of refugees must also consider the Jews and their geography. This may sound hypocritical by virtue of the fact that I am a privileged Jew.[9] Nevertheless, I believe that the Palestinian narrative of destruction and redemption as a powerful ideological mechanism must be separated from formulations of the return as a multivalent process not only intended for one specific community, or as a way to stubbornly hold on to a specific place.

Creating a just structure will require a radical transformation of the Israeli land regime: the present structure that grants Jews exclusive preference will have to change. A shared Jewish–Palestinian constitutional court, reflecting the country's heterogeneous ethnic, national and religious structure, will also be established as a mechanism defining the nature of the spatial solutions. This constitutional court will formulate general principles to be implemented, including the following: the right of return is, first and foremost, a moral right, and not only a legal right; return is not a symbolic event involving the recognition of injustice but an action that must be implemented; and the country's geography, as it existed before the 1948 war, will be taken into consideration when implementing the return. Nevertheless, redress of the moral and political injustice must not create new injustices – villages that were destroyed and resettled by Jews will not be destroyed again.

While the geography of 1948 must serve as the moral compass for the return, it cannot be reconstructed during the return. Implementing the return must take into consideration the fact that many areas have been taken over – mostly violently – by Jews. The new communal structure will take the geography of destruction into account, but will merge it with the new communities created during the refugee years. The existing refugee communities are, moreover, larger than the original village communities, a given situation that will also require a decentralized political structure.

In addition to the return of communities, individuals will also return to large cities like Jaffa, Haifa, Lod, Ramla and Jerusalem. If the building from which the refugees were expelled is still standing, they will be able to demand it. If the present residents agree, they will be generously compensated. Very large sums of money will be required to pay for such compensation and to resettle the refugees; but shortage of funds must not be an excuse for failure to implement the return, inasmuch as the return and its implementation will be fundamental principles of the regime. Disputes will be brought to the constitutional court. The court will base its decisions on liberal–individual principles as well as on political–national principles. It will have to consider all aspects of the Nakba as well as changes that have occurred in the ethnic, national and religious structure of the population since 1948.

THE POSSIBILITY OF SHARING ONESPACE

There's something utopian about the idea of a just, equitable, multinational, diverse and universalist society. There is no such political framework in real life, and there never has been. I don't expect the Jews or the Palestinians to risk their future for meaningless political promises. The hoped-for political result should be a dynamic movement that will investigate various complex possibilities for moving forward, offering territorial and governmental alternatives. Can we conceive, for instance, of a Palestinian–Israeli confederation? Division into autonomic cantons? A single bi-national state? And perhaps two states, intertwined through complex structures disclosing the fact the two people can never really part?

What matters, at this point, is not the details, but the general intention to change the way of thinking, under which we will be forced to revisit our basic premises sooner or later.

There are three analytical models for organizing governance of the space, once the 1948 question is reopened.

The first model, least preferable and most problematic, is "a state of all its citizens" stretching across the entire space, with administrative sovereignty accessible to both Jews and Arabs.[10] This model is problematic, because it assumes homogenous communities with largely individual interests, and does not consider the fact that most of the population of the area concerned is both religious and nationalist, and that there are tremendous differences within both the Jewish and the Palestinian communities. This model is also problematic because it is based on a demographic race as an inherent principle of the regime. Demography is telling, but it should be excluded from the governmental discourse as soon as a new regime is put in place.

The second model is an equitable model of a shared sovereignty that allows expression of the full religious and national rights of the two peoples. Such a model would, to a degree, preserve the existing model of the Jewish state, but would redraw its borders and be based on a new political constitution that would be shaped through just distribution of the area's resources – including land, water, access to ports, natural resources and shared cultural and economic projects.[11] I'd like to reiterate here that the UN Partition Plan is based, *inter alia*, upon an economic union between the two countries, to be administered by a shared economic council. In such a model one would be able to move easily and freely across the space, from the river to the sea. Palestinian National Council member said once that the Palestinians must guarantee the safety of the Jews coming to pray in holy places;[12] this position allows for a sovereign linkage of Jews and Palestinians to holy sites, the possibilities of which should be further explored.

The third model is that of consociational democracy,

a model of partnership that presupposes the national and religious rights of both peoples, which would be expressed through dividing the space into smaller national spaces and into religious and secular communities, canton/federation-like.[13] This is a fragmented model that allows for flexibility, and is very difficult to implement and plan; but I suppose this will be the model that will eventually become the default in the future.

Such a model would take heed of the national, economic, religious and civic considerations of both peoples, and seek to balance them out. It would include the return of refugees who desire to return, and a fair attempt to rehabilitate them as described above. In other cases, new communities may be constructed – in the Galilee, in the Negev and in the West Bank and Gaza. The refugees' resettlement would be on an individual basis (for example, in big cities like Haifa), or on a communal basis, by rebuilding some of the destroyed communities on new sites. The building of new sites would be based on a general outlined plan negotiated by the two peoples, and the redistribution of space would not harm the existing and already settled population. The refugees would be rehabilitated and afforded broad-based affirmative action. Those who choose not to return would receive financial compensation. The eradicated communities would be mentioned in all official signposting. Some communities would retain their mono-national characters if they request it. The legitimate rights of both people to exist in a shared space, with or without any variety of internal borders, would be enshrined in a shared constitution that would acquire the support of the major international powers. The consociational option does not have a single a-priori order, but a wide, flexible range of possibilities.

The new regime should be based upon a bilingual society; Hebrew and Arabic would be the official languages of all citizens. We should notice that, at this point in time, most of the Palestinians in Israel speak Hebrew, but the vast majority of Israelis do not speak Arabic. Synchronizing the times and languages of the majority and the minority is a prerequisite for a true encounter.

The new regime would afford Palestinian citizens of Israel collective rights in the political, economic, cultural and education systems of the state. Mutual collective rights for the majority and minority would also allow civic demands, such as taking part in civic service, to be made of both Jews and Palestinians.[14] This would change both the political and judiciary systems to no small degree. We can conceive of a political model which would have two parliaments: one of the Jewish majority, another of the Palestinian minority. The relationship between the two houses would be defined by the constitution and the legislative assembly, and the constitutional court would resolve their disagreements. The ethnic boundaries between the two houses could be flexible, and Palestinians and Jews would be able to get elected into either house.

Such a regime could abolish, by definition, the demographic politics. Demography would become a product of the model, not its fundamental principle. The regime would be able to deconstruct disagreements which, until now, only had binary answers, such as the questions of the Law of Return and the right of return. The laws covering immigration of Jews to Israel could be reconsidered, with agreed basic principles taken into account. The same applies to the right of return, which today moves between one radical option and another: in this model, it could be implemented through a series of decisions made by the two houses, mediated by the constitutional court, in a dynamic process.

Sovereignty is a necessity for a regime, but, as argued above, I would like to suggest considering it a multiple practice, in some cases going as far as sovereignties shared by two peoples. Tzvia Gross, former legal adviser to the Defense Ministry, has correctly observed that today's definition of sovereignty is vastly different from the classical definition – which foresees a single sovereign authority with absolute control of a given territory. The modern state, including Israel, routinely splits its sovereignty apart, by, for instance, privatizing state institutions or operation of border crossings.[15] The states of the European Union have also decided upon shared sovereignty in some areas. The shared sovereignty of Jews and Palestinians would not necessarily be based on a linear territorial continuity, but on spheres of sovereignty that would be able to serve the national, cultural, religious, economic and political desires of the different communities.

Theology would also play a pivotal role here. In the summer of 2009, an inter-religious coalition of Jews and Muslims formed in Jerusalem to challenge the construction of the city's Tolerance Museum.[16] The Museum is being built upon an ancient Muslim cemetery; Islamic movements launched protests, but to no avail. But the protest did produce a fascinating coalition between the Islamic groups, Jewish left-wing activists and members of ultra-orthodox Shas, and managed to have the place declared as halachically foul and off-limits for religious Jews. Rabbi Sheetrit, a close affiliate of Jewish Shas spiritual leader Ovadia Yossef, has secured the support of the head of the ultra-Orthodox society of holy sites – the Hevra Kadisha – Rabbi David Schmidl. Sheetrit also secured the recognition of Joseph's Tomb in Nablus as sacred to the Jews by Palestinian Authority Chairman Mahmoud Abbas.[17] In another case, Palestinians allowed settlers to retain Jewish sovereignty over the tomb of Simeon the Just, at the heart of the Palestinian neighborhood of Sheikh Jarrah in East Jerusalem.[18] Even if, in these cases, the proposals were made in colonial circumstances, this means such arrangements are not far-fetched and, if set up in a mutual manner, could expand to other areas.

We could consider Jerusalem as the model of an unpartitioned city. Israel demands Jerusalem should remain united forever, and most Israelis support that. Ruth Lapidoth has suggested several sovereignty alternatives for the Holy Basin, including Israeli administration with Palestinian autonomy, Palestinian administration with Israeli autonomy, a joint Israeli–Palestinian administration, and the administration of the Basin as a single unit by an international organization.[19] Why shouldn't we consider similar models for the entire contested space?

A program could be shaped for the entire space and enshrined in a constitution. Any constitutional model that would be mono-national and rest upon gun barrels would merely serve as an incentive for more bloodshed in the future. Since the rights of the Jews are today guaranteed primarily through violent military means, a question that should be at the basis of the constitution has been forgotten: what are the rights of the Jews, who will, inevitably, end up being a minority in the contested space? Considering the fact Jews are already a minority in the larger space of the Middle East, their prime strategic objective is to define the rights of the Jews in any future governing arrangement.

As I mentioned earlier, this discussion used to have a place within the Zionist movement. Brit Shalom and other satellite organizations maintained that the time of the small nation-state was gone, and that the period after World War II would be the time of grand federations, within which every people would be able to retain an autonomy of national distinction.[20] Intellectuals like Martin Buber, Judah Magnes and Ernest Simon have made similar proposals regarding the Jewish–Arab space.

Some of them have been affected by the cultural approach of Ahad Ha'am, who rejected the popular attitude of Zionism of the late nineteenth century, which held that "The Arabs are all desert savages, a nation resembling a donkey, which does not see or understand what is going on around it."[21] Ahad Ha'am thought that the Zionist idea did not necessarily need to be realized through a sovereign Jewish state: "The Zionist movement abroad, in its real shape ... and real force ... will go on existing even if the Land of Israel sinks tomorrow into the sea. 'Zion' for most Zionists has for a long time been a Tabernacle that can be pitched anywhere, not a Temple."[22] Ben Gurion would later dismiss this outlook, arguing that merely setting up a spiritual center was not Zionism: "A spiritual center – that would be the Hebron Yeshiva. The end of this yeshiva marks the fate of the spiritual center. No Jewish society that will serve as an example for the Jewish people will arise under the oriental Arab rule; instead, a new Yemenite diaspora will be created in Israel, perhaps the lousiest and most miserable diaspora there is."[23]

Magnes, who remained loyal to the path charted by Ahad Ha'am, saw the possibilities for an Arab–Jewish union in several circles: the first, a union between Jews and Arabs in a bi-national framework; the second, a regional semitic union between Palestine and the neighboring countries; and the third, an international circle that would take part in the local process.[24] Magnes despised violent nationalism: "Jewish nationalism tends to confuse people, not because it's secular rather than religious, but because this nationalism is regrettably chauvinist, narrow-minded and terrorist, in the finest style of eastern-European nationalism."[25] Magnes was opposed to both transfer and population swaps, and initially supported the idea of remaining in the British Commonwealth, believing such a framework would

assist in safeguarding a just administration of the area's natural resources.[26] After meeting with one of the leaders of
the Palestinian national movement, Mussa al-Alami, a draft
agreement was prepared, covering all the fundamental questions of the conflict: immigration, land and government.
The immigration laws included yearly immigration quotas.
The Jews committed to stop purchasing vast tracts of lands
from Palestinian peasants, and a cap was suggested for overall land purchases. The government envisioned included a
centralized power-sharing arrangement, with an Arab Prime
Minister and a Jewish Deputy Prime Minister, or vice versa.
Hans Cohn even composed a detailed constitution for a bi-
national entity, which he wanted to present to the British
authorities.[27] Magnes, it should be noted, stated on several
occasions that he was not anti-Zionist, pointing out that "an
anti-Zionist is someone opposed to the notion of a Jewish
national home in this land, not someone who is opposed to
the policies and methods of the Zionist Federation."[28]

Magnes also considered the para-military organizations – Haganah, Irgun and the Lehi – to be expressions of
"Nationalist Zionism."[29] Buber likened the Zionist approach
to Arabs to Israel's approach to the Givonites: they were seen
as wood-cutters and water-drawers. To Buber, the Jewish
state was a disaster and a mirage.[30] Ernst Simon foresaw as
early as 1932 that the "Israeli group" of the Jewish people
"will have to develop all the positive and negative characteristics of a warrior nation. In other words, it will have to be
the fascist chapter of the Jewish people."[31] Hans Cohn, who
despaired of Zionism and immigrated to the United States,
wrote:

> Now only two ways remain: either to oppress the Arabs and
> subjugate them through a continuous display of military
> might, of the worst kinds of imperial or colonial militarism

– or . . . to do our best to seek out paths to the Arabs and completely reshape Zionism in the light of pacifism, anti-imperialism, and democracy – all that the spirit of true Judaism actually means.[32]

Some of these thinkers did indeed meet with Palestinian leaders and try to interest them in their plans, usually to no avail. Some have changed their positions considerably over time. Many continued opposing the idea of a Jewish state even after the introduction of the Biltmore Plan in 1942. Magnes argued then a Jewish state would mean a state of constant war in the region.[33] Buber also believed that, if a Jewish state was set up, "it will find itself in a state of war for generations, which will oblige it to militant, totalitarian behavior."[34] Ghersom Scholem prophesied destruction: "It is no longer possible to rescue the movement from the forces it was sold to without a historic catastrophe . . . either it will be washed away with the waters of imperialism, or it will be burned in the revolutionary flames of the awakening East."[35]

In the meanwhile, however, these intellectuals have never forsaken what was always at the top of their priorities: the legitimate rights of the Jews in the contested space. Following the clashes between Jews and Arabs at the Western Wall on Atonement Day, 1929, Brit Shalom issued an unequivocal statement saying that the rights of the Jews must be addressed and their historical rights in the Land of Israel should be stressed.[36] It made clear that, despite its support for a democratic parliament, the question of Jewish immigration and settlement should be resolved by the Jews themselves.[37]

These statements were made before 1948, at a point in time when it was still hypothetically possible to distribute the space, to prevent the war and to create a more just, more sustainable reality. This reality is long since gone, but we may still see the proposals of Brit Shalom and Ichud as an invitation to re-imagine 1948 as an ideological revolution, a kind of a Copernican revolution that will turn around the order of things as it has been known until now. In *Critique of Pure Reason*, Kant wrote of Copernicus that when he found that he could make no progress by assuming that all the heavenly bodies revolved round the spectator, he reversed the process, and tried the experiment of assuming that the spectator revolved, while the stars remained at rest. Borrowing from Kant, we may go on and say that, after finding we could make no progress in resolving the conflict around the principle of the Green Line and the 1967 paradigm, perhaps we will meet with more success by acknowledging the disappearance of the line and looking at the political cosmology from a new perspective.

Is there a chance for this to happen non-violently? Probably not. I left important dimensions out of the utopian analysis several pages back – power, fear of change, the disengagement from the current regime of privileges, and the particular interests of each group. Leaving the power dimension outside the scope of one's analysis is a paradoxical stance to take for a sociologist trained to identify power structures in every action and discourse. The realistic position would be to state that the existing power structure will find it difficult to cope with such a vision and will prefer to ignore it. In other words, the chances for such an option to be realized voluntarily are slim. Another factor that should be taken into account in the power dimension is that the international community does not support the one-space solution, each state for its own reasons (the United States, for instance, has a strategic interest in keeping Israel Jewish.)

Considering the opposition it is certain to encounter from existing power structures, my proposition is likely to be distorted in the public discourse in Israel; the liberal public will decry it as radical leftist, and my positions may well be appropriated for the legitimization of the settlement enterprise, or legitimizing the fascist right in its work to take over more territory. I should make clear at this point that my position against the eviction of settlers does not stand on its own, but is intrinsically linked to a comprehensive solution of opening up the space and creating political justice – although this is a matter for more detailed development of the ideas proposed in this book, Israel would need to pay compensation not only for the property and land stolen from the refugees, but also for the property and the land stolen to build the settlements.

My position may also draw strong criticism from Palestinians on both sides of the Green Line who do wish to have the land partitioned by the "two states for two peoples" principle. They will argue I have no right to speak in their name, most certainly not to give up a Palestinian state in the 1967 borders, and that my positions here stem from my political privileges as a Jew. This is a justified argument and it is also linked to the positioning of this essay in the overall power matrix.

A COMMENT ON THE ROLE OF INTELLECTUALS IN TIMES OF CRISIS

My choice to present here, despite these risks, a utopian position imagining reality released from the shackles that ground it stems from my view on the role of the intellectual. We are faced with the fundamental questions: what is an intellectual? Who does he/she represent? What is the meaning of the agenda that he/she produces?[38] The critical work of the intellectual focuses on the gap between the existing and the possible, since intellectuals are expected not merely to represent a given public, but also – and even most of all – to mark out the possible and the desirable. Herbert Marcuse, in this context, suggested the intellectual should understand reality exactly as it is, and, at the same time, utterly reject the facts of it.[39] The gentle interplay between the present and the absentee, between reality and utopia, allows the rebuttal of deterministic narrations of political histories and futures. Robert Musil comments on this tension between the existing and the possible in his wonderful book, *Man Without Qualities*:

> He who seeks to easily enter open doors should take into account their frames are solid. This principle . . . is but one of the demands of a sense of reality. But if there is a sense of reality, and no one will challenge its right to exist, it would follow that there is also something called the sense of possibility . . . the sense of possibility can therefore be defined as the ability to think things that also could have been, and not to consider what exists more than that which does not exist. This creative talent can, it transpires, bring about interesting results; and, regrettably, it may also make something people admire appear wrong, and something they prohibit appear to be permitted.[40]

In this analysis, the intellectual can, and even must, represent a universal idea even if its supporters are few and far between.[41]

I remember how, in the late 1980s, protests swelled in Austria against former UN Secretary-General, Kurt Waldheim, after information on his membership of a Nazi organization in his youth came to light. The Prime Minister of Israel at the time, Yitzhak Shamir, praised the protestors for their courage. At the very same time, protests were also being held in Israel – against Israeli violence in the West Bank. Shamir dubbed these protestors "traitors."

This paradox reflects the inevitable tension between the

universal and the particular. We can take up and identify with a universalist stand when it's far away from us, but often have trouble recognizing it in our own back yard.[42] To take a stand against the regime, an intellectual must convert the symbolic capital he/she has accumulated into moral and political capital, and use it to criticize the powers that be. Yeshayahu Leibowitz didn't draw his moral strength from the complexity of his theoretical outlook on humanitarian questions, but from his symbolic capital in the field of science, which he converted into the moral field, and from the consistency and strength he had shown by repeating the principles of his faith time and time again.[43]

The fear in Israel of a regime change does not come only from the existence of a national "other" per se, but also from the fact a regime change would require many in Israel to disengage from their privileges. This is why much of the liberal audience will reject these proposals and possibly describe them as delusional. Some might say they are borderline illegitimate, because they might contradict the basic premises of the Jewish state. But neither the regime nor the law were handed down to the people on Mount Sinai, and they are based merely on what Walter Benjamin labeled "constituting violence." The task of the intellectual is to expose the mechanisms of this violence.

Michel Foucault argues that governmental arrangements on rights conceal a discourse of an unfinished war.[44] To Foucault, politics are a continuation of the war by other means, an inversion of the von Clausewitz maxim that war was a continuation of politics by other means. The war observed by Foucault is the class war, the race war, the national war – or a mix of all the above, existing before the establishment of the law and concealed by it.

Certain political terms – rights, civil liberty, civil society, democracy, the rule of law, republicanism, progress – also serve to conceal the continuation of the war. Foucault offers here a new way to understand history, not through the universal rights discourse (primordial right, natural right, right to property, right to life, right to vote, right to freedom of expression), but through the discourse of war, expressed in terms like "victory" and "conquest." In other words, Foucault challenges the modern understanding of subjugating the war to the state and retaining it as something external that happens between, rather than within, countries. For Foucault, even "peace" is a coded war, since the agreement, once signed, still inevitably bears "dry blood."

This is precisely the Israeli situation. Foucault would have described the demographic discourse in Israel as a continuation of the war by other means, because of its usage of the Schmittian distinction of "friend" and "foe." Opening up the 1948 paradigm in the Green-Line-time consciousness should come from choice, because the alternative is a violent civil war between "friends" and "foes." This is the tragedy before which we stand.[45]

The tragedy is exacerbated when we recall that, by accepting the 1967 paradigm, Israeli social democracy defends the wealthy elites and the separation solution. Its consciousness barrier does not allow it to include 1948, and it makes itself dependent on "the outcome of the war."

But the time of the Green Line is a suspended time. At some point, in the not-too-distant future, the forces that simmer underneath will burst to the front of the stage – like they did in 1967, with theological messianism; in 1977, with the overthrow of the old Labor elite; in 1987, with the first Intifada; and in 2000, with the second one – and violently undermine the 1967 paradigm. The current privileges regime and the fear of losing it – the demographic discourse is one very stark manifestation of that fear – stop the liberal elites from seeing the writing on the wall.

The thought-terrorism of the demographic discourse – which forces facts into a banal and dangerous mode of thinking – is violent towards the Palestinians, but, in the long run, it will become just as violent towards the Jews. This is the reason why opening discussion on the rights of the Jews is central to the new political program.

Today, there is no public sphere for discussing the rights of the Jews because of the asymmetry between their rights and the rights of the Palestinians: The daily, ongoing infringement of Palestinian rights obscures from discussion the legitimate rights of the Jewish residents of the area. Their rights cannot be guaranteed or sustained through violence. It is foolish to think existential security can be provided through nothing but a strong army; and that's even without mentioning the price maintaining such an army exacts upon Israel and the lifestyle to which it sentences the Israelis. And yet Israel can still use its overwhelming military might to guarantee a just and sustainable solution for both itself and the Palestinians.

The perspective I brought here is that of a utopia, for whose realization the chances are unfortunately slim. But even if the sociological conclusion is a pessimistic one, the political process of a return to 1948 is necessary, if only to include the Palestinian trauma of 1948 that has never healed and that continues to demand the repayment of its price. This process would also serve to expose the suppressed traumas of the Jews. Herbert Marcuse, despite his pessimistic sociological perspective described earlier, continued nevertheless to participate in protests and political movements. When asked about this contradiction, he replied: as a sociologist, I am pessimistic, but as a political person, I'm an optimist. I wrote this essay as a political person.

NOTES

Introduction and Overview: The Crisis Facing Zionist
Democracy

1 See, for example, Nathan Rotenstreich (1958), *The Jews and the Rights of the Jews*. Tel Aviv: Ha'Kibbutz Ha'Meuchad (Hebrew); Chaim Gans (2009), *A Just Zionism: On the Morality of the Jewish State*. Oxford: Oxford University Press.

2 Quoted in Tom Segev (2001), *1949: The First Israelis*. Jerusalem: Domino.

3 Ibid., 21.

4 Ibid., 23.

5 Ibid., 23.

6 A recorded history of the erasure of the Green Line may be found in, e.g., Peace Now's ongoing records, e.g. "Israel Erases the Green Line," "Settlement watch" : www.peacenow.org.il//data/SIP_STORAGE/files/0/3770.pdf (all URLs cited in the notes were last accessed in 2009). See also: "Where Did the Green

Line Disappear and Why Are There No Boundaries?":
www.machsomwatch.org/he/spotlight_21.

7 For a discussion of the Green Line as a cultural site
   and as a myth, see: Adriana Kemp (1999), The Mirror
   Language of Border: Territorial Borders and the
   Establishment of a National Minority in Israel, *Israeli
   Sociology*. 2 (1): 319–49 (Hebrew).

8 Michael Young (1988), *The Metronomic Society – National
   Rhythms and Human Timetables*. London: Thames and
   Hudson; see also: Hanna Herzog (2000), Every Year
   Could Be Considered the First Year: Arrangements of
   Time and Identity in Israel of the 1950s, *Theory and
   Criticism*. 17: 209–16 (Hebrew); Hanna Herzog (2007),
   Each Generation Will Tell the Following One: The
   Dialectics of Social and Political Generation Relations
   in Israel, in Hanna Herzog, Tal Kohavi and Shimshon
   Zelniker (eds.), *Generations, Spaces, Identities: Perspectives
   on the Construction of Society and Culture in Israel*. Tel Aviv
   and Jerusalem: Ha'Kibbutz Ha'Meuchad and the Van
   Leer Institute (Hebrew); Hanna Herzog (2009), Such
   and Such Generations: A Proposal for a Generational
   Perspective on Sociological Discourse, *Israeli Sociology*.
   10 (2): 259–85 (Hebrew).

9 On the notion of beginning in Palestine see: Honaida
   Ghanem (2011), The Urgency of a New Beginning in
   Palestine: An Imagined Scenario by Mahmoud Darwish
   and Hannah Arendt, *College Literature*, 38 (1): 1–20.

10 For differences between Jewish and Palestinian time, see
   Amal Jamal (2008), On the Hardships of Racialized Time,
   in Yehouda Shenhav and Yossi Yonah (eds.), *Racism in
   Israel*. Tel Aviv and Jerusalem: Ha'Kibbutz Ha'Meuchad
   and the Van Leer Institute, pp. 348–80 (Hebrew).

11 Johannes Fabian (1983), *Time and the Other: How
   Anthropology Makes Its Object*. New York: Columbia

University Press; David Harvey (2005), *A Brief History of Neo-Liberalism*. Oxford: Oxford University Press; Mikhail Bakhtin (1968/1984), *Rabelais and his World*. Bloomington: Indiana University Press.

12 In the context of the historic Palestine, Dan Rabinowitz writes: "Dozens of researchers [European scholars] . . . claim in their prefaces and introductions that their point of departure is the Bible. Their object of research – the local inhabitants they encountered during their work in Palestine – are nothing but living testaments in their path of deciphering the codes embedded in the pages of the Holy Scriptures." See Dan Rabinowitz (1988), *Anthropology and the Palestinians*. Beit Berl: The Center for the Study of Arab Society, p. 18 (Hebrew). Also note that the 9/11 events re-opened the term "secular time" and created a political paradigm defined through the Cold War, on the basis of what was called "The Clash of Civilizations." They led to the creation of new political–judicial tools and posed a new challenge to cultural studies in their judiciary, historiographical, political, philosophical and theological aspects. For discussions on the exception and state of emergency in the context of Israel, see: Yehouda Shenhav, Christoph Schmidt and Shimshon Zelinker (2009), *Beyond the Letter of the Law: The Politics of Exception and State of Emergency*. Tel Aviv and Jerusalem: Ha'Kibbutz Ha'Meuchad and the Van Leer Institute (Hebrew).

13 Jacques Alain Miller (2005), The Erotics of Time, *Lacanian Ink*. 24–25 (Spring): 8–63.

14 Thomas Kuhn (1962), *The Structure of Scientific Revolutions*. Chicago: University of Chicago Press.

15 See, for example, Tony Judt (2003), Israel: The Alternative, *The New York Review of Books*. November, 50 (2).

16 These oppositions serve to preserve the general framework of the ruling paradigm rather than to mark meaningful divides. For example, the disagreement between secular and religious Jews about the essence of the state serves ultimately to ratify the Jewish hegemony in Israel.

17 Zeev Sternhell (2009), Onwards to Save Democracy, *Haaretz*. March 6:, p.23a.

18 Yossi Harpaz (2009), Israelis and the European Passport: Understanding Dual Citizenship in an Apocalyptic Immigrant Society. MA thesis, Tel Aviv University. See also the words of Israel's Ambassador to the US, Michael Oren, who in the past wrote that Israel may turn into a "state in which Jews will not be prepared to live, nor sacrifice their life." In Akiva Eldar (2009), The Anxious Ambassador, *Haaretz*. May 12, p. 2b.

19 Herbert Marcuse (1964), *One Dimensional Society: Studies in the Ideology of Advanced Industrial Society*. Boston: Beacon.

20 The rapid migration of votes from the Labor Party and Meretz to Kadima in Israel's 2009 general elections was prime evidence of such political paralysis. Kadima, a movement characteristic of the masquerade ball of Israeli politics, blurs the traditional distinctions between left and right or coalition and opposition.

21 See: Noga Kadman (2008), *Erased from Space and Consciousness*. Tel Aviv: November Books (Hebrew).

22 See also: Lev Grinberg (2007), *Imagined Peace and War Discourse – The Failure of Leadership, Politics and Democracy in Israel 1996–2006*. Tel Aviv: Resling (Hebrew). Grinberg argues – and is right – that the Green Line enabled an imagined resolution to the conflict during the Oslo Accords.

23 See: Larissa Fleishman and Ilan Salomon (2006), The

Answer to the Question "Where is the Green Line?"
is "What is the Green Line?" *Alpayim*. 29: 26–52
(Hebrew); see also: Michael Feige (2002), *Two Maps to
the West Bank*. Jerusalem: Magnes (Hebrew).

24 At this stage I omit the question of Jerusalem and the
Temple Mount and will return to it in the last chapter.

25 See, for example, Dmitry Slaviniak's comments on the
movement of immigrants from the former Soviet Union
to the occupied territories in the West Bank: Dmitry
Slaviniak (2002), Neither Decoration of Valor Nor
Mark of Disgrace, *Eretz Acheret*. 10: 50–2 (Hebrew).

26 See, for example: Leila Farsakh (2005), Independence,
Cantons and Bantustans: Whither the Palestinian State?
Middle East Journal. 59: 1–16; Leila Farsakh (2011), The
One State Solution and the Israeli Palestinian Conflict:
Palestinian Challenges and Prospects, *Middle East
Journal*. 65: 55–71. See also the conference held on July
12, 2009, entitled "The One State Solution," organized
by Mada al-Carmel and Ibn Khaldun institutions. See
also: As'ad Ghanem (2008), Bi-National State Solution,
Israel Studies. 14 (2): 120–33; Bashir Bashir (2009),
'Bi-national State in Israel/Palestine: A Moral and
Practical Solution, in *Third Annual Conference: Towards
a Palestinian Strategy Capable of Realizing the Palestinian
National Aims*. Ramallah: Palestinian Centre for Media
and Research – Badal, pp. 132–8 (Arabic). For defense
of the two-state solution, see: Hussein Ibish (2006),
What's Wrong with the One-State Agenda? Washington
DC: American Task Force on Palestine.

27 On this politics, see, for example: Amal Jamal (2002),
Avoidance as a Form of Participation: On the Delusions
of Arab Politics in Israel, in Asher Arian and Michal
Shamir (eds.), *Elections in Israel – 2001*. Jerusalem: The
Israeli Institute for Democracy, pp. 57–100 (Hebrew).

28 Abu Mazen recently stated: "It is not my task to define the State of Israel. Call yourselves what you want – it is none of my business. All I know is that the State of Israel should exist only within the 1967 borders. Beyond that I do not accept any demand to recognize a Jewish state": Barak Ravid and Avi Issascharov (2009), Obama's Intention to Recognize the Hamas is Disappointing and Disturbing, *Haaretz*. April 28, p. 3 (Hebrew).

29 See, for example, the statement of Abu Ala, the Head of the Palestinian negotiation team (2008): We May Demand a Bi-national State Solution, *Haaretz*. August 11 (Hebrew). Regarding Israel's demands that the Palestinian recognize it as a Jewish state, Abu Ala mentioned: "We said it is none of our business. Call your state whatever you want – democratic or not, Jewish or not. It is not a fair demand, as it is tantamount to the evacuation of Israeli Arabs and predetermines the fate of the refugees, before the conclusion of negotiations. Our opposition to it is indeed firm." See: Akiva Eldar (2009), Border Control/ Peace According to Abu Ala, *Haaretz*. May 26, p. 1 (Hebrew).

30 At the "One-State Solution" conference held on July 12, 2009, organized by Mada al-Carmel and Ibn Khaldun institutions.

31 In this context, see: Yitzhak Laor (1995), *We Write You Homeland*. Tel Aviv: Ha'Kibbutz Ha'Meuchad (Hebrew); see also the works of Hannan Hever on the Hebrew literature: Hannan Hever (2001), *Producing the Modern Hebrew Canon*. New York: University of New York Press.

32 See, for example: Ruth Gabison (2002), The Jewish State: Its Principal Justification and Desirable Form,

Tchelet: 13: 50–88 (Hebrew). Gabison emphasizes the need for a moral Jewish state. She recognized the "Israeli Arabs' sense of discrimination" (p. 58), but also demands that the Palestinians accept the legitimacy of the Jewish state model, and claims that the gaps between Jews and Arabs in Israel are no wider than that of minority and majority groups elsewhere (p. 58). She argued that there is no difference between a Jewish state and a state for the Jews. She further explains that the "initial Arab insubordination following 1967 has led to the vibrant Jewish settlement enterprise in some of the territories" (p. 66). That is, the settlements were not rooted in Zionist theology and expansionism, but rather, again, in Arab "insubordination." This is a colonial position which denies the sociological and theological-political sources of the settlements, as will be elaborated further on.

Chaim Gans offers a more critical and nuanced approach in which he argues that Israel is a Jewish state in that it realizes, and should realize, the right of the Jews to self-definition. His critical stance highlights that "the right to self-definition should not be understood as the right to ownership and hegemony in all fields, especially in countries comprised of several ethno-national groups." Nevertheless, Gans ultimately argues that "it is justifiable for the Jews to aspire for a significant Jewish majority in Israel and for the state to assist in some ways, subject to the limitation decreed by the upholding of human rights. If a Palestinian State will be established, as I believe it should and is also supported by the majority of Israelis, a certain state of inequality between Jews and Arabs would be acceptable: particularly inequality pertaining to Jewish immigration and inequality justified by the force of their numerical differences or one that may be justified through numerical gaps." See Chaim Gans (2006), Particularly Jewish or Only Jewish? *Haaretz*. December 27 (Hebrew); see also Gans's important book, Chaim Gans (2008), *A Just Zionism: On the Morality of the Jewish State*. Oxford: Oxford University Press. For critique of this approach: Nadim Rouhana and Areej Sabbagh-Khoury (2006), Belligerence, the Space of Tolerance and the Privileged State, in Hanna Herzog and Kinneret Lahad (eds.), *Knowing and Keeping Silent: Silencing and Denial Mechanisms in Israeli Society*. Tel Aviv and Jerusalem: Ha'Kibbutz Ha'Meuchad and the Van Leer Institute, pp. 62–74 (Hebrew).

33 This recognition arises also among groups which are considered Zionist left. For example, Dafna Golan Agnon initially believed that only if the Israelis return to the 1967 borders can they liberate themselves from discrimination against the Palestinians. Yet, during her work as a Senior Adviser for the Minimization of Gaps at the Ministry of Education she understood that the discrimination is deeply rooted and well structured and that it was ingrained in 1948. See Dafna Golan Agnon (2005), How Loathsome We Are, *Eretz Acheret*. 27: 56–9 (Hebrew).

34 As I argue later, this will also bring the discourse on war into the society within "proper Israel." See the historical debate on the concealment of "internal" warfare in Michel Foucault (2003), *Society Must Be Defended*. New York: Picador. For analysis of Foucault's thesis, see: Andrew Neal (2004), Cutting off the King's Head: Foucault's *Society Must Be Defended* and the Problem of Sovereignty, *Alternatives: Global, Local, Political*. 29 (4): 373–98.

35 See, for example: Adi Ophir (1998), Zero Hour, *Theory and Criticism*. 12–13: 15–31 (Hebrew).

36 For a discussion on the strategies with which Israel dismissed restitution for the refugees, see: Yehouda Shenhav (2005), Arab Jews, "Population Exchange" and the Palestinian Right-of-Return, in Ann Lesch and Ian Lustick (eds.), *Exile and Return: Predicaments of Palestinians and Jews.* Pennsylvania: University of Pennsylvania Press, pp. 225–45 (reprinted in Arabic in the *Palestinian Review of History and Society.* Spring 2006, 1; reprinted in Hebrew in *Sedek.* 3: 67–80).

37 Larissa Fleishman and Ilan Salomon have shown that an increasingly large segment of Israel's population is not familiar with the Green Line. Their research further shows, as expected, that some political groups are more aware of the Green Line than others. For example, students at Bar Ilan University were less aware of the Green Line outline than those who study at the Hebrew University of Jerusalem (even if the latter did not demonstrate great knowledge). See Fleishman and Salomon (2006), The Answer to the Question "Where is the Green Line?" is "What is the Green Line?" For a survey held in the 1990s, see: Yuval Portugali (2006), *Contained Relations: Society and Space in the Israeli– Palestinian Conflict.* Tel Aviv: Ha'Kibbutz Ha'Meuchad (Hebrew).

38 Akiva Eldar and Gideon Alon (2006), Halakhic Ruling: It Is Forbidden to Study from Textbooks which Contain the Green Line, *Haaretz.* December 5 (Hebrew).

39 Zeev Sternhell (2006), The Green Line is the Border, *Haaretz.* December 15 (Hebrew).

40 This is one of the reasons why the word "occupation" should be used with caution. The word blurs occupations which have taken space in the area since 1947. Moreover, international law rules that occupation is

a situation in which a foreign army rules a territory following warfare. It is essentially defined as a temporary situation which should be resolved through the regularization of the territory in the framework of a peace agreement which will lead to the end of the war. See declaration of purpose: *Indeed a Democracy?* Jerusalem: The Association for Civil Rights in Israel, June 2007, p. 2: www.acri.org.il/pdf/democlong.pdf. The term "occupation" assumes the existence of clear borders and consecutive sovereignty which can be clearly demarcated in accordance with international law. Instead, we find perforated sovereignty, unclear borders and demands for Palestinian self-definition from "within" and "without." See: Yehouda Shenhav (2007), Why Not "Occupation," *Theory and Criticism.* 31: 13–15 (Hebrew). See: Lev Luis Greenberg (2009), Speechlessness: In Search of Language to Resist the Israeli "Thing Without a Name," *International Journal of Political Cultural Sociology.* 22: 105–16. Others have used different terms. The late Baruch Kimmerling termed it "politicide," Sari Hanafi termed it "spaciocide," whereas Hunaida Ghanem referred to it as "thanato-politics."

41 See Meir Hazan (2009), *Moderation: The Moderation of Hapoel Hatzair and Mapai 1905–1945.* Tel Aviv: Am Oved (Hebrew).

42 The absence of a significant left in Israel is not only related to the end of conflict. In the 1960s, for example, when radical youth movements arose throughout the world and protested against the nuclear bomb and the Vietnam War and supported the Civil Rights Movement, the struggle of the students and the feminist battle, the youth in Israel was busy worshipping Israeli militarism. Scholars have shown that Israel's Labor

movement never held independent leftist opinions, but only ones which were subject to the national interest. This malfunction still marks social-democratic attitudes in Israel. See: Yagil Levy (1998), The Austerity Regime, *Theory and Criticism.* 12–13: 36–46 (Hebrew); see also: Dov Khenin and Danny Filc (1998), The Strike of the Sailors, *Theory and Criticism.* 12–13: 89–98 (Hebrew), and Elkana Margalit (ed. and intro.) (1991), *The United Left: Mapam's Social Path in the Early Years of the State 1948–1954.* Collection of Studies Givat Habiba: Yad Yaari: Center for the Documentation and Research of Hashomer Hatzair (Hebrew).

Sternhell also developed this claim in his book: Ze'ev Sternhell (1995), *The Founding Myths of Israel.* Tel Aviv: Am Oved (Hebrew).

43 See Nadim Rouhana (2001), Reconciliation in Protracted National Conflict: Identity and Power in the Israeli–Palestinian Case, in A. Egly et al. (eds.), *The Social Psychology of Group Identity and Social Conflict: Theory, Application and Practice.* Washington, DC: Amer Psychological Association pp. 173–87.

44 Ari Shavit interviews Shlomo Ben-Ami (2001): The Day the Peace Died, *Haaretz.* September 14 (Hebrew). In the debates which followed the Annapolis summit, for example, the Israeli agenda seemed similar to that of Ben Ami. Saib Arikat reported that in 2008 Prime Minister Ehud Olmert offered him 5.8 percent of the territory within the Green Line in exchange for 6.5 percent of the West Bank. This proposal follows the logic of Camp David and it is therefore not surprising that it did not yield any real results. See: ww.omedia.co.il/Show_Article.asp?DynamicContentID=25152&MenuID=824&ThreadID=101401.

45 This "accountancy" language has been the language of

all peace talks since. For example, Shaul Arieli, who is associated with the "Geneva Initiative," states the following: "Like Barak, Olmert attempted to break the code of the peace agreements between Israel and Egypt and between Israel and Jordan – 'all territories in return for peace' – and reach a 1:1 territory exchange. He offered to Mahmoud Abbas 4.5 percent in return for the 6 percent that Israel would annex from the West Bank. The remaining percentage of land would be covered by the corridor from the West Bank to the Gaza Strip which would be cardinal to the Palestinian state despite its minuscule territorial weight and the fact that it would remain under Israeli sovereignty": Shaul Arieli (2009), The Space of Agreement Question, *Haaretz*. April 10, p. 12 (Hebrew).

46 Ari Shavit interviews Ehud Barak (2008): The Labor Party: Ehud Barak Again Sees Himself as a Candidate for the Office of Prime Minister, *Haaretz*. December 19 (Hebrew), www.haaretz.co.il/hasite/spages/1047831.html.

47 Yitzhak Laor writes about the leftist liberal authors Amos Oz and A. B. Yehoshua: "They ... emanated from the denial of the crimes committed against the Palestinians in 1948 and in the years that followed them, and the military regime, the expropriation of lands and the administrative detentions they brought. The issue of denial is perhaps the most striking component in the arrogance and euphoria of the supporters of Barak's fatal journey to the second Camp David Summit." Laor addresses precisely the denial of 1948, produced by the 1967 paradigm and its identity politics. See: We Call On the Palestinian Leadership to Reach a Non-Violent Settlement, in Yitzhak Laor (2002), *Things Which Should Not Be Silenced – Essays*. Tel Aviv: Babel (Hebrew).

48 In March 2009, for example, Ehud Barak stated: "Do I need to prove to anyone that I seek peace? Is there another leader in Israel who has done as much as I have to achieve peace? The issue of two states for two peoples is essential as far as I am concerned." Yossi Werter (2009), *Haaretz*. March 6, p. 3b (Hebrew). Golan Lahat describes the Zionist left in general, and Barak's moves in particular, as anchored in a "messianic secular" perception of time: Golan Lahat (2004), *The Messianic Temptation: The Rise and Fall of the Israeli Left*. Tel Aviv: Am Oved (Hebrew).

49 For a real-time critique of the Disengagement Plan, see: Yehouda Shenhav (2005), Preface, *Theory and Criticism*. 27: 5–6 (Hebrew).

50 The "problem of Gaza" is an essential part of the conflict. Israeli ideology separates Gaza from the West Bank, and by so doing increase the fractures in the national definition of the Palestinian people. I am sorry not to have devoted more room to the Gaza issue, but I wanted to keep this book as concise as possible.

51 See Tony Judt (2003), Israel: The Alternative, *The New York Review of Books*. November, 50 (2). Judt defines Zionism as "anachronistic," thereby explaining its violence. Hannan Hever also expresses concern that the possibility of genocide could become viable within the Jewish political discourse. If in 2009 Israel killed 1,400 Palestinian civilians, the numbers could increase and reach 20,000 or 30,000, and be digested by the Israeli discourse in a similar manner, as a result of self-righteousness or military rationalizations. When, in 2004, Professor Lev Grinberg of Ben Gurion University talked about a "symbolic genocide" he was assaulted for it in an unprecedented manner. From the attacks on Grinberg, one could learn about the force of thought terrorism

and the level of political paralysis within the political discourse in Israel: the Minister of Education sent a pungent letter to the President of the University, declaring her intention to boycott the university and its board of trustees as long as Greenberg remained a member. Two years earlier, in 2002, the same Minister of Education inquired with the Attorney-General whether it would be possible to take legal action against a Hebrew University professor who supported the rights of soldiers to refuse to serve in the occupied territories. In that same year she called for the establishment of a committee headed by a retired judge to investigate why the President of David Yellin College allowed Arab students to commemorate the Palestinians killed by Israeli soldiers. Yet some still believe that the state is not doing enough to silence dissident voices: Lord George Weidenfeld, Chairman of Ben Gurion University's board of trustees and one of British Jewry's greatest philanthropists, told a local journalist that, although the state should generally not interfere with the University's affairs, he was concerned that it allowed views like those expressed by Lev Grinberg to be heard. Grinberg is not alone. On March 31, 2004, the President of the Ben Gurion University received a six-page letter from the Zionist Organization of America, which expressed concern regarding the anti-Israeli activities of Neve Gordon, who was known for his firm position against the Occupation.

52 The term "Second Israel" was used, prior to 1967, to denote the poorer strata of Mizrachi Jews (Jews from Arab countries) who lived in the peripheries within the Green Line.

53 My use of the word "secular" targets the denial of the theological foundations of Zionism, which expresses affinity to the Land of Israel and its holy places.

Notwithstanding, my use of the word is only temporary – in the next chapter I will show that that which is perceived as "secular" is not necessarily so, as secularity is also embedded in theological-political Zionism.

For example, how could we explain the fact that Ehud Barak, an utterly secular Prime Minister, marshals all his political might at Camp David to claim that "The Holiest of Holies" must remain in Israel's hands? These phenomena call for post-secular perspectives. For a discussion of Jewish theology at Camp David, and its principal contradictions of the 1967 paradigm, see: Yehouda Shenhav (2006), *The Arab Jews*. Stanford: Stanford University Press, pp. 167–8. For a discussion of Israel as a post-secular society, see: Yehouda Shenhav (2008), An Invitation to a Post-Secular Sociology, *Israeli Sociology*. 10 (1): 161–88 (Hebrew). Although Amnon Raz-Krakotzkin does not use the term "post-secularism," he also adopts a non-secular stance. See Amnon Raz-Krakotzkin (2005), There Is No God, But He Promised Us the Land, *Mita'am*. 3: 71–6 (Hebrew).

54 Eliaz Cohen (2006), Talking to the Hamas, *Makor Rishon*. February 24 (Hebrew).

55 Yossi Beilin, The Most Beautiful Decade of Our Lives, see: www.arikpeace.org/Heb/Index.asp?ArticleID=619 &CategoryID=258&Page=28. In this vein, Ari Shavit (in his collected volume *The Division of the Land*. Jerusalem: Keter, 2005 [Hebrew]) called pre-1967 Israel "a gaunt and just republic." Despite its great importance, Akiva Eldar and Idit Zartal's 2005 book, *The Lords of the Land: The Settlers and the State of Israel, 1967–2004* (Tel Aiv: Kinneret, p. ii. [Hebrew]), also relies on the Green Line epistemology. "Only for nineteen years of its fifty-six

years of existence," state Eldar and Zartal, "was the State of Israel free from the curse of the Occupation." The book further presents a problematic division of responsibility, as it narrates the Occupation since 1967 only through the history of Gush Emunim (the religious settlers) and ignores the movement of the Third Israel into the West Bank and Gaza.

56 Adriana Kemp's work shows that the absorption of Mizrachi immigrants was accompanied by extreme state-induced violence. See Adriana Kemp (2002), The Wandering of Peoples or "The Great Burning": State Control and Resistance in the Israeli Periphery, in Hannan Hever, Yehouda Shenhav and Pnina Muzafi-Haller (eds.), *Mizrachim in Israel*. Tel Aviv and Jerusalem: Ha'Kibbutz Ha'Meuchad and the Van Leer Institute, pp. 36–66 (Hebrew). At the same time, Aziza Khazzoom shows that the ethnic/racial component was crucial in the dispersal of the Jewish population, rather than the year of immigration, as was previously assumed: Aziza Khazzoom (2009), Did the Israeli State Engineer Segregation? On the Placement of Jewish Immigrants in Development Towns in the 1950s, *Social Forces*. 84 (1): 115–34. See also: Smadar Sharon (2006), The Planners, the State and the Shaping of the National Space in the 1950s, *Theory and Criticism*. 29: 31–57 (Hebrew).

57 This position towards "others" held by the liberal left is further shared by Shulamit Aloni who declared, before the 2009 elections, that Shas was an illegitimate party: "The government does not represent the people because Shas decides on everything." See: www.ynet.co.il.articles/0,7340,L-3516999,00.html.

For a discussion on the Labor Party and Meretz voters' slogan "Anything But Shas," see: Amnon Raz-

Krakotzkin (2000), Rabin's Heritage: On Secularism, Nationalism and Orientalism, in Lev Greenberg (ed.), *Contested Memory: Myth, Nationalism and Democracy*. Beer-Sheba: Ben Gurion University (Hebrew); Sarah Hellman and Andre Levy (2001), Shas in the Israeli Press, in Yoav Peled (ed.), *Shas and the Challenge of Israeliness*. Tel Aviv: Maariv, pp. 390–424 (Hebrew). Haggai Ram also shows that the slogan of the Zionist left, and particularly that of Meretz – "This Is Not Iran" – not only regards Iran, but also looks into the society in Israel. He emphasized that Meretz denied Iran, but meant to say that Israel has become too similar to Iran and that if Israelis do not act quickly they may not be able to prevent the establishment of a theocratic and fundamentalist regime, similar to that of Iran, in Israel. According to this analysis, the slogan "This Is Not Iran" is closely related to Meretz's greatest fear – as well as that of the Zionist secularism from left or right – the rise of Shas to the forefront of Israel's political stage in the late 1980s. See: Haggai Ram (2010), *Iranophobia: The Logic of an Israeli Obsession*. Stanford: Stanford University Press.

58 For a detailed description of the 1950s mechanisms, see: Hillel Cohen (2006), *Good Arabs*. Jerusalem: Keter (Hebrew). Amnon Raz-Krakotzkin claimed that Israel, as described according to "The Most Beautiful Decade of Our Existence," existed only for six months (and even that was limited) – between the annulment of the military regime in 1966 and the Occupation of the new territories in June 1967: Amnon Raz-Krakotzkin (2007), The Six-Months State: Israel, Occupation and the Bi-National Stance, *Mahsom*. June 26 (Hebrew), www.arabs48.com/mahsom/article.php?id=5501 (Arabic).

59 As Michael Feige shows, Peace Now was pivotal in the defamiliarization of the occupied territories and in the construction of their extraterritoriality vis-à-vis the State of Israel. It was Tzali Reshef, one of their leaders, who adopted Robert Frost's phrase: "Good fences make good neighbors" (Feige, Judea and Samaria are Here, the Occupied Territories are There, *Theory and Criticism*. 14: 111–31 [Hebrew], p. 120). The separation expresses the wish to disengage not only from the Palestinians in the West Bank, but also from those in the State of Israel.

60 For example: Dan Shiftan (2002), The Arab MKs' New Identity: The Leaders of the Arab Sector Challenge the Foundations of the State, *Tchelet*. 13: 23–49 (Hebrew); Arnon Sofer and Gil Shalev, The De-Facto Realization of the Palestinian Demand for Return: http:// geo.haifa. ac.il/~chstrategy/publications/books/give_back_claim/ give_back_palestine_claim.pdf.

During its establishment in 1968, the Council for Peace and Security called upon the leadership not to annex the occupied territories and to return them in the framework of a security settlement. See: http://www.pas. org.il/?src=agency.co.il. Hundreds of professors, journalists, artists and writers joined this plea, among whom were Amos Kenan, A. B. Yehoshua, Amos Oz, Nathan Zach, Yehuda Amichai and Leah Goldberg. See: Alec D. Epstein (2008), From Brit Shalom to Hug 77: A Comparative Study of Political Groups Led by Hebrew University Members, in Adi Gordon (ed.), *Brit Shalom and Bi-National Zionism: The "Arab Question" as a Jewish Question*. Jerusalem: Carmel, pp. 195–224 (Hebrew).

61 When this essay was in the editing stage (in Hebrew), Ari Shavit interviewed Shmuel Hasfari and political adviser Eldad Yaniv, who were, *inter alia*, referred to

as the "Green Line Nationalists." Those I discussed it with found the interview odd, but I took the statements which appeared therein as neither strange nor provoking, but rather as a typical version of the time of the Green Line. As stated by Hasfari: "'Green Line Nationalists' sounds excellent to me. I do not wish to apologize for my country – I do not apologize for its borders nor for the Green Line, which was recognized by the whole world. This is where I live. This is my country. Green Line Nationalists? It sounds perfectly acceptable to me." Yaniv further explained: "The term we use is the 'National Left.' It was the National Left which established and built the State, but went astray after the Six-Day War": Ari Shavit (2009), An Interpretation of a Provocation, Haaretz Supplement, *Haaretz*. September 11, pp. 24–31 (Hebrew).

62 When Rabbi Menachem Furman, the spokesperson for "Rabbis for Civil Rights" and inhabitant of Tekoa, reported his plan to fly to a "large Arab country" in order to advance a meeting between rabbis and the Hamas leadership, he asked: "Pray for me to succeed in the place where politicians have failed." One of the heads of a local council in the Negev, threatened by the possibility of Furman's success, ridiculed the attempt: "The Rabbi taught us that one of the names of God is Shalom – in Hebrew as well as in Arabic. He therefore concludes that the frightening call Allahu al-Akbar is merely a promise that peace will prevail." The head of the local council further emphasized that the loss of the land policy from which he and his friends benefit was a general threat, even if it might help resolve the conflict: http://israblog.nana10.co.il/blogread.asp?blog=537016y ear=2009month=2day=0pagenum=2.

63 E.g. Himanuta, an organization established by the

JNF, purchased thousands of dunams of land in the West Bank for the sole purpose of Jewish settlement. Himanuta operates according to the ethno-racial principle in which Jewish land cannot be sold. See: Amiram Bareket (2005), Despite Its Declarations the JNF Purchases Thousands of Dunams in the Occupied Territories, *Haaretz*. February 14, p. 5a (Hebrew).

64 The local councils are similar to the old British "borough" system which originated in medieval Europe, in which towns received the authority of self-government from the monarch. The council is an administrative mechanism which enables division of space and the creation of autonomous settlements which divide the land according to a privilege regime based on Jewish ethnicity and nationalism.

65 Akiva Eldar (2009), Gush Etzion Has Trebled in Size, *Haaretz*. July 31, p. 7 (Hebrew).

66 Shoham Melamed shows the obsession with demographics and head counts, but adds that the threat does not only come from the Palestinians, but also from the Mizrachim. She calls this the "double menace." See: Shoham Melamed (2004), "Within a Few Dozen Years We Will All Be Mizrachi.": Maternity, Fertility and the Construction of the "Demographic Threat" in the Minimum Age for Marriage Law, *Theory and Criticism*. 25: 69–96 (Hebrew); Shoham Melamed and Yehouda Shenhav (2008), Beyond Nationalism: About the Neo-Malthusian Justification Regime and the Design of Israel's 1950–1966 Birth Policy, in Yossi Yonah and Adriana Kemp (eds.), *Citizenship Gaps: Migration, Birth and Identity in Israel*. Tel Aviv and Jerusalem: Ha'Kibbutz Ha'Meuchad and the Van Leer Institute, pp. 125–65 (Hebrew). Areej Sabbagh-Khoury

shows that the Palestinian press (unlike its political elite) hardly engages with the demographic question. Sabbagh focused on 1989–91, which marked the peak of immigration from the former Soviet Union, and showed that no mention of the demographic problem was made in any of two principal newspapers in Arabic. See: Areej Sabbagh-Khoury (2006), Between Return and Return: Reading in the Discourse of Palestinians in Israel. MA thesis, Tel Aviv University (Hebrew); A. Sabbagh-Khoury (2009), Palestinian Predicaments: Jewish Immigration and Palestinian Repatriation, in R. Kanaaneh and I. Nusair (eds.), *Palestinians in Israel Revisited*. New York: SUNY Press.

67 Anshel Pfeffer (2009), The Supreme Court Decreed that the Contour of the Fence is Illegal but the State Ignores Its Decision, *Haaretz*. April 19, p. 4 (Hebrew).

68 As opposed to the view of the Green Line as an (imagined) separation between Jews and Arabs, it should be remembered that Israel has never committed itself to clear borders and has never accepted the 1949 armistice borders. Throughout the years, the Green Line has served as a one-sided valve. It is supposed to block the movement from "there" to "here," but at the same time enables free flow from "here" to "there," including tours and journeys, military actions and settlements. See the model developed by Adriana Kemp to explain the cultural aspects of the term "border": Adriana Kemp (1997), Talking Borders. Ph.D. dissertation, Tel Aviv University.

69 In Haggai Segal (2009), Behind the Fence, A Portrait, *Makor Rishon*. April 8, p. 16 (Hebrew).

70 Vered Noam lives in two parallel worlds. On the one hand she is a Professor of Talmud at Tel Aviv

University, while on the other hand she is a resident of the settlement Kfar Edumim, mother of six, sister of Uri Elitzur who served as Chief Editor of the settler newspaper *Nekuda*, and the daughter of Biblical Studies Professor Yehuda Elitzur.

71 Vered Noam (1993), *Nekuda*. June: 44–59 (Hebrew).

72 Amnon Raz-Krakotzkin (2007), Bi-Nationality and Jewish Identity: Hannah Arendt and the Question of the Land of Israel, in Steven Aschheim (ed.), *Hannah Arendt in Jerusalem*. Jerusalem: Magnes, pp. 185–201 (Hebrew). See also: Honaida Ghanem (2011), The Urgency of a New Beginning in Palestine: An Imagined Scenario by Mahmoud Darwish and Hannah Arendt, *College Literature*. 38 (1): 1–20.

73 Tanya Reinhart (2002), *Israel/Palestine: How to End the War of 1948*. New York: Seven Stories Press.

74 The lack of legal Israeli sovereignty in the West Bank stems from a deep-seated fear of a bi-national reality and its demographical consequences on the continued existence of a "Jewish State." Edward Said argued that Israel's post-1967 occupations will inevitably lead us to the 1948 question – not only because the 1967 occupations enabled a certain unification between the Palestinians in Israel and those in the occupied territories, but also because they would enable a future universal demand, which might not be easily dismissed, for voting rights for each resident, from the Mediterranean Sea to the Jordan River. This would change the political configuration in the region. See Edward Said (1979/1992), *The Question of Palestine*. New York: Vintage.

75 For a discussion on "sovereignty gaps," see Yehouda Shenhav (2006), Sovereignty Gaps, the Exception and State of Emergency: Why has Imperial History Disappeared? *Theory and Criticism*. 29: 205–18 (Hebrew).

In colonial studies this phenomenon is referred to as "jurisdictional imperialism," addressing the judicial materialization of imperial needs. For a survey of the historic symptoms of British jurisdictional imperialism, see: Ross W. Johnston (1973), *Sovereignty and Protection: A Study of British Jurisdictional Imperialism in the Late Nineteenth Century*. Durham: Duke University Press.

76 Even after the assassination of Yitzhak Rabin, we find similar cleansing of consciousness among the liberal left. Ariella Azulay challenges the mythological system which enforces a decision between the "incitement" thesis of the left and the "weed" theory of the right. Azulay claims that this divide divorces the assassination from the violence-generating mechanisms which operate in Israeli society and are shared by both left and right, religious and secular, Mizrachim and Ashkenazim, men and women: Ariella Azulay (2000), *Yigal Amir's Ghost, Theory and Criticism*. 17: 9–26 (Hebrew).

77 Gadi Taub (2007), *The Settlers and the Struggle for the Importance of Zionism*. Tel Aviv: Yediot Sfarim (Hebrew).

78 Yossi Sarid (2005), I Am Sorry But I Can No Longer Feel Pain, *Haaretz*. January 24, Part II (Hebrew). For further criticism, see also: Eldar and Zartal, *The Lords of the Land*.

79 Meron Benvenisti (1988), *The Slingshot and the Club: Territories, Jews and Arabs*. Jerusalem: Kete (Hebrew). See also http://soc.haifa.ac.il/-s.smooha/download/fourmodelsandonemore.pdf. According to the data collected by Meron Benvenisti and Shlomo Hayat, the amount of Jewish land increased to 700,000 dunams in 1973. However, the principal growth took place in the early 1980s, reaching 1,800,000 dunams of state-owned

land in 1984. See Betselem report: www.betselem.org/
Downlaoad/199703_Settlements_Heb.rtf.

In an interview for *Haaretz*, Benvenisti explains the
relations between this position and his support of a bi-
national society: "Already in the early 1980s I claimed
that division of the land had become impossible and
that the construction of settlements and takeover of
lands had created an irreversible reality. There were
only 20,000 settlers then – today there are 230,000. It
is therefore obvious that the critical mass I feared, that
would not enable the status quo to change, has already
materialized. The reality we encounter today is already
bi-national and is a permanent fact. It can no longer
be ignored or denied." See: Ari Shavit (2003), Forget
Zionism, *Haaretz*. August 5.

80 *Haaretz*. May 28, 2009 (Hebrew).
81 For the commencement of such a discussion, see: Micha
    Odenheimer (2002), Self-Aware Communities, *Eretz
    Acheret*. 10: 39–41 (Hebrew).
82 Martin Buber's Address to the 12th Zionist Congress
    (1921), in *Document and Documentation*: 286–87.
83 See also: Joseph Heller (2004), *From Brit Shalom to
    Ihud*. Jerusalem: Magnes (Hebrew); Sasson Sofer
    (2001), *The Birth of Political Thought in Israel*. Tel Aviv:
    Shoken (Hebrew); Adi Gordon (ed.) (2008), *Brit Shalom
    and Bi-National Zionism: The Arab Question as a Jewish
    Question*. Jerusalem: Carmel, pp. 63–64 (Hebrew).
84 Amnon Raz-Krakotzkin (2007), The Six-Day State:
    Israel, the Occupation and the Bi-National Position,
    Mahsom, June 26; Amnon Raz-Krakotzkin (2007), *Exil
    et Souveraineté*. Paris: La Fabrique.
85 This topic is also controversial. For challenging Israeli
    sources, see: Ilan Pappe (2005), The Visible and
    Invisible in the Israeli Palestinian Conflict, in A. Lesch

and I. Lustick (eds.), *Exile and Return: Predicaments of Palestinians and Jews*. Philadelphia: University of Pennsylvania Press, pp. 279–92. See Yagil Levy (2009), Structured Bellicosity: Was the Israeli–Arab Conflict Originally Inevitable? *Journal of Historical Sociology*. 22 (3): 420–44.

1 The Roots and Consequences of the Liberal New Nostalgia

1 Ari Shavit (2005), The Next National Project, Haaretz Magazine, *Haaretz*. June 30 (Hebrew).

2 Ibid.

3 Ari Shavit (2009), Outside Both Boxes, *Haaretz*, March 19 (Hebrew).

4 Ibid.

5 For further reading, I would suggest the works of Amnon Raz-Krakotzkin, one of the first to pose this argument, as early as the mid 1990s. For example: Amnon Raz-Krakotzkin (2005), I Feel Responsible for the Victims of Zionism, February 28: http://peacepalestine.blogspot.com/2005/02/amnon-raz-krakotzkin-i-feel.html. For a collection of works on various models of bi-nationalism, see: http://oss.internetactivist.org/puosa.html.

6 An integration of his many works can be found in his book: Oren Yiftachel (2006), *Ethnocracy: Land and Identity in Israel/Palestine*. Philadelphia: University of Pennsylvania Press.

7 David Grossman (1998), *The Yellow Wind*. New York: Farrar, Straus and Giroux, p. 211.

8 Ibid., 214.

9 David Grossman (1992), *Present Absentees*. Tel Aviv: Ha'Kibbutz Ha'Meuchad, p. 244 (Hebrew).

10 Ibid.

11 Jonathan Rutherford (2000), Zombie Categories:

Interview with Ulrich Beck, *Theory and Criticism*. 16: 247–62 (Hebrew).

12 Interview with Amir Kaminer (2009), 24 Hours supplement, *Yedioth Ahronoth*. August 4.

13 Gideon Levy (2004), *Twilight Zone: Life and Death Under the Israeli Occupation*. Tel Aviv: Babel, p. 27 (Hebrew).

14 Quoted in Stephen Moses (2003), *Walter Benjamin and the Spirit of Modernism*. Tel Aviv: Resling, p. 27 (Hebrew).

15 Meir Pa'il (1986), Racism and Equality, in Hannan Hever and Ron Kuzar (eds.) (n.d.), The Written Word: A Socialist Arena, *Jerusalem: The Written Word*. 1: 41–6 (Hebrew).

16 International support was manifest in UNSC Resolution 242 in November, 1967, calling for regional peace based on Israeli withdrawal from the territories occupied "in the recent conflict," in 1967. The resolution spoke of a "just settlement of the refugee problem," but in the 1970s, Arab states sought to specifically mention "Arab refugees in the Middle East." The United States had its ambassador, Arthur Goldberg, oppose the motion. Israel, which tried pushing for the wording "Jewish refugees," also failed, and had to make do with blocking the mention of "Arab refugees."

17 Amos Elon (1972), *The Israelis: Founders and Builders*. Tel Aviv: Shocken (Hebrew), quoted in Tom Segev (2005), *1967: The Year that Changed The Middle East*. Keter (Hebrew).

18 Yossi Sarid (2008), *And So We Gather Here: An Alternative History*. Tel Aviv: Yedioth-Books, p. 174 (Hebrew).

19 Ibid., 53.

20 Ibid., 197.

21 This position has also been phrased by Fania

Oz-Zalzberger (2008), These Are Not My Children, *Haaretz*. December 7 (Hebrew). Oz-Zalzberger, like her father Amos Oz, distinguishes herself and the group she seeks to represent through formulating an artificial "rupture."

22 Quoted by Tom Segev in *1967*.

23 Ari Shavit (2005), Longing for a Yeke Paradise, Haaretz Magazine, *Haaretz* (Hebrew). See also the reactions to Amir Peretz winning the chairmanship of the Labor Party, from Galit Aliasi, Motti Gigi, Anat Yona, Vered Madar, Yuval Evri, Mati Shemoeloff and Naftali Shem-Tov (2008) in *Politics of Partition and Politics of Recognition: The 2006 General Elections as a Case Study*. Jerusalem: Identity and Status Groups, Van Leer Institute (Hebrew). This was originally presented as a paper at the Sderot Conference, 2008.

24 In his book *The End of Ashkenazi Hegemony*, Tel Aviv: Keter, 2001 (Hebrew), Baruch Kimmerling has called this hegemony "AHUSALim," the Hebrew acronym for "Ashkenazi, Secular, Veteran (residents), Socialists and Nationalists." This was his attempt (unsuccessful, to my mind) to create a local parallel for the American WASP.

25 Amos Oz (1977), From Now On, *Siman Kriaa*. May, 7: 9 (Hebrew).

26 See: Yehouda Shenhav and Yossi Yonah (eds.) (2008), *Racism in Israel*. Tel Aviv and Jerusalem: Ha'Kibbutz Ha'Meuchad and Van Leer Institute, pp. 33–7 (Hebrew).

27 Dror Mishani (2006), *There's Something Absurd about the Entire Mizrachi Affair*. Tel Aviv: Am Oved, p. 82 (Hebrew).

28 Ibid., 99.

29 Ibid., 100.

30 Amos Oz (1985), *Here and There in the Land of Israel*. Tel Aviv: Am Oved (Hebrew).

31 Anat Rimon-Or (2004), From "Death to the Arabs" to Death of the Arabs: The Modern Jew Versus the Arab Inside Him, in Yehouda Shenhav (ed.), *Colonialism and the Postcolonial Condition*. Tel Aviv and Jerusalem: Ha'Kibbutz Ha'Meuchad and Van Leer Institute, pp. 285–318 (Hebrew).

32 Shlomo Avineri (1983), Political Considerations, in Aluf Hareven (ed), *Is It Really Hard To Be Israeli?* Jerusalem: Van Leer Institute, p. 292 (Hebrew).

33 Ibid.

34 Boaz Evron (1988), *A National Reckoning*, Tel Aviv: Dvir, p. 381 (Hebrew).

35 Quoted in Haggai Ram (2010), *Iranophobia: The Logic of an Israeli Obsession*. Stanford: Stanford University Press, p. 97. See also: Haggai Ram and Yaakov Yadgar (2008), Jews Too Are Allowed To Be Anti-Semitic: "New" and "Old" Racism, the Shinui Party Case, in Yehouda Shenhav and Yossi Yonah (eds.), *Racism in Israel*. Tel Aviv and Jerusalem: Ha'Kibbutz Ha'Meuchad and Van Leer Institute, pp. 93–117 (Hebrew).

36 Nitza Harel (2006), *Without Fear or Bias: Uri Avnery and "Ha'olam Haze."* Jerusalem: Magnes (Hebrew).

37 Yaacov Shavit (1984), *From Hebrew to Canaanite*. Tel Aviv: Domino in partnership with Tel Aviv University (Hebrew).

38 There are similarities here to the "Levantine thesis" advanced by Cairo-born Israeli essayist Jacqueline Kahanov: Both yearn to abandon the principle of separation between Jews and Arabs that underlies liberal Zionism; both Kahanov and Amir saw the 1967 war as a historic opportunity to break free of the shackles of Jewish-Zionist entrenchment in the partition borders;

and in a sense, both models – the Canaanite and the Levantine – offer an alternative to the Zionist ghetto-state. For a further development of this argument, see: Tali Shif (2009), Between Minority and Majority – Jacqueline Kahanov and the Levantinism Project, 1958–1978, MA thesis, Tel Aviv University (Hebrew).

39 See: Yuval Evri (2006), To Write a Nation: On Nationalism and Ethnic Identities in the Novel "Outcast." MA thesis, Hebrew University (Hebrew).

40 Shimon Balas (1967), The Obligations of Victory, *The Nation (ha-Ouma)*. November, 2 (22): 216–23 (Hebrew).

41 Inbal Perlson (2006), *Great Happiness Tonight: Jewish–Arab Music and Mizrachi Identity*. Tel Aviv: Resling (Hebrew).

42 For a discussion of the education issues, see: Yossi Dahan and Yossi Yonah (2005), The Neoliberal Education Revolution, *Theory and Criticism*. 27: 11–38 (Hebrew); Yossi Dahan and Yossi Yonah (2006), On (the Lack of) Equality in Education, *Theory and Criticism*. 28: 101–26 (Hebrew). For a discussion of the same phenomenon in other cultural areas, see: Yossi Yonah and Yehouda Shenhav (2005), *What is Multiculturalism? On the Politics of Difference in Israel*. Tel Aviv: Babel (Hebrew).

43 See Amnon Raz-Krakotzkin (1993), Exile within Sovereignty: Toward Criticism of the "Negation of Exile" in Israeli Culture, *Theory and Criticism*. 3: 23–55 (Hebrew); Amnon Raz-Krakotzkin, Exile within Sovereignty Part B, *Theory and Criticism*. 4: 113–39 (Hebrew) .

44 See, for example: Ariel Hendel (2007), A Chronicle of the Occupation Regime 1967–2007, *Theory and Criticism*. 31: 233–46 (Hebrew).

45 Zeev Sternhell (2009), Onward to the Rescue of Democracy, *Haaretz*. March 6, p. 23A (Hebrew).

46 Zeev Sternhell (1995), *The Founding Myths of Israel*. Tel Aviv: Am Oved (Hebrew).

47 See: Chaim Gans (2006), *From Richard Wagner to The Right of Return*. Tel Aviv: Am Oved, pp. 275–6 (Hebrew). Gans also makes the interesting argument, with which I obviously disagree, that in the current historical circumstances the conquests of 1967 and the settlements project are morally worse than the ethnic cleansing of 1948.

48 Although they do determine that these methods of control cannot be fully described as merely "Occupation," or in the terms popular with the critical left, like "Colonization" and "Apartheid": Ariella Azoulay and Adi Ophir (2008), *This Regime Which is Not One*. Tel Aviv: Resling, p. 13 (Hebrew).

49 For a criticism of these arguments by Azulay and Ophir, see: Oren Yiftachel (2009), This Book Which is Not One, *Mit'am*. 17: 54–64 (Hebrew).

50 Eyal Weizman (2007), *The Hollow Land*. London: Verso.

2 Was 1967 a Revolutionary Year?

1 Yagil Levi and Yoav Peled (1993), The Rupture that Was Not: Israeli Sociology in the Mirror of the 1967 War, *Theory and Criticism*. 3: 115–28 (Hebrew). I agree with their observation, but it seems they overlook the theological-political perception that forms the continuity between 1948 and 1967. This oversight, to my mind, stems from the liberal left's denial of the theological aspect of the conquests of 1967, and the fact that the Labor Zionist movement played a significant role in the theological-political relay race.

2 Tom Segev (2005), *1967: The Year that Changed the Middle East*, pp. 191–2. All the references to this book rely on the original Hebrew edition from Keter.

3 Ibid., 199.
4 Ibid.
5 Ibid., 196. The following overview of the teleology of 1967 is based on Segev's book. Although I disagree with the book's underlying (if unstated) epistemology, his historical overview is educating.
6 Ibid., 197.
7 Ibid., 192.
8 Ibid., 191.
9 Ibid., 201.
10 Ibid., 186.
11 Ibid.
12 Ibid., 494.
13 Gershon Gorenberg (2006), *The Accidental Empire: Israel and the Birth of the Settlements 1967–1997*. New York: Times Books, p. 46.
14 Quoted by Yael Berda (2012), The Bureaucracy of the Occupation: A Study of the Permits Regime in the West Bank 2000–2006. Tel Aviv and Jerusalem: Ha'Kibbutz Ha'Meuchad and the Van Leer Institute.
15 Segev, *1967*, pp. 502–3.
16 Lev Grinberg (2005), The Unwanted Bride: The Speech Difficulties of the Opposition to the Occupation, *Theory and Criticism*. 27: 187–96 (Hebrew), quote on p. 187. The relationship between the question of territory and the question of population – the two main issues on the political agenda – is reviewed in its historical complexity by Michel Foucault, in the fourth chapter of his 2004 book: *Security, Territory, Population*. New York: Palgrave Macmillan, pp. 87–114.
17 Segev, *1967*, p. 560.
18 Ohad Zmora (ed.) (1967), *The Victory*. Tel Aviv: A. Levine-Epstein, p. 5 (Hebrew).
19 Ibid., 7.

20 For a discussion of this issue, see: Yehouda Shenhav (2008), An Invitation to a Post-secular Sociology, *Israeli Sociology*. 10 (1): 161–88 (Hebrew).

21 See: Aryeh Naor (2009), Four Models of Political Theology: The Thought of the Labor Movement Veterans on the Wholeness of the Land, 1967–1970, in Christoph Schmidt and Eli Sheinfeld (eds.), *And God Was Not Silent*. Tel Aviv and Jerusalem: Ha'Kibbutz Ha'Meuchad and the Van Leer Institute, pp. 170–202 (Hebrew).

22 This historiographic position is also expressed in the way the national ideology is conceptualized to accept the premises of the protestant history. See: Amnon Raz-Krakotzkin (1999), The Return to the History of Salvation, in S. N. Eisenstadt and M. Lisak (eds.), *Zionism and the Return to History: A Re-evaluation.* Jerusalem: Yad Yitzhak Ben Zvi (Hebrew).

23 Gershom Scholem (1989), *One More Thing: Chapters in Heritage and Revival*, vol. B, Tel Aviv: Am Oved, p. 59 (Hebrew).

24 Amnon Raz-Krakotzkin (2004), Between Brit Shalom and the Temple: The Dialectics of Salvation and Messianism, in the Footsteps of Gershom Scholem, in Yehouda Shenhav (ed.), *Colonialism and the Postcolonial Condition*, Tel Aviv and Jerusalem: Ha'Kibbutz Ha'Meuchad and the Van Leer Institute, p. 390 (Hebrew).

25 Hannan Hever (2005), In the City of Slaughter in Michael Gluzman, Hannan Hever and Dan Miron, *In the City of Slaughter, a Late Visit*. Tel Aviv: Resling, pp. 37–70 (Hebrew).

26 Adi Ophir (2001), *The Worship of the Present, Essays on Contemporary Israeli Culture*. Tel Aviv: Ha'Kibbutz Ha'Meuchad (Hebrew).

27 Shlomo Fischer (1988), Jewish Salvational Visions,

Utopias and Attitude to the Halacha, *International Journal of Comparative Sociology*. 24 (1–2): 62–75.

28 Anita Shapira (1994), The Religious Motives of the Labor Movement, in S. Almog et al. (eds.), *Zionism and Religion*. Jerusalem: Zalman Shazar Center, pp. 301–327 (Hebrew).

29 Aryeh Naor (2009), Four Models of Political Theology: The Thought of the Labor Movement Veterans on the Wholeness of the Land, 1967–1970, in Christoph Schmidt and Eli Schienfeld (eds.), *And God Was Not Silent*. Tel Aviv and Jerusalem: Ha'Kibbutz Ha'Meuchad and the Van Leer Institute, pp. 170–202 (Hebrew).

30 Ibid.

31 Ibid.

32 Ibid.

33 Yishai Rosen Zvi (2007), The Time of the Settlers, *Theory and Criticism*. 31: 275 (Hebrew).

34 Dan Miron (1987), *And If There Was To Be No Jerusalem*. Tel Aviv: Ha'Kibbutz Ha'Meuchad (Hebrew). See also: Meron Rapoport (2007), One Day, Two Petitions, *Haaretz*. June 8 (Hebrew).

35 Amit Kravitz (2007), On Zionism Caught Inextricably in the Thicket of its Own Concepts, Culture and Literature, *Haaretz*. July 13 (Hebrew).

36 Ibid.

37 Hannan Harif (2007), The Critic Who Never Stopped Battling the Priests of the Science Paper Calf, Culture and Literature, *Haaretz*. July 13 (Hebrew).

38 Quoted in Raz-Krakotzkin, Between Brit Shalom and the Temple.

3 The "Political Anomalies" of the Green Line

1 Adi Ophir (1998) Zero Hour, *Theory and Criticism*. 12–13 (48–50): 31–15 (Hebrew).

2 The first to use the term "ethnic cleansing" in this context was Ilan Pappe. Benny Morris doesn't use that term. I accept Pappe's terminology, but not the thesis that would imply this was a carefully planned operation directly administered top-down. There have been Zionist documents proposing transfer, and committees were set up and tasked with either encouraging transfer or suggesting other solutions, such as population exchange with the Arab Jews. But history is not as orderly as that, and the practice was considerably more varied than the planning: there are places where transfer was indeed carried out, complete with massacres designed to chase Palestinians out of their communities, and other places in which transfer was actually prevented, as demonstrated by Morris. But the end result was an ethnic cleansing of the Palestinians, even without attributing to one master plan. See: Benny Morris (1991), *The Birth of the Refugee Problem, 1947–1949*. Tel Aviv: Am Oved (Hebrew); Ilan Pappe (2006), *The Ethnic Cleansing of Palestine*. London: Oneworld.

3 About 15 percent of the Palestinians in Israel have been defined as "internal refugees," and call themselves "the uprooted." See: Areej Sabbagh-Khoury, "The Uprooted Palestinians of Israel," in Nadim Rouhana and Areej Sabbagh-Khoury (eds.) (2009), *The Palestinians in Israel: A Guide Book on Historical, Political and Social Issues*. Mada al-Carmel: Arab Center for Applied Social Research.

4 Michael B. Oren (2002), *The Six Days of War: June 1967 and the Making of the Modern Middle East*. Oxford: Oxford University Press, p. 306.

5 The most available information: J. Abu-Lughod (1971), The Demographic Transformation of Palestine, in

I. Abu-Lughod (ed.), *The Transformation of Palestine*. Evanston: Northwestern University Press, pp. 139–63.

6 See, for example, the debate in Sari Hanafi (2008), Palestinian Return Immigration, Lessons from the International Regime on Refugees, *Sedek*. 3: 22–31 (Hebrew).

7 For an overview, see Yaakov Tubi (2008), *On Her Doorstep: The Makings of Israel's Policy on Palestinian Refugees, 1946–1948*. Beersheba and Haifa: Ben Gurion University and Haifa University (Hebrew). For a discussion of the links between the Palestinian and Jewish refugees in Israeli policy, see: Yehouda Shenhav (2005), Arab-Jews, "Population Exchange," and the Palestinian Right of Return, in Ann Lesch and Ian Lustick (eds.), *Exile and Return: Predicaments of Palestinians and Jews*. Pennsylvania: University of Pennsylvania Press, pp. 225–45.

8 Benny Morris (1996), *Israel's Border Wars, 1949–1956*. Tel Aviv: Am Oved, p. 18 (Hebrew).

9 Ibid., 19.

10 Ibid., 276–7.

11 Ibid., 286.

12 Ibid.

13 Ibid.

14 Yagil Levi argues that Israel faced several political options, but it chose "border wars" as a military strategy: Yagil Levi (1996), War Policy, Inter-communal Relations and the Internal Spread of the State: Israel 1948–1956, *Theory and Criticism*. 8: 203–23 (Hebrew).

15 Morris, *Israel's Border Wars, 1949–1956*, p. 67.

16 Uri Ben Eliezer (1998), *The Making of Israeli Militarism*. Indiana: Indiana University Press.

17 Adriana Kemp (1992), The Mirror Language of the Borders: Territorial Borders and the Establishment

of a National Minority in Israel, *Israeli Sociology*. 2 (1): 319–24 (Hebrew).

18 Adriana Kemp (2002), The Wandering of People or the "Great Burning": State Control and Resistance in Israeli Literature, in Hannan Hever, Yehouda Shenhav and Pnina Muzaphi-Haller (eds.), *Mizrachim in Israel*. Tel Aviv and Jerusalem: Ha'Kibbutz Ha'Meuchad and the Van Leer Institute, pp. 36–66 (Hebrew).

19 For an instructive analysis of these practices, see: Mordechai Shalev (1969), Chapters in the Diary of Meir Har-Tzion, Culture and Literature, *Haaretz*, November 21. For a comprehensive review of sovereignty consciousness, see: Shimrit Peled (2008), Identity and Space in the Israeli Novel, 1967–1973. Ph.D. dissertation, Hebrew University, pp. 19–24 (Hebrew).

20 In this context, see: Gil Eyal (2006), *The Disenchantment of the Orient: Expertise in Arab Affairs and the Israeli State*. Stanford: Stanford University Press.

21 Adriana Kemp (1997), Talking Borders. Ph.D. dissertation, Tel Aviv University (Hebrew).

22 Ibid.

23 Ibid.

24 There is considerable criticism of this linkage between the Palestinian refugees and the Arab Jews, but it is largely ignored by the Jewish discourse. For a discussion of the absurdity of the equation, see: Yehouda Shenhav (2006), *The Arab Jews*. Stanford: Stanford University Press; Shenhav, Arab-Jews, "Population Exchange," and the Palestinian Right of Return; as well as the excellent historical work by Michael Fischbach (2008), *Jewish Property Claims against Arab Countries*. New York: Columbia University Press.

25 Tubi, *On Her Doorstep*, p. 2.

26 Even the most liberal position on recognizing the right of return, such as the one presented in the work of journalist Danny Rubinstein, only suggests a symbolic recognition and no more. See: Danny Rubinstein (1990), *The Fig Tree Embrace: The Palestinian "Right of Return."* Jerusalem: Keter (Hebrew).

27 Tubi, *On Her Doorstep*, p. 2.

28 Uzi Benziman and Atallah Mansour (1992), *Subletters.* Jerusalem: Keter (Hebrew).

29 Anat Leibler and Daniel Breslau (2005), The Uncounted: Citizenship and Exclusion in the Israeli Census of 1948, *Ethnic and Racial Studies.* 28 (5): 880–902; E. Zureik (2001), Constructing Palestine through Surveillance Practices, *British Journal of Middle Eastern Studies.* 8 (2): 205–8.

30 See discussion in: Dan Rabinowitz and Khawla Abu-Baker (2002), *The Stand-Tall Generation.* Tel Aviv: Keter (Hebrew); Dan Rabinowitz (1993), Oriental Nostalgia: How Palestinians Became "Israeli Arabs," *Theory and Criticism.* 4: 141–52 (Hebrew); Yoav Peled (1993), Strangers in Utopia: The Civil Status of the Palestinians in Israel, *Theory and Criticism.* 3: 21–35 (Hebrew); Dan Rabinowitz (1997), *Overlooking Nazareth.* Cambridge: Cambridge University Press. Rabinowitz describes the Arabs of 1948 as a "trapped minority."

31 On this point, it is instructive to look at the manner in which the "Arab village" was conceptualized in the discourse of Israeli orientalists, and the manner in which it is conceptualized in the dominant discourse. See Eyal, *The Disenchantment of the Orient.* It's also worth reading the analysis of the Arab village in Avner Cohen (1976), *Arab Border Villages.* Manchester: Manchester University Press. For a critical discussion of Cohen's discourse, see: Dan Rabinowitz (1998), *Anthropology and*

the Palestinians. Beit Berl: Center for Research of the Arab Society (Hebrew).

32 For the roots of this argument and the positions of Bruno Bauer and Karl Marx, see: Yoav Peled (1995), From Theology to Sociology, Marx and the Emancipation of the Jews, *Theory and Criticism.* 6: 45–59 (Hebrew).

33 David Vital (1978), *The Zionist Revolution*, vol. I: *The Beginnings of the Movement.* Tel Aviv: Am Oved and the Zionist Library, p. 183 (Hebrew).

34 This phenomenon is exacerbated by the links between Judaism and Protestantism indicated, for example, by Hermann Cohen in 1880: "When we look deeper, in all spiritual matters, we [German Jews] think and feel in the Protestant spirit. In truth, this shared religious basis is the strongest, most effective force for real national merging." Quoted in Vital, *The Zionist Revolution*, vol.1: 160.

35 The same argument is relevant for the situation of other national–religious minorities in a religious-majority society, and we could deduce from it insights regarding the status of Israel's Palestinian citizens in the Jewish space. The State of Israel, which seeks to define itself as Jewish (and Jewish only), is ready to afford the Palestinians religious freedom but not national freedom. Although the Palestinians don't have as clear an overlap between religious identity and national identity as the one in Zionism, the Israelization of the Palestinians does mean, in certain aspects, their Judaization as well. This is not as far-fetched a possibility as it would seem, and was actually proposed for discussion once by Ben Gurion himself (Cabinet meeting minutes, April 26, 1950, p. 27).

36 The author is a Catalonian journalist named Sebastian Villar Rodriguez, and the article is quoted in a translation by Danny Solar, in: The Jewish and Muslim

Problem in Europe, *News1 website*: www.news1.co.il/ archive/003–D–12411–00.htmg??tag=20–58–29.

37 One symptom is the complete and utter rejection of the Vision Documents of the Palestinian citizens of Israel. See, for example: Sarah Osetzki-Lazar and Mustafa Kabha (2008), *Between Vision and Reality: The Vision Documents of the Arabs in Israel, 2006–2007*. Jerusalem: The Citizens' Accord Forum (Hebrew). The book describes the four documents and tracks the response with which they were met.

38 For a discussion see: Peled, Strangers in Utopia. See also: Yagil Levi (2003), *Another Army for Israel*. Tel Aviv: *Yedioth Ahronoth* (Hebrew).

39 See Alison Brysk and Gershon Shafir (2004), *People out of Place: Globalization, Human Rights and the Citizenship Gap*. New York: Routledge; see also: Yossi Yonah and Adriana Kemp (2008), *Citizenship Gaps: Immigration, Fertility and Identity in Israel*. Tel Aviv and Jerusalem: Ha'Kibbutz Ha'Meuchad and the Van Leer Institute (Hebrew).

40 The amendment is known as "The Law of Citizenship and Entry into Israel" (Regulation 2003). It was motivated not by security reasons, as the state would have it, but by demographic ones. The Supreme Court upheld the amendment, proving yet again it is based on a racial approach, a product of the distorted model of a Jewish and democratic state. Yousef Jabareen argues there are at least 40 clearly racialized laws in the Israeli law book. See Altayeb Ghnaim (2007), The State Should Be Neutral Towards the National Groups within It, *Eretz Acheret*. 39: 44–8 (Hebrew).

41 See: Press release by Adalah, May, 2006: www. israel-palestinenews.org/2010/02/israel-court-to-hear-citizenship-law.html.

42 Jackie Khoury (2009), Yet Another Misgav Community Changes Its Regulation, Will Not Accept Non-Zionist Residents, *Haaretz*. June 2 (Hebrew).

43 For some of the many studies into such situations, see: Benziman and Mansour, *Subletters*, pp. 32–78; Efraim Karsh (1997), *Fabricating Israeli History*. London: Cass; Hillel Cohen (2000), *Present Absentees: The Palestinian Refugees in Israel after 1948*. Jerusalem: Center for Research of Arab Society in Israel (Hebrew); Ian Lustick (1985), *Arabs in the Jewish State*. Haifa: Mifras (Hebrew).

44 For example: Azmi Bishara (1996), The Israeli Arab: Studies in a Fragmented Political Discourse, in Pinchas Ginosar and Avi Bareli (eds), *Zionism: A Contemporary Debate*. Beersheba: Ben Gurion University, pp. 312–39 (Hebrew).

45 When the British Mandate regime issued the emergency regulations in 1945, an emergency conference of Jewish attorneys was called in Tel Aviv to protest. We would do well to recall some of the statements there, which are rarely heard in present-day Israel: "There's nothing like it in any enlightened country, even Nazi Germany didn't have such laws," said Yaakov Shapira, later Attorney General and Justice Minister, adding that the regulations amounted to "demolition of the very foundations of the justice system in the land." Dr. M Donkelblum, in years to come a Supreme Court justice, opined: "There is a violation of the elementary concepts of law, justice and trial . . . this arbitrariness, even if endorsed by a legislative body, is anarchy." Zionist leader Dov Yosef asked if it's still possible to guarantee "a citizen won't be imprisoned for life without a trial," adding: "We cannot ask a citizen to respect a law that puts him outside the law." Quoted in Sabri Jaraisi

(1966), *The Arabs in Israel*. Haifa: al-Itihad, pp. 14–15 (Arabic).

46 Some years ago it was revealed for the first time that Israel holds in remand – without trial or explanation – refugee survivors from the genocide in Darfur. It transpired that the Sudanese were detained through an emergency law passed 52 years ago as part of Israel's struggle against the Palestinian "infiltrators." See: Ruth Sinai (2006), Survivors of the Darfur Genocide in Administrative Detention at Maasiyahou, *Haaretz*. April 17, p. a5.

47 Hillel Cohen (2006), *Good Arabs*. Jerusalem: Keter (Hebrew).

48 Manar Hassan indicates patterns of cooperation between the Jewish state and the Arab patriarchy in control over Palestinian women through a problematization of discourse on what is referred to as "family honor killings." She argues that the state sought to retain the clan structure to reduce its own costs of control. "The encounter between patriarchal politics and state politics eventually cements and preserves the practice," she writes. See: Manar Hassan (1999), The Politics of Honor: Patriarchy, the State, and Family Honor Killings of Women, in Izraeli Daphna et al. (eds.) (1999), *Sex, Gender, Politics*. Tel Aviv: Ha'Kibbutz Ha'Meuchad, pp. 267–305 (Hebrew).

49 Cohen, *Good Arabs*.

50 See: Rabinowitz and Abu-Baker, *The Stand-Tall Generation*; and also Hunaida Ghanem (2006), *Rebuilding the Nation*. Jerusalem: Hebrew University, Y.L. Magnes (Hebrew).

51 Irredentism is an ideology that sees an overlap between territorial and ethnic borders. See the chapter on the Arab village in: Eyal, *The Disenchantment of the Orient*.

52 Ibid.

53 Cohen, *Good Arabs*.

54 Ibid., 47.

55 Hassan Jabareen (2004), *Haaretz* (Hebrew): www. israel-palestinenews.org/2010/02/israel-court-to-hear-citizenship-law.html.

56 Rubik Rosenthal (ed.) (2000), *Kafr Qasim, Events and a Myth*. Tel Aviv: Ha'Kibbutz Ha'Meuchad, p. 14 (Hebrew).

57 Ibid., 16.

58 Ibid., 29.

59 Quoted by Nitza Harel (2006), *Without Fear or Bias: Uri Avnery and Ha'olam Haze*. Jerusalem: Magnes, pp. 157–60 (Hebrew).

60 Peled (1993), Strangers in Utopia.

61 Cohen, *Good Arabs*, p. 48. See also the work of Areej Sabbagh-Khoury (2006), Between Return and Return: Reading in Palestinian Discourse in Israel. MA thesis, Tel Aviv University (Hebrew). Sabbagh-Khoury looks into Palestinian journalism in 1989 to 1991, the years of the great immigration wave from the crumbling Soviet Union into Israel, assuming the immigration would provoke a demographic discourse, including discussion of the right of return. Having found no such discourse in the public sphere, she explains the reticence through fear. She likens the monitoring of Israeli Palestinians to the Bentham Panopticon model as presented by Foucault, in which the task of monitoring is handed over from the monitor to the monitored themselves.

62 For example, in 2003 Ibtisam Mara'ana directed a political documentary entitled *Faradis: The Lost Paradise*, which, among other subjects, deals with the massacre in nearby Tantoura. During her research, she found out her father was one of the youths called out to bury

the victims of the massacre, but her father was afraid to be interviewed and tried talking her out of making the film, telling her: "Don't meddle in politics, be careful." Another Faradis resident told her: "Forget politics, we don't like trouble here."

63 The overview here is based on his work. See, for example: Oren Yiftachel (1998), Land Day, *Theory and Criticism*. 12–13: 279–90 (Hebrew).

64 Lev Grinberg emphasizes that the troubles of Israeli "democracy" did not begin in 1967, and that there's a link between the lack of democracy and the political structure of Israel. See: Lev Grinberg (1999), The Imagined Democracy of Israel, *Israeli Sociology*. 2 (1): 209–40 (Hebrew).

65 Zafrir Rinat (2000), "Bypass Communities," *Haaretz*. November (Hebrew).

66 Mazal Moualem (2000), "Plans for Expansion of Jewish Communities in the Galilee," *Haaretz*. November (Hebrew).

67 Supreme Court case 6698/95, *Ka'adan* v. *Israel Land Administration*, verdict no. 258(1).

68 In: Arnon Sofer and Yuval Canaan (eds.) (2004), *Geographic Processes and Developments in Israel and Abroad: A Look at Year 2020*. Haifa: Haifa University, p. 37 (Hebrew). See also Arnon Sofer and Yevgenia Bistrov (2004), *Israel, Demography 2004–2020*. Haifa: Haifa University (Hebrew); Avraham Dor (2004), *The Lookout Project in the Galilee Twenty Years Later*. Haifa: Haifa University (Hebrew).

69 In: Sofer and Canaan (eds.), *Geographic Processes and Developments in Israel and Abroad*, pp. 35–7 (Hebrew).

70 See: http://news.walla.co.il/?w=//268058.

71 Ali Waked (2002), Five Years Later: The Demographic Council is Back to Work, *Ynet*. September 2 (Hebrew).

72 Nadav Shragai, Mazal Mualem and Yoav Stern (2009), Prison Sentences for Anyone Denying Israel as a Jewish and Democratic State Passed in Preliminary Reading, *Haaretz*. May 28 (Hebrew).

73 Yiftachel, Land Day, *Theory and Criticism*. 12–13: 279–90 (Hebrew).

74 Azmi Bishara (1993), The Palestinian Minority in Israel, *Theory and Criticism*. 3: 7–20 (Hebrew).

75 Khalil Nahla (ed.) (2008), *The Future of the Palestinian Minority in Israel*. Ramallah: Madar, Palestinian Center for the Study of Israel.

76 The position of Mordechai Kremnitzer on the Vision Documents is one instructive example. See: Mordechai Kremnitzer (2007), A Strike to the Hope, *Eretz Acheret*. 39: 49–51. Also: Galit Nadav (2007), You Lost Me, *Eretz Acheret*. 39: 22–20 (Hebrew). These were the common responses in the liberal discourse for Palestinian demands for appropriate political representation.

77 On this, see: Nazir Majali (2005), The Historical Role of Israel's Arab Citizens, *Eretz Acheret*. 27: 44–6 (Hebrew). Samoha's perspective is based upon what is known as Israelization, the Green Line time approach to the Palestinians in Israel.

78 Nazir Majali (2007), Not Really Representing Us, *Eretz Acheret*. 39: 53–7 (Hebrew). For a fascinating example of a rift between the Zionist left and the Palestinian citizens of Israel in the discussion over the future of the state, see: Uzi Benziman (2006), *Whose Country Is It? A Journey to Phrasing a Jewish–Arab Treaty in Israel*. Jerusalem: Israeli Democracy Institute (Hebrew).

79 In: Sofer and Canaan (eds.), *Geographic Processes and Developments in Israel and Abroad*, pp. 35–7.

80 This is why we cannot easily distinguish left from right in Israel. Instead of left and right, we could divide the

bulk of the political map into three groups: Zionist extremists (like the National Union and Habayit Hayehoudi parties), Pragmatic Zionists (Labor, Kadima, Yisrael Beitenu, Likud) and liberal Zionists (Meretz, Peace Now). On the main national/nationalist issues, the differences between the parties are nuanced, one of the reasons why voters shift so easily from one party to another.

81 Ofer Aderet (2009), Foreign Minister Lieberman: Syria Is No Partner for Peace, *Haaretz*. April 25.

82 Vered Levi Barzilai (2001), A Home with a Garden and a Tank, *Haaretz*. October 17 (Hebrew). Sharon's plan, which was put into practice before the 1990s, made a mockery out of the Geneva Initiative. Menachem Klein (2006) shows in his book (*The Geneva Initiative: A Look from Within*. Tel Aviv: Carmel, [Hebrew]) that Sharon's plan confused the Geneva negotiators and made the entire initiative look preposterous. One of the Initiative's own team, Shaul Arieli, also admits that the Olmert government "summed up its tenure speaking with the Geneva Initiative voice. But the reality, the hands, the hands are Ariel Sharon's."

83 Zvi Bar'el criticizes the demand for eviction of settlements as an unjust prerequisite, but uses economic arguments to support his premise. "How much would it cost us and who would pay?" he asks; "The 7,000 Jews evicted from the Gaza Strip cost more than 10 billion shekels. Even if we evict only 100,000 Jews from the West Bank, it may cost us 150 billion shekels, half of the state annual budget": Zvi Bar'el (2009), Freeze to Fail, *Haaretz*. August 9, p. B1 (Hebrew).

84 Hava Pinchas Cohen (2002), Words Washing Face, *Eretz Acheret*. 10: 44–9 (Hebrew).

85 See: Edward Said (1979/1992), *The Question of Palestine*.

New York: Vintage. See also: Edward Said (2002), What Might Be the Meaning of Separation? in E. Said, *The End of the Peace Process: Oslo and Thereafter*. Beirut: Dar El-Adab.

86 The overview here is based on the work of Aviezer Ravitzky (1993), *Messianism, Zionism and Religious Radicalism in Israel*. Tel Aviv: Am Oved (Hebrew).

87 Ehud Luz (1985), *Parallels Meet*. Tel Aviv: Am Oved (Hebrew).

88 Aviezer Ravitzki (1993), *Messianism, Zionism and Religious Radicalism in Israel*. Tel Aviv: Am Oved, p. 183 (Hebrew).

89 Ibid., 187.

90 Ibid., 193. This messianic approach was further radicalized over time. Some tried to take the messianic logic to its extreme by blowing up the mosques on Temple Mount. Politically, the bombings were meant to sabotage the Camp David Accords, but they also carried a mystical meaning – breaking the foul powers of Yishmael from their suckling on the holy mount. It was also an apocalyptic attempt to create a crisis and a catastrophe to speed up the process of salvation. We should note that the leaders of the salvation camp itself were scandalized by the move: Luz, *Parallels Meet*; Dov Schwartz (1999), *Religious Zionism between Reason and Messianism*. Tel Aviv: Am Oved (Hebrew).

91 Akiva Eldar (2009), The Many-Checkpoints State, *Haaretz*. June 9 (Hebrew).

92 Haggai Segal (2009), Behind the Fence, Portrait, *Makor Rishon*. April 8, p. 12 (Hebrew).

93 Ibid.

94 Ibid.

95 Ibid.

96 See the excellent overview by Yishai Rozen Tzvi (2007),

The Time of the Settlers, *Theory and Criticism*. 31: 272–82 (Hebrew).

97 As demonstrated, for instance, by Gershon Gorenberg (2006), *The Accidental Empire: Israel and the Birth of the Settlements, 1967–1997*. New York: Times Books.

98 Yuval Azoulay (2009), Deputy Prime Minister Moshe Ya'alon: The Palestinians' Problem isn't the Occupation, *Haaretz*. May 27 (Hebrew). Other speakers at the conference suggested Jordan as a Palestinian state, a position Israeli leaders voiced frequently before the signing of the peace agreement with Jordan, which explicitly ruled out the "Jordanian Option."

99 Then-Foreign Minister of Egypt Abu al-Ghait told President Barack Obama of that demand that it was "not only damaging to the Israeli Arabs . . . but effectively wiping out any discussion of the right of return." Jordan is also wary of Israel's recognition as a Jewish state, because it would mean "expelling half a million Arabs beyond the Green Line," as noted by the Jordanian newspaper *Al Arab Al-Youm*. See: Zvi Bar'el (2009), Mubarak: No One Will Recognize a Jewish State, *Haaretz*. June 16, p. 4 (Hebrew).

100 haaretz.co.il/hasite/spages/1093064.html.

101 Chaim Levinson (2009), Ya'alon: The Prosecution Does Not Represent the Views of the Current Government on the Outposts Issue in the Supreme Court, *Haaretz*. August 18, pp. 1–3 (Hebrew).

102 Quoted in Micha Odenheimer (2002), Self-aware Communities, *Eretz Acheret*. 10: 30–41 (Hebrew).

103 Sarah Eliash (2000–2001), A Thorough Inquiry, *Eretz Acheret*. 2: 48–9 (Hebrew).

104 Vered Noam (1993), *Nekuda*. June: 44–59 (Hebrew).

105 Ibid.

106 Ibid.

107 Avi Gisser (2005), If You Take Your Fate in Your Hands, *Eretz Acheret*. 28: 68–73 (Hebrew).

108 Meron Rappoport (2006), The Settler Who Heard Ishmael, *Haaretz*. March 17 (Hebrew).

109 Ibid.

110 Eyal Meged (2005), The Conscience Cleaners, Diary, *Makor Rishon*. August 12, p. 11 (Hebrew).

111 In a conversation with Emmanuel Halperin, Knesset Channel, March 23, 2009.

112 Odenheimer, Self-aware Communities.

113 Gadi Taub (2007), *The Settlers and the Struggle for the Meaning of Zionism*. Tel Aviv: Yediot Books, p. 87 (Hebrew). This is an argument so embarrassing even the radical right does not employ it frequently.

114 Rosen-Zvi, The Time of the Settlers.

115 See the work of Michael Feige (2002), *Two Maps for the West Bank: Gush Emunim, Peace Now and Shaping the Space in Israel*. Jerusalem: Magnes (Hebrew).

116 Segal, Behind the Fence, Portrait, p. 12.

117 Rivi Gillis (2009) Now They Are Also Settlers: The Ethnic Morphology of the Settlements. MA thesis, Tel Aviv University (Hebrew).

118 Shlomo Fischer (2002), Very Modern, *Eretz Acheret*. 10: 39–41 (Hebrew).

119 Noam, *Nekuda*.

120 Odenheimer, Self-aware Communities.

121 See: Uriel Abulof (2006), Son of Abraham, *Eretz Acheret*. 32: 80–4 (Hebrew).

122 The first to formulate this was Daniel Gutwein (2004), Comments on the Class Foundations of the Occupation, *Theory and Criticism*. 24: 203–11 (Hebrew).

123 Dmitry Slivniak (2002), Neither a Medal Nor a Mark of Cain, *Eretz Acheret*. 10: 50–2 (Hebrew).

124 Gillis, Now They Are Also Settlers.

125 Rafi Vaknin (1985), The Right to Cry Out Section: We've Prevented Massive Settlement of Judea, Samaria and Gaza with Our Own Hands, *Nekuda*. July, 89: 26 (Hebrew). Quoted in Gillis, Now They Are Also Settlers.

126 Gadi Algazi (2006) Matrix in Bilin: A Story of Colonial Capitalism in Modern-day Israel, *Theory and Criticism*. 29: 173–92 (Hebrew).

127 Shir Hever (2009), *The Political Economy of Israel's Occupation beyond Mere Exploitation*. London: Pluto Press. Hever analyzes the integration of the two economies, and shows the borders between them are artificial.

128 Uri Blau and Jotam Feldman (2009), The Nightmare Merchants, Haaretz Magazine, *Haaretz*. June 12, pp. 18–24 (Hebrew).

129 For detailed data, see an article by Sandy Keidar and Oren Yiftachel (2003), On Power and Land: The Israeli Lands Regime, in Yehouda Shenhav (ed.), *Space, Land, Home*. Tel Aviv, pp. 18–52 (Hebrew).

130 Land and Social Justice. A position paper by the Mizrachi Democratic Rainbow, November 2000.

131 Haim Yaakobi and Shelly Cohen (eds.) (2007), *Separation – The Politics of Space in Israel*. Tel Aviv: Hargol (Hebrew).

132 The Adalah monthly e-newsletter, September 2007, 40.

133 These data are based on the work of Ravit Hananel, who also prepared a work-paper for the Mizrachi Democratic Rainbow on the same issue: The Mizrachi Democratic Rainbow for Reform in the Process of Changing Municipal Borders. Tel Aviv, November, 2004.

134 Shelly.org.il/%3fp%3d2645.

135 Peled, Strangers in Utopia.

136 See Mati Shmeuloff's analysis of the privatization of Shfaim land (2009), *Ynet*. March 29 (Hebrew).

137 See, for example: Algazi, Matrix in Bil'in.

138 For a discussion of the links between the "Occupation" (the 1967 paradigm) and the ethnic and class inequality, see: Gutwein, Comments on the Class Foundations of the Occupation.

139 Danny Filc (2006), *Populism and Hegemony in Israel*. Tel Aviv: Resling (Hebrew).

140 See: Bernard Semmel (1968), *Imperialism and Social Reform: English Social Imperial Thought, 1895–1914*. New York: Anchor Books.

141 For a discussion of the mechanisms of occupation within the Green Line, see: Yehouda Shenhav (2006), The Occupation Does Not Stop at the Checkpoint, in Yisahi Menuhin (ed.), *Occupation and Refusal*. Tel Aviv: November Books, pp. 12–21 (Hebrew).

4 1948 and the Return to the Rights of the Palestinians

1 Ghassan Kanafani (1970), *Return to Haifa*. Beirut: Dar al-Awda (Arabic).

2 Ibid.

3 This approach was revealed in a rather fascinating way in the international criticism leveled at Israel during the Eichmann trial in 1961. The main argument – except that it's inappropriate for victims to try the killers – was that the State of Israel did not exist when the crimes were carried out, and that they were carried out elsewhere. Israel argued that this was not a retroactive trial, and the eternity of the Jewish nation existed even while the Nazi crimes were being carried out. The use of the argument of the eternity of a nation is paradoxical and ironic, resembling as it does an argument in the Nazis' own law on the eternity of the German nation.

4 Sasson Sofer (2001), *The Birth of Israeli Political Thought*. Tel Aviv: Shoken, p. 396 (Hebrew).

5 Yfaat Weiss (2008) Central European Ethnonationalism and Zionist Bi-nationalism, in Adi Gordon (ed.), *"Brit Shalom" and Binational Zionism: The Arab Question as a Jewish Question*. Jerusalem: Carmel, pp. 43–66 (Hebrew); Zohar Maor, The Unattainable Land: On the Central-European Roots of Brit Shalom, in Gordon (ed.), *"Brit Shalom" and Binational Zionism*, pp. 93–110.

6 In Sofer, *The Birth of Israeli Political Thought*, p. 396.

7 See Bernard Reich (1995), *Arab–Israeli Conflict and Conciliation: A Documentary History*. London: Praeger.

8 Ibid.

9 In: Sofer, *The Birth of Israeli Political Thought*, p. 396.

10 Ibid., 404.

11 Sarah Strassberg-Dayan (2008), Zion: Kingdom of Heaven or Kingdom of Israel? Between Brith Shalom and Brith Habiryonim, in Gordon (ed.), *"Brit Shalom" and Binational Zionism*, p. 185.

12 E. Kedar (1981), Brit Shalom, *The Jerusalem Quarterly*. 18: 55–64.

13 For example, Magnes met in 1937 in Beirut with Iraqi Prime Minister Nuri Said, to discuss the possibility of establishing a confederative model. In the summer of the same year, Chaim Klowirski met with members of the Istiqlal Party, winning criticism from then head of the Jewish Agency political department and future Prime Minister, Moshe Sharett. See Sofer, *The Birth of Israeli Political Thought*, p. 396.

14 Constantin Zreik (1948), *The Meaning of the Nakba*. Beirut: Dar Alem Lalmalyan (Arabic).

15 Hunaida Ghanem shows how central the concept of the Nakba is in establishing the history of 1948, and

in the perception of the year as a point of fracture for Palestinian intellectuals in Israel: Hunaida Ghanem (2004), The Role and Status of Palestinian Intellectuals in Israel. Ph.D. dissertation, Hebrew University.

16 For a thorough discussion, see: Noga Kadman (2008), *Erased from Space and Consciousness*. Tel Aviv: November Books (Hebrew).

17 Hillel Cohen (2000) *Absent Presentees: Palestinian Refugees in Israel since 1948*. Jerusalem: Van Leer Institute (Hebrew).

18 See: Aadel Manaa (forthcoming), *Politics of Survival: A History of the Arabs in Israel in the First Decade, 1948–1958*. Tel Aviv and Jerusalem: Ha'Kibbutz Ha'Meuchad and Van Leer Institute (Hebrew).

19 Benny Morris (1991), *The Birth of the Palestinian Refugees Problem 1947–1949*. Tel Aviv: Am Oved (Hebrew). See also: Anita Shapira (2004), *Yigal Alon: A Biography*. Tel Aviv: Ha'Kibbutz Ha'Meuchad (Hebrew).

20 Morris, *The Birth of the Palestinian Refugees Problem 1947–1949*. See also: Shapira, *Yigal Alon*.

21 Dan Zaks (1996), Historiography and National Identity: The New Historian in Israel and the Historians' Quarrel in Germany, *Theory and Criticism*. 8: 73–89 (Hebrew).

22 Ibid.

23 In 2007, the Education Ministry approved a geography book entitled *Living Together in Israel* for third-grade students (ages seven to eight). The book included the following phrase: "At the end of the war, the Jews overcame the Arabs; ceasefire agreements were signed between Israel and its neighbors. The Arabs call the war Nakba, or catastrophe and loss, while the Jews call it the War of Independence." This minimalistic, entirely non-committal phrase created a political firestorm in the Knesset.

24 Esther Yogev and Eyal Naveh (2002), *Histories: Toward a Dialog with the Yesterday*. Tel Aviv: Babel (Hebrew).

25 Or Kashti (2004), History Ends in 1948, *NRG*. September 29 (Hebrew).

26 For a comprehensive analysis of the obliterated memory of the Palestinian Nakba in Israeli discourse, see: Uri Ram (2011), *Israeli Nationalism: Social Conflicts and the Politics of Knowledge*. London and New York: Routledge, pp. 89–110.

27 Dan Horowitz and Moshe Lisak (1990), *Distress in Utopia: Israel – An Overloaded Society*. Tel Aviv: Am Oved, p. 69 (Hebrew).

28 Hannan Hever (1999), *Literature Written from Here*. Tel Aviv: Yedioth Books, p. 12 (Hebrew); Hannan Hever (2001), *Producing the Modern Hebrew Canon*. New York: University of New York Press.

29 See: Azmi Bishara (1998), One Hundred Years of Zionism, *Theory and Criticism*. 12–13: 507–22 (Hebrew).

30 Emile Habibi (1984), *The Pessoptimist*. Tel Aviv: Ha'Kibbutz Ha'Meuchad, p. 148 (Hebrew).

31 This discussion is based on my joint work with Hannan Hever. See: Yehouda Shenhav and Hannan Hever (2000), The Postcolonial Gaze, *Theory and Criticism*. 20: 9–21 (Hebrew).

32 I rely here on some of the important points raised by Faisal Daraj (1998), Ghassan Kanafani, *Theory and Criticism*. 12–13: 215–27 (Hebrew).

33 See: Yfaat Weiss (2007), *Wadi Sali — The Present and the Absentee*. Tel Aviv and Jerusalem: Ha'Kibbutz Ha'meuchad and the Van Leer Institute (Hebrew).

34 Daraj, Ghassan Kanafani.

35 Ibid.

36 Hever, *Producing the Modern Hebrew Canon*, p. 317.

37 Ibid.

38 Hannan Hever (1991), Hebrew under the Arab Pen: Six Chapters on *Arabesques* by Anton Shamas, *Theory and Criticism*. 1: 23–38 (Hebrew).

39 Ibid.

40 Ibid.

41 Ibid.

42 Kadman, *Erased from Space and Consciousness*, p. 11.

43 Meron Benvenishti (1997), The Hebrew Map, *Theory and Criticism*. 11: 7–29 (Hebrew).

44 Ibid.

45 Hannan Hever demonstrates how the trauma of 1948 is contained in Hebrew literary writing. For example, poet Nathan Alterman demonstrates in his poem "The War of the Cities" the trauma of the Nakba following the exodus and expulsion from Jaffa in April 1948, but neutralizes it by putting it into the context of a national struggle and the Arab threat to the Jews. See Hannan Hever (forthcoming), Trauma and Responsibility in Nathan Alterman's *War of the Cities*, in N. Davidovich, R. Zleshik and M. Alberstein (eds.), *Trauma and Memory in Israel: Between the Individual and the Collective* (Hebrew).

46 See Effi Ziv (forthcoming), The Stubbornness of Insidious Trauma, in Davidovich et al. (eds.), *Trauma and Memory in Israel*.

47 Qassem Fatma (2006) Language, History and Women: Palestinian Women in Israel Describe the Nakba, *Theory and Criticism*. 29: 59–80.

48 Dan Rabinowich and Khawla Abu-Baker (2002), *The Stand-Tall Generation*. Jerusalem: Keter, pp. 153–4.

49 Ibid.

50 Ibid.

51 Edward Said's (1999) autobiography, *Out of Place*, can also be read in this context.

52 Zochrot, How do you say "Nakba" in Hebrew? A Nakba Teaching Kit, p. 1.
53 Salim Tamari and Rima Hamami (2007), Imagined Returns, *Sedek*. 1: 33–44 (Hebrew). See Walid Khalidi (1998), *In Order Not to Forget: The Palestinians Villages that Israel Destroyed in the Year 1948*. Beirut: Institute for The Study of Palestine (Arabic).
54 Tomer Gardi (2008), I Didn't Go Deep into this At All, *Sedek*. 2: 33–4 (Hebrew).
55 Ofer Kahana and Hagar Goren (2008), To Distance the Approaching Holocaust, *Sedek*. 2: 13–15 (Hebrew).
56 Ariella Azoulay (2009), *Constituting Violence, 1947–1950*. Tel Aviv: Resling (Hebrew).
57 Kadman, *Erased from Space and Consciousness*.
58 Ibid., 14.
59 Ibid., 128.
60 For a critique of the Zochrot project, see: Ronit Lentin (ed.) (2008), *Thinking Palestine*. London: Zen Books, pp. 211–18.
61 For a more nuanced analysis, I suggest the work of Chaim Gans, especially the last chapter of his book, in which he considers the various options of return: Haim Gantz (2006), *From Richard Wagner to the Right of Return*. Tel Aviv: Am Oved (Hebrew).
62 State archives preserve voluminous Foreign Ministry correspondence regarding the property of Iraqi Jews, in folders under the candid title of "Protecting the Property of Israel." See: Yehouda Shenhav (1999), The Jews of Iraq, Zionist Ideology, and the Property of the Palestinian Refugees of 1948: An Anomaly of National Accounting, *International Journal of Middle East Studies*. 31: 605–30.
63 For a discussion of this issue, see: Yehouda Shenhav (2005), Arab Jews, "Population Exchange" and the

Palestinian Right-of-Return, in Ann Lesch and Ian Lustick (eds.), *Exile and Return: Predicaments of Palestinians and Jews*. Pennsylvania: University of Pennsylvania Press, pp. 225–45.

64 Zochrot, How do you say "Nakba" in Hebrew? p. 1.

65 Ariella Azoulay and Adi Ophir (2008), *This Regime Which Is Not One*. Tel Aviv: Resling (Hebrew).

66 Elazar Barkan, who researched discourse structures in both societies, shows that one of the main phenomena of the history of the Nakba – if not the central one – is the prevention of the return of the refugees after the war and their definition as "infiltrators." This observation is shared by both sides of the conflict. See: http://historyandreconciliation.org/mideast

67 Even historians clearly associated with the national wing, like Yoav Gelber, admit that "none of the problems that arose in the relationship between Jews and Arabs during and following the 1948 war was ever solved": Yoav Gelber (2004), *Independence and Nakba*. Tel Aviv: Dvir (Hebrew).

68 Tamar Herman (2008), The Binational Idea in Israel/Palestine, Past and Present, in Gordon (ed.), *"Brith Shalom" and Binational Zionism*, pp. 19–41.

69 For example: Amnon Raz-Krakotzkin (2005), Post-Zionism and the Binational Challenge, *New Horizons*. August 25, p. 24.

70 For example: Ali Abunimah (2006), *One Country: A Bold Proposal to End the Israeli–Palestinian Conflict*. Metropolitan Books.

71 See, for example, a statement made by Palestinian chief negotiator Abu Ala: "We may demand a binational state solution": *Haaretz*. August 11, 2008 (Hebrew).

72 Tony Judt (2003), Israel: The Alternative, *New York Review of Books*. November 2, 50.

73 See: Eviatar Zerubavel (1982), The Standardization of Time: A Sociohistorical Perspective, *American Journal of Sociology*. 88: 1–24.

74 Ibid.

75 Emile Durkheim (1965), *The Elementary Forms of Religious Life*. New York: Free Press.

76 Jacques Alain Miller (2005), The Erotics of Time, *Lacanian Ink*. 24–5 (Spring): 8–63.

77 Michael R. Fischbach (2006), *The Peace Process and the Palestinian Refugee Claims*. Washington: USIP Press Books.

5 The Return to the Rights of the Jews

1 Zeev Chiff and Ehud Yaari tell us just how stunned the security establishment was by the Palestinian uprising in the territories, and point out the conceptual disconnect between that and the Lebanon War of 1982. See Zeev Schiff and Ehud Yaari (1990), *Intifada*. Tel Aviv: Shocken (Hebrew).

2 See Hanna Herzog, Inna Laikin and Smadar Sharon (2008), Us? Racist? The Racist Discourse on Palestinian Citizens of Israel as Reflected in Printed Hebrew Journalism 1949–2000, in Yehouda Shenhav and Yossi Yonah (eds.), *Racism in Israel*. Tel Aviv and Jerusalem: Ha'Kibbutz Ha'Meuchad and Van Leer Institute, pp. 48–75 (Hebrew).

3 José Casanova (2007), Religion, European Secular Identities and European Integration, *Eurozine*: www.eurozine.com/authors/casanova.html.

4 Yagil Levi (1993), The War of the Peripheries: The Social Mapping of the IDF Casualties in the Second Intifada, *Theory and Criticism*. 3: 7–20 (Hebrew).

5 The Westphalian model preserves the European advantage in sovereignty and conceals the racial disputes that

accompanied its establishment not only in Europe but also in the conflict between Europe and non-European societies. For a critique of the Westphalian sovereignty model in the colonial context, see Antony Anghie (2004), *Imperialism, Sovereignty and the Making of International Law*. Cambridge: Cambridge University Press.

6 Gross refers to Jerusalem, but her point is also valid with respect to other locations.

7 Mathias Mossberg (2010), One Land, Two States? Parallel States as an Example of "Out of the Box" Thinking on Israel/Palestine, *Journal of Palestine Studies*. 39 (2): 1–7.

8 Lev Grinberg (2010), The Israeli–Palestine Union: The 1-2-7 States Vision of the Future, *Journal of Palestine Studies*. 39 (2): 8–15.

9 For a discussion of "Jewish privileges," cf. Ruhana and Sabbagh Khouri 2006

10 The first and foremost speaker for this model in the past two decades in Israel was Azmi Bishara. See: Azmi Bishara (1993), On the Question of the Palestinian Minority in Israel, *Theory and Criticism*. 3: 7–20 (Hebrew).

11 For more information on the manner in which Israel selfishly and unjustly took over Palestinian water resources, see: Jotam Feldman and Uri Blau (2009), Thirst, Haaretz Magazine, *Haaretz*. August 7, pp. 34–42 (Hebrew).

12 Altayeb Ghnaim (2006), Leave the Bleeding Issues Behind Us and Move On, *Eretz Acheret*. 32: 68–70 (Hebrew).

13 For a discussion of this model, see: Yoav Peled (1993), Strangers in Utopia: The Civil Status of the Palestinians in Israel, *Theory and Criticism*. 3: 21–35 (Hebrew).

14 Azmi Bishara wrote on this that a model in which the Palestinians are not committed to military, national

or civic service is convenient for the Jewish state in a vicious circle whereby civic service cements the Israeli republicanism and vice versa: Azmi Bishara (1993), On the Question of the Palestinian Minority in Israel, *Theory and Criticism*. 3: 7–20 (Hebrew).

15 Tzvia Gross (2009), Sovereignty-light in Jerusalem, *Haaretz*. July 6, p. B2 (Hebrew). The same idea can be applied to other theologically contested places across the space.

16 Nir Hasson (2009), A Boycott on the Tolerance Museum in Exchange for Recognition of Joseph's Tomb, *Haaretz*. July 1 (Hebrew).

17 Ibid.

18 See, for example: Akiva Eldar (2009), The Americans Demand Israel Prevents the Eviction of Sheikh Jarrah Residents, *Haaretz*. April 19, p. 2 (Hebrew).

19 Aluf Benn (2009), Cracked Basin, *Haaretz*. June 26, p. 2 (Hebrew).

20 Sasson Sofer (2001), *The Birth of Israeli Political Thought*. Tel Aviv: Shocken, p. 396 (Hebrew).

21 Joseph Heller (2004), *From Brit Shalom to Ihud*. Jerusalem: Magnes, p. 42 (Hebrew).

22 Zohar Maor (2008) The Unattainable Land: On the Central-European Roots of Brit Shalom, in Adi Gordon (ed.), *Brith Shalom and Binational Zionism: The Arab Question as a Jewish Question*. Jerusalem: Carmel, p. 95 (Hebrew).

23 Heller, *From Brit Shalom to Ihud*, p. 54.

24 Sofer, *The Birth of Israeli Political Thought*, pp. 399–400.

25 Heller, *From Brit Shalom to Ihud*, p. 234.

26 Ibid., 138.

27 Hedva Ben Israel (2008), Magnes and Brith Shalom, in Gordon (ed.), *"Brit Shalom" and Binational Zionism*, p. 71.

28 Heller, *From Brit Shalom to Ihud*, p. 246.

29 Ibid., 272.

30 Ibid.

31 Ibid., 72.

32 Adi Gordon (2008), This Is About Unrequited Love: The Retirement of Hans Cohn from the Zionist Movement, in Gordon (ed.), *"Brit Shalom" and Binational Zionism*, p. 71.

33 Heller, *From Brit Shalom to Ihud*, p. 6.

34 Ibid., 244.

35 Ibid., 21.

36 Ibid., 63.

37 Ibid., 76.

38 On the ways in which intellectuals deny the political structure and the political immorality of the Israeli state, see: Yehouda Shenhav (2006), The Political Is Into You: Intellectuals, Power and Politics, in Hanna Herzog and Kinneret Lahad (eds.), *Knowing and Keeping Silent: Mechanisms of Silencing and Denial in Israeli Society.* Tel Aviv and Jerusalem: Ha'Kibbutz Ha'Meuchad and Van Leer Institute, 168–78 (Hebrew).

39 Herbert Marcuse (1941), *Reason and Revolution: Hegel and the Rise of Social Theory.* Quoted from the Hebrew edition, Tel Aviv: Ha'Kibbutz Ha'Meuchad, 1951.

40 Robert Musil (1988), *Man Without Qualities.* Tel Aviv: Shocken, p. 28 (Hebrew).

41 For a more detailed discussion of this issue, see: Hannan Hever (2000), A Comment on the Position of the Israeli Intellectual, in Adi Ophir (ed.), *Real Time.* Jerusalem: Keter, pp. 191–6 (Hebrew).

42 Ibid.

43 We should note intellectuals who justified their status as such, including Martin Buber, Judah Magnes, Shimon Balas and Yaakov Talmon, who predicted the establish-

ment of ghettos in the occupied territories as early as 1970. These should be compared to Amnon Rubinstein, a pronounced liberal, who noted in *Haaretz* (Hebrew) on June 10, 1967, that time works for us, and therefore we shouldn't rush to leave the territories, so that Arabs understand what power means.

44 Michel Foucault (2003), *Society Must Be Defended*. New York: Picador.

45 For a fascinating discussion of these questions, see: Andrew Neal (2004), Cutting off the King's Head: Foucault's *Society Must Be Defended* and the Problem of Sovereignty, *Alternatives: Global, Local, Political*. 29 (4): 373–98.

INDEX